THE CITIZEN

Exploring the future of universal asset policies

Edited by Will Paxton and Stuart White

with Dominic Maxwell

First published in Great Britain in January 2006 by

The Policy Press
University of Bristol
Fourth Floor
Beacon House
Queen's Road
Bristol BS8 1QU
UK

Tel +44 (0)117 331 4054
Fax +44 (0)117 331 4093
e-mail tpp-info@bristol.ac.uk
www.policypress.org.uk

British Library Cataloguing in Publication Data
A catalogue record for this book is available from the British Library.

Library of Congress Cataloging-in-Publication Data
A catalog record for this book has been requested.

ISBN-10 1 86134 699 9 paperback
ISBN-13 978 186134 699 5

A hardcover version of this book is also available

Cover design by Qube Design Associates, Bristol.
Printed and bound in Great Britain by Hobbs the Printers Ltd, Southampton

Contents

List of tables, figures and boxes

Tables

Figures

Boxes

Acknowledgements

The editors would like to give deep thanks to the Leverhulme Trust for its financial support for the project on which this book is based (grant F/01 087/A, 'The new politics of ownership: policy options and public opinion'). We are also very grateful for supplementary support from the Department of Politics and International Relations, Oxford University, and ARCO. Core funding for the Centre for Asset-Based Welfare at the Institute for Public Policy Research (ippr) is generously provided by The Children's Mutual. At ippr, we give big thanks to Dominic Maxwell for his superlative contribution, which included intensive help with the editing of all chapters as well as the chapter of his own. We also give big thanks to Miranda Lewis and Laura Edwards of the public involvement team at ippr, who ran the deliberative workshops on inheritance tax and crucially guided us in their design. Thanks also to Nick Pearce, Howard Reed and Kate Stanley. Howard and Kate provided very helpful feedback on the book as a whole. At Oxford, we give grateful thanks to Bridget Taylor and Andrew Fairweather-Tall for their vital help and support. Warm thanks also to Alexandra Couto for her research into the state of the debate on asset-based social policy in Germany and France (which we draw upon and refer to in Chapter Twelve); and also to Robert Jubb and Karl Widerquist. First drafts of most of the chapters of this book were presented at two day-long seminars at Oxford, and we would like to thank everyone who participated in these (plus extra thanks for those who contributed papers). In addition to Dominic, Miranda and Karl they include: Fran Bennett, David Bollier, Linda Boyes, Samuel Brittan, Keith Dowding, Andrew Gamble, Howard Glennerster, Jane Lewis, Jim McCormick, Abigail McKnight, Iain McLean, Jane Millar, David Miller, Michael Orton, Christopher Pierson, Rajiv Prabhakar, Andrew Reeve, Karen Rowlingson, Adam Swift, David White. We thank Anne Alstott for contributing a key chapter at very short notice. Many seminar participants also provided critical written feedback on the various chapters, for which we are very grateful. We also thank Richard Brooks, Janie Cowling, John Cunliffe, Gösta Esping-Andersen, Richenda Gambles, Sarah Gillinson, Peter Robinson, Karen Rowlingson and Michael Sherraden for providing helpful comments on one or more chapters. Not least, we thank Dawn Rushen and Emily Watt at The Policy Press for their support. Stuart White would also like to thank

Katherine Wedell for her love, and Isaac Wedell White for helping to remind him on a daily basis of what this project is ultimately all about.

List of contributors

Anne L. Alstott is the Jacquin D. Bierman Professor of Taxation at Yale Law School.

David Bollier is Editor of OntheCommons.org, a Fellow at the Tomales Bay Institute (Point Reyes, California), and Senior Fellow at the Norman Lear Center at the University of Southern California's Annenberg School for Communication.

Linda Boyes is a Policy Manager at the Scottish Council Foundation.

Andrew Gamble is Professor of Politics at Sheffield University.

Howard Glennester is Emeritus Professor of Social Policy at the London School of Economics and Political Science, and Co-Director of the Centre for Analysis of Social Exclusion.

Jane Lewis is Professor of Social Policy at the London School of Economics and Political Science.

Miranda Lewis is a Senior Research Fellow at the Institute for Public Policy Research.

Dominic Maxwell is a Research Fellow at the Institute for Public Policy Research.

Jim McCormick is Director of the Scottish Council Foundation.

Abigail McKnight is Toyota Research Fellow at the Centre for Analysis of Social Exclusion, London School of Economics and Political Science.

Iain McLean is Official Fellow in Politics, Nuffield College and Professor of Politics, University of Oxford.

Will Paxton is a Senior Research Fellow at the Institute for Public Policy Research.

Nick Pearce is Director of the Institute for Public Policy Research.

Rajiv Prabhakar is Ludwig M. Lachmann Research Fellow at the London School of Economics and Political Science.

Stuart White is a Fellow in Politics, Jesus College, Oxford University.

ONE

Introduction: the new politics of ownership

Will Paxton and Stuart White

When a young couple begin the world, the difference is exceedingly great whether they begin the world with nothing or with fifteen pounds apiece. With this aid they could buy a cow, and implements to cultivate a few acres of land; and instead of becoming burdens upon society ... would be put in the way of becoming useful and profitable citizens. (Thomas Paine, 1987 [1797], p 483)

Introduction

Market economies are crucial for efficiency. But market economies also tend to generate significant inequality. In recent years, Britain has experienced not only an increase in income inequality, but an increase of inequality in wealth; not only a rise in income poverty, but a rise in asset poverty (Paxton and Dixon, 2004). Since the birth of industrial capitalism towards the end of the 18th century, however, one idea has insistently resurfaced as a proposal for moderating inequality of wealth in market economies. This is the proposal to endow all citizens on maturity with a generous capital grant as of right, or what we term a *citizen's stake*. For Thomas Paine, writing in the 1790s, the goal was to endow each adult on maturity with the sum of £15, with which they could buy a cow and implements to cultivate a few acres of land (Paine, 1987 [1797]). The Child Trust Fund, recently introduced by the Labour government in Britain, represents a modest variant on this idea of a citizen's stake. In this book, we explore how (if at all) the principle of the citizen's stake might be further developed.

This introduction does three things. First, in section 1, we clarify the normative arguments which support the idea of a citizen's stake. Second, in section 2, we briefly explain the recently introduced Child

Trust Fund. Section 3 then sets out the concrete policy questions we intend to explore in this book, and explains how each chapter relates to them.

The motivation for the citizen's stake

Why should we be interested in establishing a ▇▇▇▇▇▇▇'s stake? What arguments, historically, and in our own ▇▇▇▇▇▇▇▇ support the proposal? Into what wider vision of socie▇▇▇▇▇▇ ▇▇sal fit? Philosophically, four ideas play a key role in arguments for a citizen's stake: natural rights; freedom; welfare; and equality of opportunity (see Dowding et al, 2003, for a related discussion that informs that here).

1. *Natural rights.* The idea of a natural right to property is one with a long history. A common view, for example, is that the labourer has a natural right to the product of his or her labour (for variations on this idea, see Locke, 1960 [1682], ch 5; Nozick, 1974). But of course as a community we inherit some resources from nature and/or from past generations. What kind of rights do we have with respect to these resources, which exist (to some extent) prior to or independently of our labour or the labour of anyone else living? One answer to which many philosophers have been drawn is that these resources are common property. Morally speaking, they belong to us all. If, for reasons of economic efficiency, we find it advisable to individuate claims to the resources (I get to hold this piece of land, you get to hold that piece of land), then everyone has a right to be included in this share-out. Each citizen has a right to her or his share of those resources that represent a common inheritance to us all; a shared national (or, indeed, global) patrimony. As Thomas Paine put it, in setting out his case for a citizen's stake in his 1797 work, *Agrarian justice*, raw natural resources are the 'common property of the human race' and, where private property has been adopted as a basis for economic life, this is legitimate only if all are guaranteed their share of this 'natural inheritance' or an equivalent sum (Paine, 1987 [1797]). 'No man made the land,' Mill writes, echoing Paine, 'It is the original inheritance of the whole species' (Mill, 1970 [1848], p 384). Following Paine's lead, some philosophers defend the introduction of a citizen's stake as a way of ensuring that people get their rightful share of a collective inheritance, or a fair equivalent (see, for example, Steiner, 1994; Van Parijs, 1995; Steiner and Vallentyne, 2000).

2. *Freedom.* A second idea that plays an important role in arguments for a citizen's stake is that of freedom. The basic intuition is that the

status of being a free person depends on having one's own wealth; hence, if we think people ought to be free, we ought also to be concerned to ensure that they can access wealth. This basic intuition can be elaborated in a number of different ways. In some accounts, the key consideration is being able to avoid relationships in which one is dominated by others: an unfree person is someone who lives at the mercy of another (Pettit, 1997; Skinner, 1998). With one's own wealth at one's disposal it is that much easier to walk out on the bullying boss or the bullying spouse. As James Meade puts it: 'A man with ... property has ... bargaining strength and a sense of security, independence, and freedom.... He can snap his fingers at those on whom he must rely for income, for he can always rely for a time on his capital' (quoted in Ackerman and Alstott, 1999, p 25). A related worry is that a lack of wealth will undermine political freedom and citizenship. If Smith's lack of wealth makes her dependent for a living on the goodwill of Jones, then Jones has a power over her that can be used to compromise her political independence. This is why radical democrats such as Jean-Jacques Rousseau have argued that 'no citizen should be rich enough to be able to buy another, and none so poor that he has to sell himself' (Rousseau, 1993 [1762], p 87). Another theme, which we think especially important, concerns the way in which wealth enables people to think creatively about what to do with their lives, enhancing personal autonomy. This idea is emphasised by Bruce Ackerman and Anne Alstott in their recent defence of the citizen's stake proposal, *The stakeholder society* (1999). In their view, a society that takes freedom seriously is one in which every young person can ask themselves seriously: 'What do I want to do with my life?' But, they argue, a lack of wealth in early adulthood undermines people's ability to pose this question in a meaningful way:

> Our present arrangements impose an unnecessary moral dilemma: just at the moment we expect young adults to make responsible life-shaping decisions, we do not afford them the resources that they need to take a responsible long-term perspective. Forced to put bread on the table ... almost all young adults are squeezed into short-term thinking.... (Ackerman and Alstott, 1999, p 35)

The empirical literature on the so-called 'asset effect' offers some support for this sort of argument (for reviews of this literature, see Boshara, 2001; Paxton, 2002b). For example, those who start adult life with some assets are more likely to form their own businesses

(Blanchflower and Oswald, 1998). People with savings at age 23 are less likely to be ill or unemployed at age 33 (Bynner, 2001). People who own their own homes are more likely to negotiate successfully stressful events such as losing a job (Page-Adams and Vosler, 1996). These results are all consistent with the image of wealth-holders as people with more control over their lives, and who perhaps perform better because they are and feel more in control.

3. *Welfare.* This reference to the empirical literature on the 'asset-effect' points to another, related argument that can be made for citizen's stake policies: that they enhance welfare or well-being. If holding assets has a positive impact on variables such as health, employment, self-esteem, and so on, then perhaps citizen's stake policies that enact a right to wealth for all citizens will have beneficial effects on welfare. That said, the empirical evidence on the 'asset effect' must be treated with some circumspection. For one thing, it is always difficult in such studies to be absolutely sure that one has identified a true causal relationship between some asset variable and some welfare variable. For example, perhaps it is not having savings at 23 that explains why people with savings at 23 are more likely to be healthy and employed when they are 33. Perhaps there is some third factor, as yet undiscovered, that explains both why these people hold savings at 23 and are also more likely to be healthy and employed at 33. Statistical analyses such as that reported above take into account a wide range of other variables, but it is impossible ever fully to exclude the possibility of an unknown or unobservable characteristic. Second, one must distinguish between the putative welfare effects of *holding* or *inheriting* assets and the putative effects of *accumulating* assets. If the main welfare effects come through the experience of accumulating assets, for example through matched savings programmes like Individual Development Accounts in the US, then merely *giving* people an asset endowment will not necessarily have these welfare effects. (As we explain below, the British government's Child Trust Fund combines the two approaches, giving all children a modest initial asset at birth to help stimulate saving by their parents and themselves.) One must accept, then, that the nature and extent of the 'asset effect' is not yet fully understood, although the evidence we have is consistent with the thesis that a citizen's stake policy, securing everyone a decent sum of capital in early adulthood, will have a positive effect on the welfare of those who would otherwise lack such capital.

4. *Equality of opportunity.* A fourth argument for a citizen's stake policy appeals to the value of equality of opportunity. What we have in mind here, more exactly, is John Rawls's idea of 'fair equality of opportunity'

(Rawls, 1999 [1971], 2001). This obtains when two people with roughly similar natural endowments and motivation have roughly equal chances of developing their talents and of succeeding in getting jobs and holding offices, regardless of their initial social background. (It should be noted that, for Rawls, there is more to social justice than equality of opportunity in this sense. Justice also requires, he argues, that if there is inequality in reward this should work to maximise the prospects of the least rewarded group.) One of the forces working against equality of opportunity in societies like our own is inequality in the wealth that people have access to at the start of their adult lives. Wealth inequality at this stage can affect opportunities for education, training, travel, enterprise and a host of other things, with potentially large consequences for the further opportunities that people have later in life. A citizen's stake policy ensures that each young adult has at least some capital as they begin life and so can help to reduce the inequality of opportunity that otherwise arises at this time (Ackerman and Alstott, 1999; Nissan and Le Grand, 2000; see also Haveman, 1988; Le Grand, 1989). Rawls himself is clear that the commitment to fair equality of opportunity, along with the commitment to maintain the fair value of political freedom, requires urgent attention to the distribution of financial and human capital, a claim fully in keeping with the spirit of the citizen's stake proposal. For Rawls, fair equality of opportunity and effective political freedom require not merely a 'welfare state' but a 'property-owning democracy'. He elaborates this as follows:

> ... the background institutions of property-owning democracy, with its system of (workably) competitive markets, tries to disperse the ownership of wealth and capital, and thus to prevent a small part of society from controlling the economy and indirectly political life itself. Property-owning democracy avoids this, not by redistributing income to those with less at the end of each period, so to speak, but rather by ensuring the widespread ownership of productive assets and human capital ... at the beginning of each period.... The idea is not simply to assist those who lose out through accident or misfortune (although this must be done), but instead to put all citizens in a position to manage their own affairs and to take part in social cooperation on a footing of mutual respect under appropriately equal conditions. (Rawls, 1999 [1971], p xv; see also pp 242-51)

Needless to say, a citizen's stake is hardly sufficient by itself to secure fair equality of opportunity. The point, rather, is that such a policy may be one of a range of policies that is needed to help achieve equality of opportunity. We certainly should not put all of our eggs in this basket. But a balanced strategy for increasing equality of opportunity probably requires that we do not leave this particular basket empty.

Enter the Child Trust Fund

From the basic arguments behind the idea of a citizen's stake, we can turn to concrete and immediate policy. In Britain, 2005 has witnessed the introduction of the Child Trust Fund (CTF), which is a form of citizen's stake. With the CTF, all newborn children receive an endowment from the state, paid into their own individual account. This fund then increases with additional state top-ups at specific ages and contributions from the child's family, until they have access to the financial asset at the age of 18 (see Box 1.1 for further details). The primary objective is to ensure that, after the first cohort of account holders reaches 18, all citizens start their adult life with a financial asset that, it is hoped, will improve their life chances. Policy makers thought that an account that starts at birth and stays with the child as they grow up would maximise the positive behavioural and attitudinal effects of holding an asset (see Bynner, 2001, for further details).

The CTF establishes an important principle: the right of the individual, as a citizen, to capital. However, the sums presently involved might seem rather modest when set against the high ambition of, say, Ackerman and Alstott with their radical vision of a society that assures each young person of a citizen's stake in the region of £50,000. Even if one thinks it unnecessary, or undesirable, to go this far, many supporters of the CTF see it as a first step. It is, to be sure, a vitally important first step. But the issue arises as to how the existing CTF might be developed or complemented so as to establish a more generous and effective citizen's stake.

Discussion of this issue has relevance well beyond Britain. For while the CTF is at present a unique policy internationally, there is a widening debate about policies of this kind across the world (Regan and Paxton, 2001). On the face of it, this debate is concentrated in the nations of what is sometimes called 'Anglo-Saxon' capitalism: the US, Canada, New Zealand and Australia. However, somewhat parallel discussions are underway in continental Europe. The language of 'asset-based welfare' has not yet been exported to France or Germany, but policy makers there are increasingly interested in ideas such as 'social drawing

Box 1.1: The Child Trust Fund

Every child born since 1 September 2002 will have a Child Trust Fund, kick-started by an initial government endowment. Every child will receive at least £250, and children in the poorest 40% of families will receive £500. Further endowments will be made at the age of seven.

The endowment will be given in the form of a voucher that parents can take to a wide range of financial institutions, investing in cash, shares, or special 'stakeholder accounts' that have charge caps, a low minimum contribution, and other extra protections for consumers. If after a year the parents have not opened a CTF for their child, the government will open a stakeholder account for them.

Parents, family and friends will be encouraged to contribute – up to £1,200 can be given each year, and any interest on the account will be free of tax. Every birthday the child will receive an annual statement on their account, and accounts will also be linked to financial education classes in schools. After the age of 16, children themselves can choose how the money should be invested.

The account matures at 18, and until then there can be no withdrawals. But once the child is 18 there are no restrictions on how the money is spent. The initial government endowments, contributions from parents, and all the interest can be spent however the child feels fit, or invested for a rainy day.

See HM Treasury and Inland Revenue (2003) and Financial Services Authority (2004), for further details.

rights' and 'sabbatical accounts', which have some of the features of capital grant policies like the CTF. So our discussion, while focused primarily on the future of citizen's stake policy in Britain, is part of a much wider, international discussion concerned with finding ways of empowering individuals through the creation of individual capital (or capital-like) accounts.

The key questions and how we address them

In thinking about the continued development of the citizen's stake, there are a number of questions that call out for consideration. First, how can we afford a more generous citizen's stake? This question is addressed in Part One of the book, 'Financing a citizen's stake'. Second, what form should a possible expanded citizen's stake take? Should it be simply a more generous CTF? Should restrictions be placed on how a CTF can be spent? Should an expanded citizen's stake take a different form to the CTF? These questions are addressed in Part Two of the book, 'Forms of a citizen's stake'. Here we provide a brief overview of the chapters that fit into these respective parts of the book.

1. *Financing a citizen's stake.* The case for a citizen's stake is strongest when there is a clear link between its funding and benefits. Philosophical arguments based on natural rights, as outlined above, identify specific assets – inherited wealth, natural resources – as funding sources for a citizen's stake. More pragmatic arguments might consider how an expanded citizen's stake could be financed from savings in other government expenditures. All of these possibilities are explored in Part One of the book (although these possibilities are clearly not exhaustive).

We begin with the idea of linking the citizen's stake with inheritance tax, a link advocated in a number of recent works (Ackerman and Alstott, 1999; Nissan and Le Grand, 2000). Indeed, this link is also explicit in Paine's presentation of the citizen's stake policy. Inheritance tax and the citizen's stake are often seen as two sides of the same coin, the tax and spend sides of a system of socialised inheritance in which a portion of the nation's patrimony is appropriated by the state and passed back to individuals in a way that promotes greater equality of capital endowments. But how receptive is public opinion in Britain to this idea of socialised inheritance? Could a reformed inheritance tax provide the basis for an expanded citizen's stake policy? Should inheritance tax be reformed? If so, in what direction?

These questions are explored in Chapters Two and Three. In Chapter Two, Miranda Lewis and Stuart White confront two key questions: To what extent are popular attitudes likely to constrain reform of inheritance tax? And how responsive is popular opinion to arguments concerning fairness in inheritance and wealth distribution? They report the results of two deliberative workshops undertaken to explore public attitudes on these questions. Drawing on the findings of this research, in Chapter Three, Dominic Maxwell presents a strategy for reform of the tax. He argues that an ideal tax would be more progressive, would raise more revenue and would have fewer negative impacts on the welfare of taxpayers, but that any suggested improvements must be accompanied by a vigorous defence of the principles behind inheritance tax. A relatively modest reform could spread the burden of taxation more fairly and still raise some additional revenue. This could be used to increase the generosity of the CTF, which in turn might help the tax gain public support. The author admits that this falls short of some of the more ambitious calls to socialise inheritance, but argues that raising larger sums of money is only possible with extremely high rates, or by extending inheritance tax to those less well off. Both, he argues, are economically questionable and, for the foreseeable future, politically implausible.

Chapters Four and Five then consider two further possible funding sources: 'common assets' and land value taxation. Philosophically, both proposals can be seen as expressing the intuition behind the natural rights argument that certain assets (particularly natural resources) are, as Paine put it, properly the 'inheritance of the species', and should hence be appropriated for universal benefit. In Chapter Four, David Bollier explores in depth the concept of 'common assets'. He argues that if new revenues could be drawn from these common assets, they could be used to improve the economic security of millions of citizens and reduce inequalities of wealth. In Chapter Five, Iain McLean discusses land value taxation. He provides an overview of the history of ideas on land value taxation from the writings of Thomas Paine to the Land Campaign of Lloyd George. But can land tax reform in the spirit of these thinkers work today? McLean thinks so, arguing that the potential benefits from land tax reform are so great that this could help fund a citizen's stake and much more besides. There are existing taxes that act as bad substitutes for proper land value taxation, and these have a high yield; but as the reformed land taxes they would stimulate rather than suppress real economic activity, and suppress rather than encourage bubbles in the housing market; proper land value taxation could yield more while costing less.

For some philosophers of a libertarian persuasion, a citizen's stake policy is desirable as an alternative to more conventional welfare policies. From this libertarian perspective, it would make sense to shift some of the funds currently used for cash transfers or public services into a citizen's stake. To what extent should we try to finance an expanded citizen's stake in this way? In Chapter Six, Howard Glennerster and Abigail McKnight examine how desirable it would be to follow this libertarian proposal and 'roll up' existing welfare expenditures into a capital grant policy. Drawing on well-established arguments from public economics they argue that such a proposal is largely undesirable, although they do identify one or two policy areas in which the case for rolling up existing provision into some kind of individual grant or account is strong. Since the CTF was first mooted in 2001, its supporters on the 'centre-left' in Britain have been at pains to emphasise that it should be seen largely as a complement to existing welfare policy, not as a substitute. This chapter is one of the first efforts to explore this issue systematically, and to consider in an open-minded way the extent to which the CTF or similar policies should be seen as a complement to or a substitute for conventional welfare expenditures.

2. *Forms of a citizen's stake.* Assuming we had the resources to finance it, what form should an expanded citizen's stake take? Key questions here include that of how a citizen's stake policy can be designed to tackle the problem of responsible use. Should account-holders be free to use their funds however they like? Should funds be restricted, perhaps even limited to very specific purposes such as meeting the costs of training or taking time out from employment to provide care?

A concern about the responsible use of citizen stakes emerges clearly from the discussion in Chapter Seven, in which Andrew Gamble and Rajiv Prabhakar report findings from some research they have conducted recently into young people's attitudes to the CTF and similar citizen's stake policies. Probing young people's attitudes to a range of such policies, they find that young people are sceptical about very generous stakes of the size advocated by Ackerman and Alstott. In addition, young people voice concern over the lack of any restrictions on how CTF accounts can be used. This reflects the concern about responsible use, which also came out clearly in the deliberative workshops that White, Lewis and Edwards ran to explore public attitudes towards the idea of socialised inheritance (Chapter Two).

This sets the stage for Chapter Eight, in which Will Paxton and Stuart White consider how the issue of responsible use might effectively be addressed. They argue that the philosophical case for setting conditions on how citizen's stakes can be used are stronger than is often thought. Nevertheless, the practical barriers to policing the use of CTF funds would be considerable: 700,000 people reach maturity each year in the UK, and it would be a major challenge to police closely how each of these individuals uses their CTF. In addition, there is the problem that any attempt to stipulate a fixed list of supposedly 'responsible' uses for the grant would almost certainly fail to be sufficiently sensitive to the circumstances and needs of different groups. In the case of the CTF, the chapter argues that the responsible use issue is probably best addressed through the provision of advice, information and mentoring.

Another option that Paxton and White mention, but do not discuss in depth, would be to see the CTF as just one part of the citizen's stake, to be complemented by other kinds of individual accounts that are smaller but more narrowly targeted at specific needs. In virtue of being so targeted, the issue of responsible use can to some extent be assuaged (although the flip side of this is that the accounts might cost more to administer). This approach has more in common with the idea of 'social drawing rights' under discussion in continental Europe: accounts that individuals can draw from at their discretion to cover specific costs, such as learning accounts to meet training costs and sabbatical accounts to provide income support in periods of time-off from employment. To what extent would it be desirable to develop a system of more use-specific accounts of this kind alongside the CTF (or, perhaps, instead of it)?

This question lies at the centre of Chapters Nine to Eleven. Anne Alstott, co-author of *The stakeholder society*, a book that did much to stimulate interest in citizen's stake ideas, kicks off in Chapter Nine with a proposal for 'caretaker resource accounts', a proposal developed in her more recent work, *No exit* (2004). Under this scheme, which Alstott initially set out for the US, each caretaker-parent with a child under 13 would receive an annual grant of $5,000. They would be free to spend this on childcare, education, or retirement saving. Alstott argues that this asset-based approach best supports each caretaker's autonomy to plan their life over time, with appropriate state support but minimal state intrusion.

In Chapter Ten, Jane Lewis argues that there are significant limitations to this approach. Lewis questions two related claims that she argues are made by supporters of caretaker resource accounts: first, the alleged importance, possibly superiority, of cash provision relative to services; and second, the opportunities that asset accounts present for exercising greater individual choice. Women's freedom to choose between employment and carework is restricted by the needs and choices of others, Lewis argues. Care accounts would privatise the issue to the individual account holder, who may not otherwise have the power to exercise genuine choice. Lewis argues that while Alstott's proposal might be a reasonable way forward in the specific context of the US, it is unsuitable for Western Europe, where the baseline we start from in care policy is radically different.

In Chapter Eleven, Linda Boyes and Jim McCormick outline some realistic proposals for what continental European policy thinkers would call sabbatical accounts: individual accounts that can be used to give the individual more freedom in distributing working time over their life. The scheme they describe involves banking and buying time off from employers. A similar approach, they argue, could be used to facilitate more flexible working prior to retirement.

In the final chapter, Nick Pearce, Will Paxton and Stuart White provide a concluding overview of the discussion. They develop the point that, in considering possible futures for the citizen's stake, it is vital to clarify one's underlying philosophical perspective or social ideal. They set out some of the different (partly competing, partly complementary) philosophical perspectives that are currently in play in the debate over the future of the citizen's stake. Second, and related to this, they explore in more depth than here the potential relevance of British debates over the future of the citizen's stake to other countries, and the potential relevance of parallel debates in other countries, including France and Germany, to citizen's stake discussions in Britain. Lastly, drawing on the insights of the book as a whole, they discuss a series of immediate policy challenges that confront those wishing to develop further the principle of the citizen's stake.

Part One:
Financing a citizen's stake

TWO

Inheritance tax: what do the people think? Evidence from deliberative workshops

Miranda Lewis and Stuart White

Introduction: context and questions

The Child Trust Fund (CTF) is meant to ensure that all citizens have capital on maturity. As the editors note in the Introduction, since the days of Thomas Paine, proposals for universal capital grants have been linked with proposals to reform inheritance tax (IHT). The idea is to move towards a new system of inheritance in which more of the wealth that passes across generations is socialised via IHT and distributed to all as a 'citizen's inheritance'. So, might an egalitarian reform of IHT today provide a way to develop a more generous CTF?

One apparent obstacle to such reform is public opinion. In a recent poll commissioned by the Fabian Society's Commission on Taxation and Citizenship, 51% of those surveyed agreed with the proposition that 'no inheritances should be taxed' (Commission on Taxation and Citizenship, 2000, table 2.5, p 55). In order to explore public opinion on this issue in more depth, we used deliberative workshops in which a small group of people, chosen as broadly representative of the national population, were brought together to discuss a subject in the light of information and argument provided by facilitators and invited experts. Using the workshops we sought to shed light on four main questions:

1) What are people's initial views about IHT? In particular, what are people's initial views about the fairness of IHT?
2) To what extent (if at all), do views change after a significant period of discussion in which people have been presented with relevant information and exposed to the key normative arguments surrounding IHT?

3) To what extent (if at all) does the proposal to hypothecate IHT for specific spending purposes increase support for the tax or for an increase in the tax? In particular, does support increase if the tax – or a proposed increase in the tax – is explicitly linked to policies like the CTF (as the Fabian Society's Commission on Taxation and Citizenship speculated: Commission on Taxation and Citizenship, 2000, pp 286-7)?

4) If people could change the existing IHT in Britain, what features of it would they alter, and how?

In what follows, we explain our methodology in more depth and describe our main findings. Specifically, section 1 sets out the details of the deliberative workshops. Sections 2-5 present our findings with respect to the four questions listed above. Finally there is a conclusion, with a brief discussion of the implications of our findings for egalitarian tax reformers.

The deliberative workshops

To explore public opinion about IHT we employed the method of deliberative workshops. A clear inspiration here is James Fishkin's work using 'deliberative opinion polls' to explore public attitudes on policy issues (Fishkin, 1995). Like Fishkin, we were concerned that conventional polling data reveals 'what the people think' when people are in an uninformed state, without having given issues significant reflection. A deliberative method allows one to get some sense of how fixed public views are, of the overall potential for change, and of the specific arguments and considerations that both underpin existing viewpoints and that are likely to move existing viewpoints one way or the other. In this way, a deliberative approach can give a fuller, richer sense of the terrain of public opinion on which egalitarian (or other) policy makers have to work.

Each deliberative workshop took place over two consecutive three-hour evening sessions in early 2004. Each had 16 participants recruited by a market research organisation so as to be broadly representative of the British population in terms of social class, gender, ethnicity and age. All participants were paid. Each participant was asked at the start of the first session to answer a survey that included a range of questions about inheritance, IHT, and taxation more generally. To track how (if at all) opinion had changed, they were asked to complete the same survey at the end of the second evening session. In the first session, after completing the survey, participants were asked to say what they knew about IHT and to state any initial views they had about its desirability. They were then presented in turn with information about how IHT works, about the incidence of IHT, and about wealth distribution, and were asked to discuss this information. Exposure to the key normative arguments for and against IHT was then structured by staging a debate between two academic experts: Mark Pennington presented arguments for abolishing IHT, while Stuart White presented arguments for increasing IHT. After the experts had completed their presentations, workshop participants were able to question the experts and discuss the arguments. In the second three-hour session, the following evening, workshop participants reviewed some material from the previous session and then discussed various reform proposals in small groups and in plenary sessions. We conducted two such workshops: one in a northern English location (Stockport) and one in a southern English location (Oxford), on the grounds that differences in house prices in these areas might affect people's views about IHT.

So constructed, the deliberative workshops we employed had two key features in common with a Fishkin-style deliberative opinion poll. First, as in a deliberative poll, we sought to expose participants to information about the policy issue under discussion, and, not least, to the normative arguments on each side of the debate. Second, as in a deliberative poll, we tested opinion before and after deliberation. The main difference with a deliberative poll is the relatively low number of participants in the workshops. The small size of the groups enabled us to follow the discussion very closely and so to get in detail at the attitudes and beliefs underlying people's opinions about IHT. It enabled us to observe their response to specific pieces of information, normative arguments and policy proposals. However, while our surveys did provide some indication as to the fixity of people's views about IHT, the small size of our groups also required that we be circumspect about drawing firm conclusions about the exact shape of public opinion from them (more circumspect than one needs to be with a deliberative poll). The timescale of the workshops is also somewhat shorter than is usual for a deliberative poll, although an effort was made to allow participants time to mull over information and arguments by holding the workshops over two evening sessions, rather than squeezing everything into one session.

Clearly, in a deliberative approach of this kind, the information presented to the participants is very important. The four main arguments presented on each side of the expert debate, exploring the philosophy of IHT, are summarised in Table 2.1.

Table 2.1: Arguments in the expert debate

(A) Pennington's arguments against IHT (preferred policy is abolition)

1. *Who can say what distribution is fair?* The idea of a fair distribution of goods is too ambiguous to be the basis for government policy making. Its contestability makes it a dangerous idea that politicians can manipulate to suit their own agendas. So any arguments for IHT that appeal to notions of fair distribution should be disregarded.

2. *Double taxation.* IHT represents double taxation and is therefore unfair.

3. *Avoidance.* Because it lacks legitimacy, people will try to avoid IHT if they can. Many will succeed, most of all the rich who can afford the best advisers. In practice, therefore, the tax burden will not be shared equitably among people.

4. *Tax on love.* Many people wish to help their children or other loved ones by passing wealth on to them when they die. IHT is undesirable because it taxes people who act in this loving way.

(B) White's arguments for IHT (preferred policy is increase in IHT in part to fund CTF)

1. *Fair start.* Inherited wealth is distributed between people in a very unequal way. But the wealth that people inherit can make a big difference to the opportunities they have in life. To make sure that every young person gets a fair start, we should tax inheritances more than we do now and use the funds to give everyone a decent capital sum on maturity.

2. *Viewpoint of the worst-off.* The people who are worst off under the present system of inheritance are those who receive nothing. If you put yourself in their shoes, and think what it must be like to receive nothing when others receive so much, can you really say that the present system is fair? This evident unfairness would be lessened under a system of citizen's inheritance.

3. *Lack of merit or desert.* Under the present system of inheritance, people who make little useful contribution to society can end up comfortably off if they get a big inheritance, while people who do make a contribution end up worse off if they get no inheritance. Thus, the system weakens the link between wealth and merit.

4. *Family values.* Under the present system of inheritance, people rely wholly on family and friends to get an inheritance. This can put family members under too much pressure to leave an inheritance. It can also lead to some family members manipulating other members by threatening to withdraw a possible inheritance. Both problems would be reduced under a system of citizen's inheritance.

Baseline views about inheritance and IHT

As noted, conventional poll data reports quite a high level of hostility to IHT (Commission on Taxation and Citizenship, 2000, pp 44-56). A comparable level of hostility was reflected in the replies to our first survey. In response to the question, 'Do you think that tax should be paid when someone dies and leaves an estate?', 50% of workshop participants answered with a straightforward 'No'. (This figure is similar to the 51% who agreed that 'no inheritances should be taxed' in the poll commissioned by the Commission on Taxation and Citizenship, 2000.) Of the 32 participants in the workshops, only one person was prepared to give a clear, unequivocal 'Yes' to this question at the start of the two evening sessions. Ten participants gave a more equivocal, 'Depends on estate' as their answer, while a significant number, five, answered 'Don't know'.

The discussion in the workshops provided plenty of clues as to the considerations underpinning this high level of hostility to IHT. Here we group the considerations into three categories: (1) initial perceptions of the fairness of IHT; (2) perceptions of economic self-interest; and (3) important background beliefs about the nature of society and government.

Initial perceptions of the fairness of IHT

In the discussion groups they ran for the Fabian Society's Commission on Taxation and Citizenship, Alan Hedges and Catherine Bromley found that concerns about 'double taxation' played a large part in people's thinking about the fairness of the tax system in general and about IHT in particular (Hedges and Bromley, 2000). This was also a major concern for the participants at the start of our workshops. In both workshops, before any information or arguments had been presented for the participants to reflect on, a number of them quickly came forward with the opinion that IHT is a particularly unfair tax because it represents *double taxation*, and this view was repeated later in the workshops:

> 'We're taxed all the way through our lives, and now what we're going to do is when you're dead, we're going to tax you.' (male, 36, Stockport)

> 'Inheritance tax seems to be targeting the wrong people and it's taxing people twice.' (male, 38, Stockport)

'You're taxed when you earn, save, pay for things, then again when you die.' (female, 21, Stockport)

'We just shouldn't pay inheritance tax as it's a double tax.' (female, 48, Stockport)

'How many times do you get taxed on a salary or wage? You get taxed on work, you get taxed on petrol or clothes – then if you die you get taxed on your property!' (female, 39, Oxford)

Initial perceptions of unfairness were not confined to double taxation, however. Most participants felt strongly that there is something right in being able to transmit advantage, in the form of wealth, to one's children, viewing this as a natural expression of love that IHT constrains or even punishes: hence IHT was seen as a *tax on love*. In the first survey, 22 out of 32 participants agreed strongly with the proposition that 'it is important for parents to be able to pass on their wealth and property to their children, regardless of how well-off their children are', and only two participants disagreed with this. As one participant put it: 'People only want to give a gift to their children to give them a better lifestyle' (female, 60, Stockport).

Participants also invoked notions of *desert* and *entitlement* in their responses to IHT (not distinguishing the two notions as most philosophers would). In part, the thought here seemed to be that if you have earned money legally, then part of its being yours includes the right to give it away as you wish (entitlement). In part, the thought was that the right to give away one's wealth is part of the proper reward for the work involved in building up this wealth (desert). One participant in the Stockport workshop commented on how he wanted to pass on a sum to his children, adding in justification, 'If I've worked hard, why should that be denied?' (male, 36, Stockport). As other participants put it: 'If you work hard you should be able to pass on wealth earned to your kids' (male, 52, Stockport), and 'If you've worked hard all your life it's just wrong to tax you' (male, 29, Oxford).

There was a tendency in both workshops to claim that richer people generally deserve their wealth as a result of hard work (in the Stockport workshop, Richard Branson was cited as a clear example of the deserving rich). In both workshops, there was also a concern that taxation of the wealthy (for example through IHT) is undesirable as it might discourage enterprise. (While philosophers would clearly distinguish this *efficiency* concern from a concern about desert, the two were connected in many participants' minds.)

Perceptions of economic self-interest

As one would perhaps expect, concerns about IHT were also clearly connected with people's perceptions of their economic position and sense of what would best serve their economic interests. In both locations, rising house prices came up as a relevant consideration almost immediately in both groups. When participants were made aware of the threshold for IHT prevailing at the time of the workshops in 2004 (£263,000), this did not strike them as particularly high. Participants quickly suggested that rising house prices would make more estates liable to IHT, and some were concerned that their estates would be more likely to be liable to IHT as a result of this. There was a degree of resentment about this, despite the windfall character of the benefit some people were getting from higher house prices. One participant spoke for many when he said of IHT: 'It's become a property tax on location' (male, 49, Oxford). Some participants also expressed concern that with house prices rising so much, their children or grandchildren would have a hard time getting their feet on the housing ladder. They looked at passing on an inheritance as a way of protecting the interests of their children in this situation: 'People worry more about their mortgages and their futures now – in the old days people could save' (female, 49, Oxford).

A further economic concern that seemed to be influencing opinions was uncertainty about pensions. According to one participant, pension provision today is a 'whole load of jumble' (female, 49, Stockport). 'It's hard for young people to trust pension funds these days', she commented. Another participant: 'Pensions aren't going to pay for old age, the world just isn't like that' (female, 45, Oxford). Given these fears, some older participants looked to an inheritance as a way of providing some retirement security for their children, while participants a little younger looked to the receipt of an inheritance as a way of topping up their pensions.

However, while these economic considerations clearly influenced baseline views of IHT, we did not find that hostility was greater among people from social classes more likely to receive an inheritance. In both workshop groups, those initially willing to defend IHT were drawn from social classes A and B, while the most vocally opposed were from classes C2, D and E. This corresponds with the findings from recent larger surveys that have found that the people least likely to pay IHT are more likely to be hostile to it than people in higher social classes (Hedges and Bromley, 2000; Patrick and Jacobs, 2003). A kind of 'class consciousness' did find voice in the workshops, but this was constructed in terms of a middle-class group getting hit hard to support the less prudent while the very rich managed to escape tax:

> 'The middle bracket is hit hard whatever. The third of people with no savings are the cleverest, those who live on credit, pay the minimum amount and continually increase their credit limit. They have no worry about inheritance tax. It's always the middle bracket affected.' (female, 60, Stockport)

Background beliefs about society and government

In the course of the workshops, it became clear that participants' initial views about IHT were also affected by some general background beliefs about British society and government. Two viewpoints seemed especially prevalent and influential in shaping people's judgements: that government is untrustworthy and/or incompetent (*distrust*); and that basic social relations and public policies can't be changed in a radical way, that social arrangements just are as they are and this should be accepted (*fatalism*). In addition, two other viewpoints seemed to be exerting some influence: that modern society is such that everyone just has to look after themselves and their own family (*individualism*); and, somewhat at odds with the first three perspectives, the viewpoint that taxation and public spending can in some cases provide genuine goods for people (*moderate welfarism*).

The distrust viewpoint was particularly strong in both workshops. A lack of trust in government to use tax monies appropriately underpinned a general aversion to tax. Participants both perceived a lack of control over how tax money is spent, and expressed a lack of confidence in government's capacity to spend tax money effectively. Once again, there is a clear echo of the discussion groups on tax conducted by Hedges and Bromley for the Fabian Society, which identified a stong sense of 'disconnection' from tax in these two respects (Commission on Taxation and Citizenship, 2000; Hedges and Bromley, 2000). There is a clear echo too of findings from the 2002 British Social Attitudes survey on trust in government and public services (Park et al, 2002; Taylor-Gooby, 2004). Typical comments include:

'Supposing we lived in a real democracy, would Tony Blair have been able to spend all that money dropping bombs on Iraq? That's all paid for by the taxpayer – supposing we had the choice as to where it's spent, we have no control, we complain about fascists in other countries but we elect our own fascists.' (male, 52, Stockport)

'You elect a government and then lose control.' (male, 68, Stockport)

'I think the government wastes a lot of money, the NHS wastes a lot on research for the sake of it.' (female, 49, Oxford)

'They want more from us, but we're getting less and less.' (female, 58, Stockport)

Perhaps connected with this strong distrust of government, many participants expressed in the course of the workshops somewhat fatalistic attitudes about the possibility of achieving major social changes:

'Idealism is not practical, you should just leave the money with those that have it.' (male, 67, Stockport)

'You need a government that's willing to tackle the problem. You'd never get a revolution in this country, people are too busy watching Coronation Street, they are more interested in what their football team's doing and how the lottery's going.' (male, 67, Stockport)

'You're living in a dream world. It's not real, is it?' (female, 21, Stockport; addressed to Stuart White's advocacy of a citizen's inheritance).

'There's always going to be a gap between rich and poor, I'm never going to be rich unless I win the lottery.' (female, 48, Stockport)

Some participants expressed a view that contemporary society is individualistic, making it either impractical or undesirable to think in terms of trying to share out wealth more evenly through IHT: 'These days everyone lives for number one and lives for their own – and that's what I want to happen, it should go to my own. That choice shouldn't be made for me' (female, 23, Oxford). As already noted, these viewpoints emerged in the course of the discussion at the workshops, not necessarily at the beginning. However, they might help to explain the relatively high baseline level of hostility towards IHT.

However, at times some participants also expressed more positive views about taxation and public spending. At the Stockport workshop, two participants gave concrete examples early on of how public money had supported them (while remaining suspicious of the amount of taxes being paid). The first, a 36-year-old man, had suffered a stroke and described how he'd received very good and quick treatment from the NHS, while a 21-year-old woman described how as a single mother on benefits she gets help from tax-financed welfare benefits: 'I don't pay tax, I get Working Families Tax Credit, so I get a really good deal out of your money' (female, 21, Stockport).

During the course of the Oxford workshop, some positive views about public spending were also expressed. Given this viewpoint of moderate welfarism, participants were somewhat receptive to arguments about the good that might come from IHT, although this welfarism was heavily qualified by the viewpoints of distrust, fatalism and individualism already described.

How do people's views about IHT develop?

A central aim of the deliberative approach is to explore whether, and how, people's views develop as a result of acquiring more information and balanced exposure to competing arguments. So how did participants' views develop over the course of the workshops?

The aggregate view at the start and end of the workshops

A comparison of the first and second surveys suggests a modest but definite increase in support for taxation in general and IHT in particular. Looking at Table 2.2 below, one can see that 50% of participants were opposed to any taxation of inheritance at the end of the workshops – exactly the same proportion as at the beginning. However, there was also a clear increase in the number of participants willing to give an unequivocal 'Yes' to the principle of taxing inheritance.

Turning to the more general questions about tax, we see an aggregate rise in the number of participants agreeing that higher taxes are a price worth paying for better public services, and a modest fall in the

Table 2.2: Views about taxation and distribution at the start and end of the workshops

(1) Question: *Do you think that tax should be paid when someone dies and leaves an estate?*

	Start	End
Yes	1	9
No	16	16
Depends on estate	10	6
Don't know	5	1

(2) Statement: *'Higher taxes are a price worth paying for better public services.'*

	Start	End
Agree strongly	1	4
Tend to agree	18	22
Tend to disagree	7	4
Disagree strongly	3	2
Don't know	3	0

(3) Statement: *'I pay more tax than I want to.'*

	Start	End
Agree strongly	13	9
Tend to agree	11	11
Tend to disagree	7	7
Disagree strongly	0	2
Don't know	1	3

number agreeing that they themselves currently pay more tax than they would wish. On the other hand, it must be acknowledged that at the end of the workshops there remains a clear majority of firm opponents of the principle of taxing inheritance over firm supporters of this principle (although the majority is cut from 15 to seven). Moreover, so far as taxation in general is concerned, there apparently remains a clear difference at the end, as at the start, between the numbers who support higher taxation in principle (26) and the numbers who seem to be willing to pay more tax themselves (nine).

Specific points and concerns emerging in the discussion

Our surveys provide a snapshot of opinion at the start and end of the workshops, but tell us nothing about the specific points made and concerns arising in the course of the discussion. Here we note some of the more salient points and concerns. We also offer some thoughts on what might have caused the modest shift in opinion noted above.

As they became better informed about the structure of the present IHT system in Britain, some of our participants were struck by what they perceived as the unnecessary complexity of IHT, particularly in regard to exemption clauses and the seven-year rule about gifts. Expressing (and perhaps reinforcing) the distrust viewpoint noted above, some even suggested that this perceived complexity might be a government ploy to obscure what was going on: 'I think the detail is ridiculous....' (male, 68, Stockport); 'They make it so intricate that no one understands, or wants to....' (female, 60, Stockport) and '... they [the government] bore us to tears....' (male, 52, Stockport).

Participants also had strong views on the substance of the exemption clauses. In both workshops there was near universal concern that while wealth transfers between married couples are exempt from IHT, those between unmarried partners apparently are not: 'A lot of people now have common-law spouses and so on, so why hasn't that been changed?' (female, 45, Oxford). Some participants also expressed concern at the exemption for donations to political parties, particularly as this is restricted to parties with representation in Parliament. Again, this feature of IHT was framed in terms of, and possibly reinforced, the distrust viewpoint described above.

An important feature of the workshops was the effort to engage participants with the key normative arguments surrounding IHT. A number of Pennington's arguments clearly echoed ideas that the participants themselves had brought into the discussion prior to the expert debate. Pennington's arguments that IHT is unfair because it represents double taxation and a tax on love were both received sympathetically by the two groups. Pennington's point about likely evasion also struck a chord, particularly as data presented earlier in the workshop concerning the incidence of IHT was interpreted by many participants as evidencing evasion by the very rich, reinforcing the sense of unfairness to the 'middle bracket'.

On the other hand, most participants were not persuaded by the strongly egalitarian conception of fairness that motivated White's arguments for an increased IHT linked to a citizen's inheritance. Most participants viewed equality of opportunity as impractical and possibly not even desirable:

'It wouldn't be good if everyone was born the same way.' (female, 49, Oxford)

'I disagree, we do need to worry about the haves and have nots.' (female, 23, Oxford)

'... two babies aged two don't have the same opportunities [so there's not much point trying to make opportunities equal]....' (male, 67, Stockport)

'... society has different levels of wealth, it should stay like this.' (female, 25, Stockport)

This is not to say, however, that participants were unconcerned about the plight of those with very limited opportunity. But the prevailing sense of justice was 'sufficientarian' rather than egalitarian: what matters is *adequacy*, rather than *equality*, of opportunity.

White contested the desert-based defence of inheritance by arguing that inheritance can break the link between contribution to society and reward. However, this argument was not very compelling to participants. Confronted with this argument, participants in effect replied that it is the family rather than the individual that is the relevant unit of reward when it comes to wealth. Hence, wealth should be permitted to stay within families as they have worked to deserve it.

Egalitarian redistribution of inherited wealth was also seen as potentially unfair because it could lead to the hard-working and thrifty subsidising the life-styles of other lazier, less thrifty people. If one has worked hard to save for one's children, why should this wealth be taxed away to assist the children of other families in which people have squandered their income? This viewpoint was associated with the perception of unfairness towards middle-income groups that, as noted above, emerged quite early on in the workshop discussion.

'I know someone the same age and background as me who lived life to the full and always spent their money. But we decided to buy our own home. They're still living in a council house and getting free spectacles and so on, and you're telling me I should pay more tax to pay for them? ... I would hate to see another child disadvantaged, but I don't see how I should pay tax all my life for another child as well.' (female, 68, Oxford)

'There are too many spongers in this country - taking everything and giving nothing.' (male, 45, Stockport)

Nevertheless, as we have seen, in the aggregate, opinion did shift over the course of the workshops in a direction that was more favourable to IHT. Why might this have occurred?

A first possibility is that participants may have initially been more familiar with the normative arguments against IHT, over the two evenings they may have come to weigh these against other arguments, for IHT, that they were initially less familiar with. Someone might start off viewing IHT, considered in the abstract and in isolation, as unfair. But when they then consider what might replace it, or what spending might be cut to pay for its abolition, they might see abolition of IHT as also risking unfairness, and so might come round in favour of IHT on this basis. At least one of the comments below (female, 23, Oxford) can be read in this way. A second possibility is that discussion of hypothecation in the second session of the workshops (see this page) might have helped to give participants a more positive feel for what could be done with the revenues from IHT that, in turn, made them more supportive of the tax itself. It is possible that this discussion might have worked to temper the underlying viewpoints of distrust and fatalism, and to strengthen the moderate welfarism that was also apparent in participants' comments from an early stage.

A third possibility is that the viewpoint we have described as fatalism ultimately worked to bring some people round to IHT, albeit somewhat reluctantly. Fatalism easily shades into a conservatism from which standpoint *any* idea for radical change – whether it be to increase IHT to pay for a generous citizen's inheritance (as proposed by White), *or* to abolish IHT (as proposed by Pennington) – seems unrealistic:

> 'They'd have to find the 2.4 billion elsewhere [if we abolished IHT].' (female, 23, Oxford)

> 'In an ideal world I'd like to abolish it, but it's better than finding 2.4 billion from other taxes. I'm still in two minds.' (female, 49, Oxford)

> 'Initially I thought you should abolish it, but then had concerns about the 2.4 billion, I wouldn't want people to be hurt by stopping what comes from a few.' (female, 23, Oxford)

> 'I'm definitely more accepting of the need for it now.' (male, 29, Oxford)

Does hypothecation increase support for IHT?

Does the baseline hostility to IHT reduce if IHT is explicitly linked to specific expenditures? In particular, do people become more supportive of IHT if it is linked to policies such as the CTF? Table 2.3 reports the responses to the first and second surveys on the basic hypothecation issue.

Table 2.3: Views on hypothecation at the start and end of the workshops

(1) Question: *Do you think it's a good idea to target the money raised by IHT to spend on particular public services?*

	Start	End
Yes	21	24
No	7	4
Don't know	4	4

(2) Question: *Would you be more willing to support higher IHT if it were put aside to spend on a particular area of public services?*

	Start	End
Yes	10	19
No	16	9
Don't know	6	4

As we see, a substantial majority favoured the basic idea of explicit linkage to specific spending purposes, a majority that increased slightly over the workshop sessions. However, perhaps more interesting is the aggregate shift in declared willingness to support a higher IHT if it were hypothecated to a specific, preferred spending purpose. In the first survey, those saying 'No' to this question were in a clear majority over those answering 'Yes' (16 to 10). But in the second survey, the clear majority was with those answering 'Yes' (19 to nine). In the discussions, representative comments on this topic included:

> 'I might be more inclined [to support IHT] if I knew it was going on something, but at the moment where's it all going? If the government says where it's going perhaps you'd be more inclined to pay it?' (female, 58, Stockport)

> 'I don't believe we should be taxed but if it were to go to good causes then I've not got a problem with that at all.' (male, 36, Stockport)

> 'In principle I'd agree [with a hypothecated increase], but I'd need figures.' (female, 49, Oxford)

> '… I think people accept taxes much more readily if they can identify where the hypothecation is….' (male, 57, Stockport)

That said, the two groups differed somewhat in their views about hypothecation, with the Stockport group more supportive than the Oxford group, perhaps because there was someone very vocal and articulate (male, 57) in favour in the Stockport group. Hypothecation addresses directly the issue of distrust in government, but in the Oxford workshop the distrust viewpoint was so strong that people were distrustful of hypothecation itself: 'The question [in the survey] asked if the money should go towards something specific. I wrote down that we'd never know if they did it' (female, 39, Oxford).

As Maxwell points out in the following chapter, such a suspicion of hypothecation is not necessarily misplaced. Moreover, even if there is majority support for a hypothecated increase in IHT, this does not mean much if people cannot agree on what the extra IHT should be spent on (also a point raised against hypothecation in the Oxford group). In the workshops, we presented the participants with three options for hypothecation: the CTF; early-years support policies akin to Sure Start; and long-term care for older people.

In the expert debate, White argued for a linkage between increased IHT and the CTF. He argued that by taxing inheritance more and using the proceeds to fund policies like the CTF society could assure every young person an adequate 'citizen's inheritance'. Appealing directly to the ideas of political theorists like Bruce Ackerman and Anne Alstott, he claimed that: 'At a time when young people could launch their life ... every young person would have real freedom to decide what to do with their lives. Our present inheritance system doesn't give us that' (White, in discussion, Stockport).

Confronted with this argument, judgements about the CTF itself differed somewhat between the Stockport and Oxford groups. The Stockport group was basically favourable to the CTF, viewing it as a potentially useful way of expanding opportunity: in a vote at the end of the workshop, 11 supported the CTF with three against and two undecided. That said, there was considerable concern about how some young people might use their accounts irresponsibly (perhaps especially from participants from social classes C2, D and E). Comments from the Stockport workshop included:

> 'Stuart's principle is fantastic, but one person would buy a pen and another will buy a gun.... Giving people cash is not a good idea....' (male, 38, Stockport)

> 'If you give the money out to just anybody some people would just go the pub. We need to put the money into education.' (male, 36, Stockport)

'Until I was 24 I would have blown the money. What restrictions should be in place to prevent this?' (female, 24, Stockport)

'I don't like the idea of just giving people money.... But I like the idea of helping all young people.' (male, 17, Stockport)

On the other hand, other participants expressed their views: 'It's only a small group who would not use it constructively' (male, 57, Stockport), and 'You have to take a risk to help the youngest people' (female, 58, Stockport).

Grappling with these concerns, participants in the Stockport group considered a range of ways to increase the likelihood that the capital grant would be well used, including linking the grant to sound business plans, to investment in housing, and complementing it with financial education: 'We need teaching, in school, how to invest, we're not taught anything like that ... we're not taught how to spend that money.... You're not taught how to live' (male, 38, Stockport).

The issue of responsible use was also very strong in the Oxford workshops. Indeed, while the bulk of public opinion research on the CTF and similar policies shows people generally supportive of the policy, in this specific workshop the responsible use concern was so strong that it seemed to sink support for the policy altogether: 'If you give 20K to 18-year-olds the roads would be full of BMWs' (male, 39, Oxford), and 'You can't make a child grasp an opportunity – they might get in with the wacky baccy' (female, 68, Oxford). Concern was also expressed about 'giving something for nothing' or 'giving money for nothing' (male, 20, Oxford and female, 21, Stockport), and about the value of any likely capital grant based on the CTF: 'What can you get for £18,000 these days?' (female, 23, Oxford).

Given this lack of enthusiasm for the CTF as a policy, the Oxford group was, unsurprisingly, unsupportive of linking an increase in IHT to this policy. The reservations voiced in the Stockport group perhaps explain why they too were less enthusiastic about linking an IHT increase to CTFs compared to the other policies. While academic political theorists who advocate CTF-style policies find the link with IHT perfectly logical, seeing them as two aspects of a new model of socialised inheritance, the participants in these workshops did not find the link at all intuitive. The fatalism viewpoint was also evident here, in comments such as:

'I like the idea of the Child Trust Fund, but I can't see it working. It's better to get rid of inheritance tax.' (female, 40, Stockport)

'Stuart's idea is nice, but it's not very realistic....' (male, 17, Stockport)

'Who's gonna give you 20 grand? It's pathetic, it's just an absurd thought. If your parents are rich then, 'Wahoo!', if they're not, then, 'Shit happens'.' (female, 21, Stockport)

The proposal to link IHT reform with early-years support met with greater approval in both groups, reflecting a general view about the relative superiority of securing adequate opportunity through the development of human capital rather than through financial capital. However, by the far strongest support was for linking IHT reform with spending on long-term care for older people. Long-term care was picked up by both groups as an issue that needs urgently addressing, with a lot of concern about the use of means-testing to decide who receives state assistance. Moreover, in this case, many participants thought they did see an intuitive connection between the nature of the tax and the nature of the spending commitment. A number of participants argued that it is older people who pay IHT, hence it is only fair that the revenue be used on something that benefits them: 'I believe in early-years support, it's a bloody good idea, but if old people are paying inheritance tax it seems fairer that the elderly should benefit' (female, 49, Oxford); and 'The elderly tend to pay most inheritance tax so it really should benefit them' (male, 29, Oxford).

Views on other reform proposals

The workshops provided an opportunity to explore participants' views about other reform options for IHT. Options discussed included: changing the threshold above which IHT is paid; changing and/or tapering the rate at which IHT is paid; moving from a tax on estates to a tax on capital receipts. Participants were also asked to consider the issue of avoidance.

On the question of changing the threshold for IHT, views were, of course, strongly affected by participants' views about the basic desirability of IHT. Concern over recent increases in house prices led some to argue that the threshold should be raised, and this was certainly the majority view. However, by the end of the workshop a few participants in each group were prepared to defend a policy of lowering the threshold so as to increase the overall yield from IHT. For those in favour of raising the threshold, a figure of around £400,000 to £500,000 drew a lot of support. Those in favour of lowering the threshold tended also to support the introduction of a lower starting rate of IHT.

On the issue of IHT rates, there was very little support for the current system of a flat rate of 40% over the threshold. Opinion was fairly evenly split between those who supported a shift to a tapered system in which the rate would be higher for larger estates, and those who supported a shift to a lower flat rate – possibly paid on all inheritances if the rate were low enough. In the absence of figures showing the likely effects of alternative reforms on yields, however, views on this topic were tentative. Comments on the related issues of thresholds and rates included:

> 'If you've got an inheritance, depending on your situation, 100 [ie 100,000] is plenty, and anything above that should get taxed on it at a tapered level. The way it is at the moment, I think that 100 [100,000] is plenty to receive.' (female, 21, Stockport)

> 'If this [tapering] would be fairer then perhaps there would be less avoidance.' (male, 68, Stockport)

> '... a lower starting threshold and a taper would be better. A flat rate of 40% is thought of as penal therefore people try to avoid it.' (male, 57, Stockport)

Among tax experts, there has long been support for the idea of shifting from a tax on estates to a tax on capital receipts (Meade, 1964; Sandford et al, 1973; Commission on Taxation and Citizenship, 2000; Nissan and Le Grand, 2000; Patrick and Jacobs, 2003). Thus, individuals might be allowed a certain lifetime quota of capital receipts, and then face taxation on all gifts and inheritances above this quota. We found a degree of support for this idea. In the Stockport group especially, most thought this would be a fairer system in principle. On the other hand, taxing the recipient was seen as harder to administer, particularly in relation to lifetime gifts. Opinion was also divided as to whether a capital receipts tax would create an effective incentive to transfer wealth to the disadvantaged, and, if so, whether creating such an incentive was actually desirable:

'I'm thinking it might be possible to persuade people to spread their wealth more widely, ie, to leave smaller sums so you might leave it all to your grandchildren as well as your children. Certainly people will do that to avoid paying the tax.' (male, 57, Stockport)

'Surely when you're writing your will you give it to who you want to give it to.' (male, 29, Oxford)

'Aren't we getting away from the fact that the person that's died, they're leaving it to their children that they've treated equally…. If you start to say, 'Well, I'll give you three thousand of that because you're not earning as much as your brother', aren't you splitting a family?' (female, 48, Stockport)

Some participants, particularly in the Oxford group, also felt that a capital receipts tax is inherently wrong because it means that in providing someone with a gift one automatically creates a tax burden for them: 'It's wrong. It's like giving a 15-year-old a gift and then saying, 'By the way, I want 40% back'. So it's not really a gift' (female, 39, Oxford), and 'It's like something you've got on your shoulder permanently….' (female, 48, Stockport).

Finally, there was also some discussion of the issue of avoidance of IHT. While participants generally agreed that this was regrettable in principle, they did not wholly agree that action should be taken to close 'loopholes' and prevent avoidance: 'This is difficult to achieve but in principle it should be done' (male, 57, Stockport), and 'It will just increase the amount of civil servants needed and will waste more money than it will save' (male, 68, Stockport).

Conclusion: lessons for egalitarian tax reformers

According to the political scientist, Robert Goodin, IHTs are 'the 'third rail' of tax policy – touch them, and you are dead, politically' (Goodin, 2003, p 70). Our research indicates that there is indeed a high level of baseline hostility to IHT in Britain, a hostility connected not only with perceptions of economic self-interest but with latent ideas about fairness and influential underlying viewpoints about the nature of government and society. However, opinions are not wholly fixed. At the end of the workshops, after discussion of relevant facts, normative arguments, and of possible ways of spending the funds from

IHT, opinion had shifted modestly towards greater support for IHT, although the shift *was* modest and from a starting point of strong opposition to IHT.

Thus, while a little deliberation does not convert people into egalitarians supportive of socialised inheritance, we do not think egalitarian tax reformers should despair. So far as the short to medium term is concerned, egalitarian reformers can use our findings to try to anticipate the main concerns likely to be excited by modest proposals for egalitarian reform of IHT. Aside from the basic desire to be able to pass wealth on to one's loved ones, these include: the perception of double taxation; rising house prices (which may be perceived by a homeowner as a source of insecurity for their children as much as a windfall gain to themself); and the uncertainty of pension provision. Against a background of distrust in government, our findings support the thesis that earmarking the revenue from any IHT reform to specific purposes is a means of building support for reform, although people's priorities for earmarking might differ from those who support the idea of a citizen's stake. If policy makers were to press a connection between IHT reform and an expanded citizen's stake, then our findings suggest that they would probably also have to address the concerns about responsible use of the CTF that emerged in our workshops (and which are echoed in Gamble and Prabhakar's research described in Chapter Seven). In addition, we found people to be somewhat receptive to the idea of shifting to a tapered system of IHT rates, and it might be possible to design a shift to a tapered system in a way that simultaneously addresses concerns about IHT related to rising house prices *and raises* more revenue. This possibility is explored by Dominic Maxwell in Chapter Three, together with the ideas to move to a tax on capital receipts, and other policy options. Beyond this, there are clearly some reforms, such as changes to the spousal exemption clauses to include unmarried partners, that would be very popular and which do fit with egalitarian values (although this type of reform would reduce the tax yield from IHT).

Looking to the long term, the distrust and fatalism viewpoints we have identified suggest a widespread cynicism about political life that is hardly compatible with stable support for an activist, equality-promoting state. To make radical advance over the long term, proponents of asset-based egalitarianism may need to think about how reform of our basic structures of governance could counter these feelings of futility and alienation.

THREE

Towards a citizen's inheritance: reforming inheritance tax

Dominic Maxwell

Introduction

Tarnished by emotive phrases, labelled the 'death tax' and 'the tax on love', inheritance tax (IHT) has become the bogeyman of British taxes. Add a link to house prices, the favourite topic of certain British newspapers, and a regular place in the headlines seems assured. But, like the bogeyman, many of the flaws of IHT are more talked about than real, and contain a large dose of myth and misunderstanding. This chapter argues that we need to defend the principle of a strong IHT, while at the same time recognising that there are some genuine problems with the current system. We must address the two together: to defend a strong tax, we need to reform its errors; to reform its errors, we must defend its principles. In reforming IHT, it may also be possible to raise modest revenues for an expanded citizens' stake such as the Child Trust Fund (CTF)

Debate on the future of IHT is active and aggressive. At its gentlest, reform is led by the Treasury, steadily closing loopholes, introducing new rules to prevent avoidance, and, in the pre-election budget of 2005, increasing the threshold. Raising the temperature slightly, the Fabian Society's Commission on Taxation and Citizenship in 2000 proposed that the formal incidence be shifted from the estate to the recipient – this is discussed in Section 2 of this chapter, at p 43. In August 2004 the headlines were briefly filled by the preliminary publication of this paper, suggesting that IHT should be banded in a way similar to income tax. The press commentary, dividing relatively clearly between left and right, showed again that IHT provokes interest far beyond its size in terms of revenue or number of taxpayers. It demonstrated a clear appetite for reform, but also that the cost of opening the debate may be to unleash abolitionist forces that would otherwise remain dormant. At its most aggressive, argument on IHT was taken up by the Conservative Party ahead of the 2005 general election, and put at the centre of the party's tax-cutting proposals.

America's phasing out of estate tax, as part of George W. Bush, Jr's 2001 tax package, has added a sense of momentum to reform. With Canada, Australia and New Zealand also having abolished it, Britain now feels unusual among developed English-speaking nations. But we are not alone. Ireland retains a strong capital acquisition tax, as does Japan and many European nations including Germany and France. The Bush tax cuts of 2001 are frequently held to be unfairly and irresponsibly skewed towards the rich. On IHT, as in other ways, they are not something to which Britain should aspire.

The current system in the UK is a 40% tax on every £1 of estate over £263,000 (2004-05), but there are important exemptions and additions. First of all, the *net estate* is calculated by taking away debts and funeral expenses, and adding in a percentage of certain gifts that were made up to seven years before death (with the rate depending on how long ago they were given). Certain *exemptions* are also removed from the net estate, including charitable donations, 'heritage assets', agricultural land, unquoted shares and anything inherited by a surviving spouse. If after all this the net estate after exemptions is less than £263,000, no tax is paid. If the net estate after exemptions is worth £263,000 or over, 40p tax is charged for every £1 that exceeds the threshold. As mentioned above, the threshold at which IHT becomes payable was increased in the 2005 budget to £275,000 in 2005-06, £285,000 in 2006-07 and £300,000 in 2007-08.

Structure of this chapter

The rest of the chapter is laid out as follows. The first section starts with the basics: why should we defend the principles of IHT? Given that defence, why should we reform the details? Section 2 presents some major options for reform: either replacing the tax on estates with a tax on capital receipts, or creating bands, with higher rates for larger estates.

Qualitative research, presented in this volume by Lewis and White, suggests that earmarking IHT could increase support for it. Section 3 explores this argument. After summarising the theoretical arguments for and against earmarking, it examines the case for linking any increased revenue directly to CTFs. Finally, there is a conclusion, identifying questions for future research.

Defend and reform

Why tax inheritance?

Periodic cries from the right call for 'euthanasia for death duties' (Bracewell-Milnes, 2002), but IHT should be defended. A strong case can be built on the grounds of efficiency, stability and fiscal neutrality; on powerful egalitarian arguments; and on the nature of a bequest.

We should tax inheritance to reduce the burden of other, less desirable, taxes. If IHT were abolished, other taxes would have to rise in response, and these would distort other incentives in more damaging ways. Income tax can penalise work, and VAT penalises spending and thus earning, but the distortionary impact of IHT is thought to be smaller.

Exactly how much smaller depends largely on the motive for bequests (see Masson and Pestieau, 1997, for a survey of the literature). To the extent that bequests are 'accidental' – the result of savings held as a precaution by older people and intended primarily for that purpose – then the taxation of inheritance can in theory have a zero efficiency cost. In other words, there is no excess burden or substitution effect, which together reduce the efficiency of taxes. Several facts suggest that accidental bequests are common, and donors are not motivated solely by the desire to improve the welfare of their heirs: there is a strong need for precautionary savings, given an uncertain length of life and uncertain health costs; how an estate is split does not normally take account of inheritors' different incomes, whereas gifts during the lifetime do, and the distribution of wealth within extended families is highly dependent on the distribution of income within that family. Thus extended families are not a single unit, with resources shared selflessly within them. This is certainly not to say that all bequests are accidental. But 'accident' is a sufficient motivation that a strong IHT should be levied as part of a broad tax base, allowing lower marginal rates, more stability and less artificial distortion of incentives.

An alternative way of viewing the argument for a broad tax base is to see IHT as a way of deferring lifetime taxation until death, and so allowing people to use their assets rather than sell them. Pensioners, for example, can continue to live in their own houses. Higher consumption tax, income tax, capital tax or user charges (such as for long-term care) would all reduce their living standards in a way that IHT does not. Thus there are good administrative reasons for taxing inheritance. There are also convincing egalitarian arguments.

Inheritance and wealth are very unequally distributed. IHT is a small but important counter-balance. The gini coefficient, a measure of inequality that gives total equality a score of zero and total inequality a score of one, marks the distribution of wealth as twice as unequal as income, at 0.7 compared to 0.35 (Inland Revenue, 2005, table 13.5). Only some of this can be explained by the distribution between age groups, and what is worse, the situation appears to be deteriorating: the gini coefficient of wealth has been rising steadily since 1992, and the percentage of wealth held by the richest 1% increased from 18% to 23% between 1992 and 2002 (Inland Revenue, 2005).

Inheritance adds to the problem. One study of America suggested that 35-45% of total wealth has been inherited (Davies and Shorrocks, 2000, quoted in Blumkin and Sadka, 2003), and Britons who inherit the most are likely to be the richest (Banks et al, 2002). Against this background, IHT can only ever make a small difference. But it is still important. IHT acts as a once-a-generation wealth tax, marginally reducing the transmission of inequality.

Property rights are weakest when wealth has been inherited, so tax on inheritance is more legitimate than on other forms of wealth. If one accepts that the right to control one's property is fundamental (as, for example, John Locke), then all taxation is to that extent unsatisfactory. But IHT is the least unsatisfactory, because one's right to property ends at death. Theorists from William Blackstone (1942 [1769]) to Thomas Jefferson and Tom Paine, among others, have argued that government therefore has a right to regulate transfers of property from the dead to the living (see also McLean, Chapter Five).

Why reform IHT?

So, if IHT is worth preserving, why should we reform it? The public opinion research by Lewis and White revealed a large degree of hostility towards IHT, but some of this was incoherent or based on misunderstandings. For example, many initially objected to the idea that it takes 40% of the entire estate, rather than 40% of the extra pound above the threshold. The tax was accused of penalising the average homeowner, when in fact only 3.5-4% pay any IHT at all (Inland Revenue, 2005, Introductory note, C14; table 12.3, note). Many people objected to IHT as a 'double taxation', because much of the estate may have been taxed when it was earned – although unrealised capital gains and, in particular, gains from house price inflation will not have been previously taxed. Certainly, no tax will have been paid by the person who receives the bequest. Even when IHT is double taxation, that does not mean it is a bad thing. Sales tax, for example, is also double taxation. In order to achieve a broad tax base, wealth is already taxed many times as it passes through the system, including when it is earned, saved, or spent. A system with low marginal taxes at many points is more stable, fair and neutral to incentives than one that has only one point of tax, but at a very high rate.

One of the criticisms that was damaging, and forms the first of our headline goals, is that IHT is increasingly hitting the 'wrong' people, being effectively optional for the super-rich. Complaints were also made that IHT imposes a greater burden than other taxes. The third goal, which motivates not just this chapter but much of the book, is to release more funding for a larger citizen's stake. All three headline goals are elaborated below, as well as some economic and administrative criteria for reform.

IHT could be more progressive. A 'progressive' tax is one in which the proportion of income or wealth that is taken in tax increases with income or wealth: the rich pay a larger slice of their inheritance. In this technical sense IHT is already progressive, but it could and should be more so. Simply to be progressive is a low standard, and is satisfied whenever the marginal tax rate is above the effective tax rate. That is always true if there is a nil-rate band followed by an unchanging rate of tax. In the case of IHT, the first £263,000 is exempt, so the tax rate over the whole estate will increase as estates rise, but never quite reach the marginal rate of 40%.

Nevertheless, more progressivity is an important objective of reform because of tax avoidance at the top, and fiscal drag at the bottom. The use of trusts, lifetime gifts and careful planning allow the very wealthy to avoid a large tax bill. Meanwhile those of more moderate wealth – either unaccustomed or unable to use the same loopholes – are caught in the net. If your main asset is your family home, you cannot give it away before death, and trading down to a smaller house imposes a large transaction cost.

At the bottom, the number of taxpayers has increased through fiscal drag: the tax-free threshold is indexed to consumer inflation, rather than growth in the stock of wealth or in house prices. Between 1994 and 2004 the threshold increased by 75%, while house prices increased 150% (HBOS, 2004). A more progressive IHT would therefore place a heavier burden on the very wealthy who are comfortably over the threshold, and a lighter one on reasonably wealthy homeowners. It is worth remembering, however, that the poorest IHT-payers are still far from poor: an estate of £263,000 is considerable, even given recent house price increases. An ideal IHT would also be progressive in the sense of encouraging progressive behaviour and recognising progressive ideals. Thus we might expect IHT to promote wider asset ownership and recognise same-sex as well as married couples.

IHT should minimise the welfare cost to taxpayers. Not every pound of tax is as painful to pay. Minimising the welfare cost should be of interest to any benevolent tax reformer, but is doubly important in the emotive and politically sensitive case of IHT.

In the interim publication of this chapter (Maxwell 2004), reforms were proposed that could ease the burden of IHT when it is most onerous. Recipients of a family home could be allowed to postpone payment of the tax until the home is sold, particularly in cases of unmarried partners and long-term dependants of the deceased, such as adult but severely disabled offspring. There may also be room for improvement in the probate process, to allow bereaved relatives more time to grieve without worrying about a tax bill. These ideas are not discussed further here, but large-scale reforms would gain wider public support if they were accompanied by improvements to the collection process.

Finally, an ideal IHT would raise more revenue. Even as wealth inequality is rising, the Inland Revenue estimates that only 6% of the total value bequeathed per year is taken in tax. Furthermore the contribution of wealth transfer taxes to the total tax revenue has fallen from 2% in 1971 to 0.65% in 2001 (OECD, 2003a, quoted in Duff, 2004). At first glance, this seems like a possible way to raise money for policies that will spread asset ownership and the life-changing opportunities that go with it.

The overall aim, then, is a more progressive, amenable and lucrative IHT: a bigger pill that is easier to swallow. These political aims must be combined with administrative and economic ones. The most important of these are 'horizontal equity', which states that similar people should be treated in similar ways; 'vertical equity', or treating relevantly different people in different ways; and minimal distortion of incentives (see Atkinson and Stiglitz, 1980; and Kay and King, 1990).

Options for reform

We now have our criteria. How can we meet them? The two major possible reforms of IHT would be to replace it with a capital receipts tax (CRT); or to introduce a progressive banding structure.

Replace tax on estates with tax on inheritance

What we call IHT is not really a tax on inheritance at all: it is really an estates tax, calculated and levied on the total estate, regardless of who inherits it. A true tax on inheritance could take account of the individual circumstances of the legatee.

The proposal is not new. John Stuart Mill, in 1848, argued that a strongly progressive tax on inheritances would help erode 'enormous fortunes' by creating the incentive to spread wealth more widely (Mill 1970 [1848]). The Institute for Fiscal Studies (Sandford et al, 1973), and more recently the Fabian Society's Commission on Taxation and Citizenship (2000), argued in favour of a tax based on the amount received, also including gifts during the lifetime – a capital receipts tax (CRT). The exemptions and rate of tax paid would depend on the cumulative total of gifts received by the individual over their lifetime, with no tax on the first £80,000, rising to a 40% rate after £240,000. Since 1976 Ireland has had a similar scheme, the capital acquisition tax. Tax is levied on recipients rather than donors, with the tax rate dependent on the relationship between the donor and the recipient.

In theory a similar change in Britain could reduce tax avoidance and clarify a key principle of IHT, as linking tax to the recipient suggests that this is the taxation of unearned income, rather than accumulated wealth. More importantly, it could close the biggest loophole facing British IHT: the very wealthy are able to dispose of a large proportion of their assets during their lifetime. They avoid tax completely if they do so seven years or more before death. As already noted, those with more moderate wealth are generally unable to take advantage of this because they rely on their assets for housing, security, or income.

But whether the new system would produce a more even distribution of inheritance, as suggested, is not clear, and this goes to the heart of the CRT proposals. Would people choose their legatee for tax reasons? Hard evidence is scarce, but the response in Institute of Public Policy Research (ippr) deliberative workshops was unequivocally discouraging. Patrick and Jacobs, in 2003, suggested that CRT 'might in theory lead to donors leaving their wealth to a larger number of people ... [but] evidence from tax practitioners suggests that donors' behaviour is unlikely to change' (p xiv). This is certainly the opinion of John Battersby, a KPMG tax partner who analysed the proposals in the same volume. What one might expect is that the incentive would change behaviour most when the donor is almost indifferent between two possible recipients, such as children versus grandchildren. The

CRT could then encourage assets to skip a generation, so that people receive inheritances earlier in life.

Either way, a CRT would impose an additional burden on both the Inland Revenue and individuals. All taxpayers would be required to retain detailed records of gifts received, keeping a running total *even if* they are well below the level at which the tax would start. For administrative reasons, it may be necessary for individuals to retain complete gift-by-gift records, rather than just a running total: the Inland Revenue must be able to check declarations, and checks would then range over the entire history of receipts, rather than just the most recent. Finally, the tax on gifts is harder to justify than a tax on inheritance, and should not be seen as equivalent. In the case of gifts, the tax *would* have a significant effect on incentives, and the arguments based on the nature of property rights after death do not apply.

A CRT that excludes lifetime gifts is possible, and is already in place in Japan. One system might be for each individual to be able to receive £100,000 tax-free from each estate, and any inheritance after that would be treated as marginal income and taxed accordingly. This would mean that IHT rates would track income tax rates, with a similar banding structure. As a benefit, the extra administration of tracking lifetime gifts would be removed, and the large incentive to divide estates would remain, with potentially progressive results. The social waste associated with the tax could reduce, as avoiding tax may be easier to do by splitting the estate rather than hiring accountants and solicitors who could be better employed elsewhere. On the downside, lifetime gifts would still provide easy tax avoidance for the very wealthy, and total tax revenue could fall considerably. People who are the sole inheritors of a large estate would lose, as they would have a much lower tax-free threshold: if the personal allowance is set at £100,000, then a sole inheritor of £263,000 or more would pay £65,000 extra tax.

This analysis is mostly negative. We cannot rule out a beneficial and desirable CRT, and more research is needed, in particular on the effect on yield and the possibility of a CRT that does not include lifetime gifts. But the arguments presented so far suggest that an effective CRT would be a difficult challenge. In particular, a CRT on lifetime gifts should not be seen as a reform of IHT, but a new tax on a different category of activity. The medicine may be worse than the disease.

Introduce bands

Breaking IHT rates down into different bands is one of the simplest of possible IHT reforms. It could have a big impact. While it is the average tax rate that is reflected in the cheque sent to the Inland Revenue, the most visible summary of the tax is the marginal rate. It was to this that most people referred in the deliberative workshops organised by ippr and Oxford University.

What would a banded IHT look like? The unpopularity and misunderstandings of IHT, and the rising number of taxpayers, suggest that it should be loosened at the bottom if its future is to be secured. But equally, the robust egalitarian reasons for taxing the transmission of inequality, and the increasingly unequal distribution of wealth, among other reasons, suggest a higher tax rate could be desirable for very large estates.

So the basic rate should be kept at 40%, but an easier starting rate should be adopted at the bottom, and a tougher one at the top. Thus the first part of a large estate would be charged at 0%, the next part would be charged at a starting rate of, say, 30%, the middle at 40%, and the top slice at, say, 45%. Only the largest estates would be big enough to reach the top band, and many would be charged only at the starting rate.

The limiting factor for a top rate is that a high marginal rate drives tax avoidance. This has traditionally been taken to mean that the tax rate should be low and the base broad, but the distributional consequences of applying this to IHT, not to mention the tax's unique role in addressing inequality, makes that inapplicable. A 20% IHT with a low tax-free allowance would give vast gains to multi-millionaires and sizeable losses to the majority. It would do a worse job at combating inequality, not a better one.

Some possible bands are shown in Table 3.1 below, with their estimated effect on revenue. The first set has been designed to be revenue-neutral to within £10 million. The second set gives a small increase, but just enough to justify the tax by linking it to a popular spending programme (see section 3). The final set raises several hundred million pounds each. The bands given refer to the size of the estate *after* the deduction of the tax-free allowance, which was £263,000 in 2004-05, and £242,000 in 2001-02 (the most recent year for which data on estate sizes are available).

We can take some general points from the examples above. The concentration of estates towards the bottom means that changing the rate has a greater effect on yield the closer it is to the starting rate. So, for example, cutting the rate from 40% to 30% for the first £40,000 costs £80 million, but the cost of applying it to the next £40,000 is only £62 million. The size of the band is doubled, but the cost increases by only three quarters.

Table 3.1: Some ideas for banded IHT

Starting rate/ top rate (%)	Lower band	Upper band	Revenue change
No significant change in revenue			
A. 22/45	22% on chargeable estate below £25,000	45% on chargeable estate above £500,000	– £3 million
B. 22/50	22% on chargeable estate below £25,000	50% on chargeable estate above £1 million	+ £4 million
C. 30/50	30% on chargeable estate below £25,000	50% on chargeable estate above £2 million	– £7 million
Small increases in revenue			
D. 22/45	22% on chargeable estate below £25,000	45% on chargeable estate above £200,000	+ £67 million
E. 22/50	22% on chargeable estate below £25,000	50% on chargeable estate above £300,000	+ £167 million
F. 30/50	30% on chargeable estate below £25,000	50% on chargeable estate above 500,000	+ £132 million
Larger increases in revenue			
G. 22/60	22% on chargeable estate below £25,000	60% on chargeable estate above £500,000	+ £274 million
H. 30/60	30% on chargeable estate below £25,000	60% on chargeable estate above £300,000	+ £472 million

Notes: 1. Estate figures refer to *chargeable* estate, not net estate. That is, they refer to the net estate after the deduction of the nil-rate threshold. In 2001-02 this was £242,000, so the first £25,000 of chargeable estate would be from £242,000 to £267,000. In 2003-04 the threshold was £263,000. 2. All packages assume a middle rate of 40%. 3. For source data and method of calculation, see Appendix on pp 52-3.

A corollary of this is that the gain from increasing the top rate is much less than the cost of an equivalent tax cut at the bottom, so most packages generally sound more aggressive than they are. To increase the yield by £500 million, approximately enough to pay for the entire CTF programme with top-ups at seven, would require a top rate of 60% starting £300,000 above the nil-rate threshold. Given the large drawbacks of such a rate – the high incentive to avoid taxes, the political pressure, the huge cost to some individuals – it seems very unlikely that IHT on the very wealthy can pay for a much-expanded citizen's stake.

So very large increases in yield are implausible, but it is possible to make changes that more than counter-balance the changes at the bottom and provide modest extra resources: packages D, E and F increase the yield by £67-167 million.

It is worth looking at these three in more detail. Introducing a 22% rate on the first £25,000, would save estates up to £4,500, and introducing a 30% rate would save up to £2,500. Because of this saving on the first part of each estate, the point at which estates become worse off as a result of the banding structure is well above the point at which the higher rate starts: packages D, E and F would increase the tax bill for net estates worth more than £538,000, £587,000, and £767,000 respectively. This uses 2001-02 figures. The figures for 2004-05 would be £21,000 higher, but data on the distribution of estates for this year is not yet available so the changes in yield cannot be calculated. These break-even points, where a tax saving turns into a tax loss, are illustrated in Figure 3.1.

Figure 3.1 also shows how the tax bill changes much less at the bottom than at the top. This poses a difficult problem: if the yield to the state is more sensitive at the bottom, but the bill to the individual is more sensitive to the top, then any revenue-neutral banding will produce many small winners and a few big losers. The problems of coordinating a large group may mean that the small group of losers is better able to assert itself (Olson, 1965), particularly when, as in this case, they are likely to be among the wealthiest in the country.

Which package is preferable?

Given that the reasons for introducing a lower rate are partly symbolic and psychological, removing the false notion of a 40% effective rate, it seems preferable to introduce a lower rate in a shorter band, rather than a higher one for longer. The rate of 22% has a strong magnetism. Using the same rate as income tax would help people to frame inheritance as windfall income, the taxation of which is thus comparable to income tax. It also gives a reasonable gain to smaller estates: almost 20% of estates that pay IHT would pay only the starting rate, and their tax bill would fall by 45%. Those people whose estate falls in the 40% category would save exactly £4,500, with the size of this group determined by what point the higher rate starts. If the top rate starts £300,000 after the first threshold, then 7% would save £4,500; if it starts £500,000 above, then 11% would.

At the top, the psychological effect of breaching 50% may be considerable, and making it much higher than that would put it out of line with the rest of the tax system. The package with a top rate of 45%, however, is unable to raise sufficient sums of money for a citizen's

Figure 3.1: Winners and losers under a banded IHT

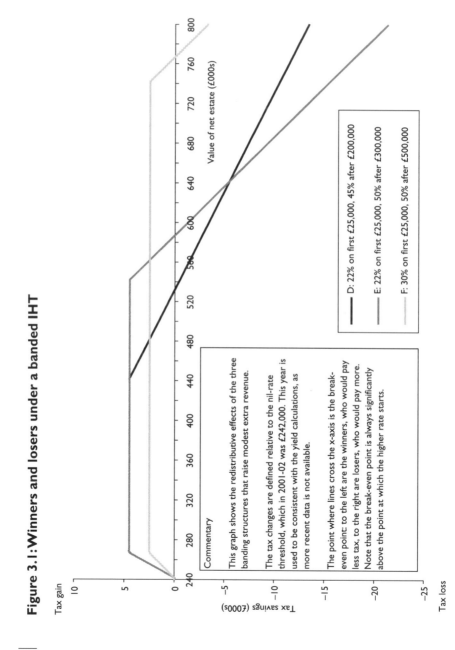

stake. Package E gives an excellent compromise. The first £25,000 of chargeable estate would be charged at 22%, and after £300,000 the rate would be 50%. Using 2001–02 figures, 5,000 estates (21%) would be worse off, as they would be larger than the break-even point of £587,000 after debts and allowances.

This package is a modest, progressive change to IHT. It could increase public support and revenue in one go. It gives an easy 'win' to middle-income groups, and lays in place a structure that, if desired, could be incrementally tightened through fiscal drag. It is modest, but effective: it is strongly recommended.

Spending it: should we earmark IHT?

Reforming IHT to pay for a citizen's stake may be more successful if the two are explicitly linked. Evidence from the deliberative workshops showed that earmarking IHT for a particular purpose can substantially increase support for it, and for revenue-enhancing reforms.

But earmarking tax is a dangerous thing. On the one hand, it can help reconnect taxation with expenditure, win popular support for new revenue streams, and make funding appear transparent (Mulgan and Murray, 1993). On the other hand, there is no reason to suppose that an earmarked tax will provide the optimal revenue: a depressed tax base can prevent sufficient expenditure, and a buoyant tax base can result in waste. Furthermore, the fungibility of tax revenue means that earmarking can be illusory. Over time, it becomes harder to provide a counter-factual that shows a certain tax increase has provided more revenue for a certain expenditure programme. Unless that programme is funded entirely by the hypothecated tax, it becomes impossible to provide a benchmark.

So, strict hypothecation is only advisable when the tax pays entirely and only for that spending programme, and there is a clear link between the amounted needed and the amount that can be raised – as in the case of the BBC licence fee. An *increase* in tax can never provide this clear relationship, so instead the link could be an informal earmarking; a way of explaining why the tax is increasing, rather than a way of deciding how much to spend. Given our starting objectives – remaking the case for a strong IHT, and if possible raising more revenue for a citizen's stake – there appears to be a good case for it.

First, linking an IHT increase to the CTF is administratively appropriate: there is a very clear baseline of pre-tax rise expenditure, a well-defined spending programme and relatively easy public auditing and accounting. The size of the revenue raised roughly matches the size required, although this does depend on how ambitious a citizen's stake should be. The total package of reforms proposed above would raise up to £167 million, which would provide every child with an additional £175, and £350 for the poorest 40%. After 18 years of investment, this would grow to £385 and £770 respectively, using the Inland Revenue illustrative assumption of 4.5% real growth.

This would tangibly expand the impact of CTFs, but it could not provide for the more radical increases, such as the £10,000 proposed by Nissan and Le Grand (2000). As discussed above, such sums cannot plausibly be raised from increasing IHT on large estates. Importantly, there is also a good intuitive link between IHT and CTFs, as both programmes are based on the notion that wealth should cascade down the generations a little more equally. Again, however, this is not entirely without problems. The qualitative research by Lewis and White gave a poor reception to arguments based on inheritance as a social construct, and to the very idea that inheritance currently transmits inequality and disadvantage. The fair unit of analysis was thought by most to be the family, rather than the individual, so that any distribution between generations should not be of concern to the state. The interim publication of this chapter did propose that the two should be linked, but in the public discussion that followed it became clear that the newspapers and commentators most hostile to IHT were also the most hostile to CTFs. The problem may be that the link between IHT and CTFs is actually *too* strong: they share some of the same premises, so a rejection of IHT is likely to imply a rejection of CTFs, and the one can never convince a sceptic of the need for the other. A less political cause, such as long-term care for older people, may do more to increase the popularity of IHT (but see Maxwell, 2004, for a discussion of why long-term care in particular may be problematic).

Linking the CTF with IHT reform is thus attractive, but the reforms proposed will not provide the level of resources hoped for by more ambitious advocates of a citizen's stake. Linking the two must also overcome the serious stumbling block of weak public support.

Conclusion

Introducing progressive tax bands, with a starting rate of 22% and a top rate of 50%, would spread IHT more fairly; would benefit 79% of tax paying estates and would raise about £170 million for a citizen's stake. Paying for a more radical expansion through the top rate of IHT could be done only through very severe increases in the rate.

A CRT, on the other hand, would not necessarily encourage a more equal distribution of estates, would impost extra compliance and collection costs, and should be seen not just as a reform of IHT, but as a new, additional tax on lifetime gifts. Adopting an inheritance-based tax rather than an estate-based tax could be desirable, and in many ways would be easier to justify, but would fail to address the tax avoidance of lifetime giving.

On the spending side, the CTF could be linked to reforms of IHT. It would help spread ownership of wealth more widely, and the idea of socialised inheritance provides an intellectually robust link between tax and revenue. However, it could not provide enough revenue to finance a very large expansion of a citizen's stake, and the deliberative workshops run by Oxford University and ippr show that public support for these ideas cannot be assumed.

Together these reforms would produce a fairer, more progressive IHT. They would help address complaints that IHT primarily targets those with moderate wealth – enough to be above the tax-free allowance, but not enough to use tax-avoidance tools. At the same time, these reforms would help contribute to a more equal distribution of wealth. They are modest changes, and deliberately so, but they show that a more progressive structure is possible and desirable.

Some broader questions for discussion remain.

Rescuing a CRT. Tax-free lifetime gifts are the biggest loophole in IHT. Is there a way to tax these, while avoiding the problems of the Fabian CRT? Should we move from an estate-based system to an inheritance-based system without including lifetime gifts? Should we look at an annual tax on the value of trusts, as in Ireland?

IHT by stealth. Could the introduction of new bands in IHT ease the way for a future tightening of the thresholds? If that is what we want, is this the best way to go about it?

House prices and regional variation. Rising house prices give a windfall to homeowners. Does this mean we should tax it more, or, because homeowners' income and other wealth are moderate, should we tax it less? The regional diversity in house prices introduces another element: an Inland Revenue Exercise in 2001 and 2002 revealed that 40% of taxpayers, accounting for half of IHT, reside in London and the southeast (Inland Revenue, 2005, table 12.6). How, if at all, should IHT respond?

Linking reform of IHT with a new spending programme. Earmarking a tax may provide only a temporary increase in its support. This being so, are we ducking the argument if we use a spending programme to reform IHT? Would it be braver, and more successful in the long term, to make the case for IHT directly?

IHT and charitable giving. What new incentives could be created to encourage bequests to charities?

Appendix

Table 3.2: Chargeable estate by band: estates notified for probate, numbers and tax by range of estate for years of death (2001-02)

Range of net estate (lower limit) (£)	Total net value of estates passing on death (£)	Value of estates passing on death after deduction of reliefs and IHT threshold (£)	Number of estates passing on death after deduction of reliefs and IHT threshold
0	28.2	8.4	1,951
10,000	430.2	36.9	2,177
25,000	609.6	62.3	1,946
40,000	449.7	40.6	903
50,000	615.3	62.6	1,134
60,000	1,378.9	121.7	1,741
80,000	1,643.1	128.6	1,432
100,000	9,703.5	684.8	4,747
200,000	6,354.7	550.5	2,241
300,000	3,703.3	486.7	1,407
400,000	2,451.6	407.3	913
500,000	1,774.3	346.7	633
600,000	1,244.6	318.1	491
700,000	1,014.3	267.9	360
800,000	871.6	225.3	266
900,000	714.7	154.3	163
1,000,000	2,082.1	627.7	521
1,500,000	1,277.0	333.1	196
2,000,000	4,238.3	1,027.9	282
Total	40,585.1	5,891.4	23,501

Source: Inland Revenue

Table 3.3: The effects on revenue of changing IHT (£ million)

	Tax cuts (by upper limit)				Tax rises (by lower limit)		
	0.22	0.3	0.35	0.4	0.45	0.5	0.6
Upper/ lower limit (£)							
0				0	295	589	1,178
10,000	−40	−22	−11	0	283	567	1,133
25,000	−95	−53	−26	0	268	536	1,072
40,000	−145	−80	−40	0	254	509	1,017
50,000	−175	−97	−49	0	246	492	983
60,000	−204	−113	−57	0	238	476	951
80,000	−256	−142	−71	0	223	447	893
100,000	−303	−168	−84	0	210	421	842
200,000	−475	−264	−132	0	163	325	650
300,000	−588	−327	−163	0	131	263	525
400,000	−668	−371	−186	0	109	218	436
500,000	−728	−405	−202	0	92	185	369
600,000	−775	−430	−215	0	79	159	317
700,000	−811	−451	−225	0	69	138	277
800,000	−840	−467	−233	0	61	123	245
900,000	−863	−479	−240	0	55	110	219
1,000,000	−882	−490	−245	0	49	99	198
1,500,000	−945	−525	−262	0	32	64	129
2,000,000	−977	−543	−271	0	23	46	93

Notes: Table 3.2 was used to generate Table 3.3. For tax cuts at the bottom, the formula used is:

[(change in tax rate)

x (value of net estates not exceeding the upper limit after deduction of reliefs and IHT threshold)]

+ [(change in tax rate) x (value of upper limit) x (number of estates exceeding the upper limit)]

For tax increases at the top, the formula is:

[(change in tax rate) x (value of estates exceeding the lower limit)]

− [(change in tax rate) x (lower limit) x (number of estates exceeding the lower limit)]

FOUR

Using stakeholder trusts to reclaim common assets

David Bollier

Introduction

Most private wealth is owned by a fraction of the population, prompting one wag to lament that the trouble with capitalism is that it does not create enough capitalists (Gates, 1998). How can a genuinely popular form of capitalism be created? Inheritance tax (IHT) is clearly an important tool. But in this chapter I argue that we should also look to a more imaginative and equitable management of what I call 'common assets' as a route to greater equality.

Common assets are a class of resources that have been created collectively or naturally, and so, morally speaking, are the property of all citizens collectively. Many are now being privatised by business or mismanaged by government, or both. If new revenues could be drawn from these common assets, they could generate new streams of non-wage income for the average citizen. The funds would improve the economic security of millions of citizens and reduce gross inequalities of wealth.

This chapter elaborates both the basic idea of common assets and the mechanisms to manage them to benefit the ordinary citizen. I argue that the preeminent mechanism for using and preserving common assets is the *trust*. The corporation competing in the market tends to favour short-term, economic exploitation of resources. Government tends to have its own political and financial limitations as a steward of common assets. By contrast, the trust is a time-tested legal mechanism for assuring that the interests of beneficiaries are adequately protected. It should be adapted and expanded to serve the commons. *The commons* is a generic term that refers to creations of nature and society. They are freely inherited, collectively used and shared, and held in trust for future generations. Many of these are natural resources such as the atmosphere, agricultural seeds, fresh water supplies, wildlife, ecosystems and the humane genome. Other commons are socially created resources such as national parks, academic communities and public spaces.

While any innovations in the use of common assets will require some leaps into the novel and untested, there are many compelling precedents and models that can be built upon.

The importance of common assets

Politicians and economists have long assumed that there are really only two sectors of power and value: markets and the state. Markets are supposed to be the vehicle for economic progress while government is supposed to take care of everything else. Increasingly, however, it is becoming clear that the commons is at least as important to our well being.

Because common assets are naturally or socially created, the sector is (ideally) typified by social governance for the benefit of the general public or specific social communities. They tend to be open and accessible to the relevant community, often for free. The management goals are not those of the market, which rely upon private property rights and contracts in pursuit of profit. The commons also has different dynamics than the democratic state, which is generally too large, bureaucratic or politicised to manage resources responsively. The commons refers to a more direct, social and sometimes informal governance of a shared resource, especially those that we wish to endure from one generation to the next. A large literature about management of the commons has developed over the past 15 years, focusing especially on commons management of natural resources in developing countries (Ostrom, 1990; McCay and Acheson, 1996; Burger et al, 2001; plus the websites of the International Association for the Study of Common Property at www.iascp.org, and the Digital Library of the Commons at http://dlc.dlib.indiana.edu).

My focus here is on a particular subset of the commons that I call *common assets*. Not all the resources of the commons are to be considered as marketable assets. Resources are more often shared and distributed in their 'natural' state, rather than as a 'market value'. A scientific community, for example, does not exchange its research findings based upon a market price or contracts, but rather through a complex set of social and ethical protocols. An indigenous tribe that assigns irrigation rights to its members does not 'sell' water, but rather allocates it based on social considerations. Nonetheless, some common resources can be treated as marketable assets without harming the community that has a claim on the resources.

John Locke famously asserted that the moral justification for appropriating something from nature as private property is the labour value that a person expends in making it useful (Locke, 1960 [1682]). But proponents of this theory often fail to acknowledge an important proviso that Locke added: that (in a pre-monetary world, at least) appropriation is justified only where 'enough and as good' is left for others. The neglect of this proviso in practice has not been good for the commons. Essentially, Locke's labour theory of property has been used to justify private market appropriation of natural wealth while minimising or ignoring the impact on the natural resources that we share. The companies that use or deplete the air, water, soil, fisheries and wildlife do *not* leave them intact for others, but deplete them for private gain.

To talk about the commons, then, is to reassert the value of common resources, over and above any market valuations of them. It is to raise the question that perhaps the market is not the most responsible steward of the resource over the long term. Historically, government has been the countervailing force to intervene when markets overstep ecological or ethical boundaries. Government often acts as a public trustee for public resources. It often funds public goods such as schools and libraries because markets are generally incapable of funding such resources.

Unfortunately, government is often an unreliable and even corrupt steward of common assets. It is also a notoriously reluctant funder of many public goods. It is all too common for public assets to be used to subsidise companies and to bolster the power of government or politicians. For example, government often gives companies cheap, direct access to oil and minerals, or the rights to government-funded scientific research. Revenues from broadcasters who buy the right to use the airwaves may or may not benefit the people.

That is why it is useful to distinguish *public assets* from *common assets*. The former are resources that the government owns and manages, ostensibly for the benefit of the people. The latter are resources that belong to the people, and can never be truly owned by government. The distinction between government-owned property and 'the people's property' goes back to Roman law, which recognised that some property belongs to the government and some inherently belongs to the people (Wilkinson, 1989; Dowie, 2003). The air, the human genome and fresh water are common assets that do not belong to the government. By their very nature, these resources belong to all of us, and should never be privately owned by corporations or mismanaged by government.

In the US, there is a common-law doctrine of environmental law called the 'public trust' that carries on this tradition in Roman law. The public trust doctrine holds that the unorganised public is the sovereign owner of certain resources, and that government has no authority to seize or give away such resources (Sax, 1970). The concept has a particular resonance in the American political system, which is predicated on the preeminence of 'We, the people', as the Declaration of Independence puts it, and not on the supremacy of government authority.

Talking about common assets instead of public assets serves two important goals: (a) it underscores the fact that the people, not the government, are the rightful owners and beneficiaries of certain assets; and (b) it associates these assets with the indispensable third sector of life – the commons – which is distinct from government and the market. The taxonomy for understanding the commons is still evolving. Still, it is possible to identify some basic classes of commons:

1) *Zero-use commons.* Some resources are fundamentally changed and diminished in value if they are opened to commercial development. Wilderness areas are an example. By social agreement, therefore, we declare that certain commons are inappropriate places for marketplace activity and should not be used in any irreversible or depletable ways.
2) *Infinite-use commons.* Some commons can be used to an infinite degree without a degradation or depletion of their resources. Cultural commons such as literature or the internet are examples. They are infinitely extensible and face no physical limits on their use. The goal in these commons should be to encourage maximum use, because the more people are participating, the greater the value likely to be created.
3) *Partial-use commons.* Many natural commons can be used to some extent without depleting the resource. Usage cannot be infinite, but neither does it make sense to ban all usage. *Some* usage is ecologically and socially acceptable. We therefore allow timber to be cut from forests, but not so much that it destroys the local ecology. We allow the electro-magnetic spectrum to be used by a finite number of broadcasters, but not so many that it would cause signal interference.

Another important analytic distinction that should be made about commons is whether their resources should be exploited as revenue sources. Should the resources of a commons be alienable for market use, or should they be kept intact? In talking about common assets, we accept the judgement that certain shared resources are appropriately alienated for 'export' to the market. Answering the question of what should be alienable is a matter of moral judgement, social consensus and political debate. It is possible to imagine different societies coming to different conclusions about which of their resources should be considered private property or convertible into money. In any case, the answers will say a great deal about the identity of that society and the ideals of human development that they endorse.

Using common assets to address inequality

If a resource can be assetised in an ecologically and socially benign way, we should explore the best institutional vehicles for doing so. We should adopt a basic principle: that any monetary value should be captured for public use and shared with as many citizens as possible. Cash value should not be diverted for private gain without a corresponding public benefit.

British economist James Robertson, a cofounder of the New Economics Foundation, calls this strategy 'pre-distribution' and contrasts it with 'redistributionist' policies. He writes:

> Whereas redistribution aims to correct the outcomes of economic activity after the event, predistribution shares the value of essential inputs to economic activity. Whereas redistribution is dependency-reinforcing, predistribution is enabling. Because it addresses the underlying causes of economic injustice, inequality and exclusion, predistribution is an essential feature of a prosperous economy in an inclusive society. It reverses the private 'enclosure' of common resources on which so much conventional economic development has been based – and still is. (Robertson, 2000, p 10)

Corporations have a long history of expropriating the commons and then privatising the surplus gains for themselves (The Ecologist, 1993; Bollier, 2002). Certainly, most industrialised nations have bravely tried to ease some of the resulting hardships through the welfare state. But in societies based on the supremacy of the market, welfare programmes are often reviled and politically vulnerable. Government funding is frequently portrayed as a 'subsidy' that distorts the 'free market'. Or it is cast as a morally tainted 'giveaway' that erodes people's 'work ethic'.

The virtue of a common assets approach is that it restores some measure of equity to commoners without becoming entangled in the familiar politics of 'redistribution'. The moral burden is shifted. The politics of the commons is about ordinary people reclaiming what rightfully belongs to them. By asserting collective ownership over their common assets and sharing the dividends, citizens do not need to recoil in shame that they are receiving a 'government handout'. They are proudly claiming dividends due to them as a civic entitlement. Such dividends provide citizens with a valuable, regular supplement to wage income, enhancing their personal security and enabling them to 'invest in themselves' through education or entrepreneurial ventures.

The benefits of predistribution from common assets are especially important to today's young people and, odd as this may sound, babies. As Bruce Ackerman and Anne Alstott have shown in their book, *The stakeholder society* (1999), one of the preeminent obstacles facing young people is acquiring the capital to finance their education or start a business. The burdens of debt on young people can be crushing, which means that those children who come from affluent families and inherit money have much greater opportunities (Koerner, 2004). Inequity replicates itself from one generation to the next, and indeed grows worse. That is why it is certainly encouraging to see the British government implementing Child Trust Funds (CTFs) as a fresh approach to this problem.

In general, common assets represent a politically attractive financial base for a new set of universal grants. However, there is a danger, as mentioned earlier, that our enthusiasm for new revenue sources could drive policy makers to over-exploit fragile or depletable natural resources. This is why the *institutional governance* of common assets is so critical. Equitable benefits and long-term preservation must be twin goals in managing common assets.

The stakeholder trust and the commons

In thinking about how to manage a common asset and distribute its revenues, our first reflex might be to assign such responsibilities to a government agency. Indeed, government tends to be the default trustee of the public's resources. But the history of government stewardship of common assets should give us pause. Government regulation is fraught with the deep, enduring problems of politics, bureaucratic (mis)management, secrecy, and barriers to democratic participation. Many of these are structural issues, not isolated problems of agency leadership or under-funding. This is not to reject summarily government as a potential steward of common assets, but rather to raise the question: are there superior alternatives? In many instances, I believe there are.

The nonprofit *trust* is a time-tested institutional structure that could be adapted to manage a great many common assets in effective, accountable ways. My colleague Peter Barnes argues that if the corporation is the preeminent institution of the market sector, the *trust* is the preeminent institution of the commons (Barnes, 2001, 2003). The main arguments for trusts as an alternative to government stewardship are the following:

1) Government has been the default trustee of common resources for several hundred years and has clearly failed to protect the assets in question, much less assure that stakeholders receive the benefits owed to them.
2) Sound government policy making and regulatory enforcement have been irredeemably corrupted by profit-maximising corporations.
3) While stakeholder trusts could conceivably be corrupted as well, their institutional structure has stronger safeguards. Specifically, trusts are explicitly charged with preservation of the asset and trustees have clearly defined fiduciary responsibilities. In trusts, decision making is more transparent and accountability more easily enforced than in government.
4) Finally, trusts have a more focused mission than government. This makes it easier to see where revenues and expenditures are going, which improves financial accountability. Government simply has too many complex, intermingled revenue streams for the general public or the press to monitor. Government also has so many complex tasks to perform at once – scientific research, administrative coordination, the political brokering of interests, law enforcement, and so on – that corporations with political clout are far better positioned to advance their own interests at the expense of citizens'.

Trusts with well-defined missions are less likely to suffer from these problems. They have distinct beneficiaries who have a keen self-interest in monitoring a trust's performance and clearer legal standards for responsible performance. The most familiar forms of trusts may be *preservation trusts* where the goal is to preserve the integrity of the asset over time for the benefit of the named beneficiaries. An excellent example is the National Trust, whose basic mission is to preserve the natural resources of the British people in perpetuity. It is the trustee for more than 200 historic homes, 612,000 acres of countryside, and 600 miles of unspoiled natural coastline.

In the US, land trusts are a popular vehicle for preserving forests, farmlands, beaches and other priceless natural resources. Two of the leading private land trusts in the US are the Nature Conservancy and the Trust for Public Land. There are also agricultural land trusts, which buy conservation easements from farmers to prevent development of the land, preserve the countryside and bolster the farm economy. At the local level, community gardens are a form of trust that rejuvenate neighbourhoods and let city dwellers enjoy gardening.

Preservation trusts are generally not structured to generate revenues, but rather to preserve the asset and ensure fair access and use of it. But if the goal is to generate non-wage income streams for citizens, the *stakeholder trust* offers an excellent vehicle for doing so.

In the US, state land trusts generate revenues from the more than 150 million acres that they administer. Much of this land is leased for timber, grazing or oil production, with revenues going to public schools. One example is the Texas Permanent School Fund, which gives the proceeds from oil and gas leases on submerged Gulf Coast lands to local schools. The overall sums generated from these lands are huge. In 1996, 22 states earned $3 billion from the leasing of 135 million acres of land (Watt, 1999, p 16). At the national level, the Land and Water Conservation Fund has used revenues from offshore oil and gas leases to acquire about seven million acres of wilderness, park land and open spaces, and to fund development in more than 37,000 state parks and recreation projects (see the home page of the Land and Water Conservation Fund at www.nps.gov/lwcf).

One of the more ingenious revenue-generating trusts is the Music Performance Trust Fund, which was formed in 1948 through an agreement between the recording industry and the musicians' union (see the home page of the Music Performance Trust at www.mptf.org/home). Musicians who played in live performances were worried that the expansion of recorded music would weaken the musical communities that nurture and sustain musicians. Under the agreement, a small percentage of record sales goes into a fund that pays for free concerts in schools, parks and hospitals, as well as for musical appreciation and education programmes.

Perhaps the biggest, most successful stakeholder trust is the Alaska Permanent Fund, a state-run investment savings account that pays equal annual dividends to every Alaskan citizen; in 2005 each citizen received $845.76. The fund was established in 1976 by a voter-approved amendment to the state constitution requiring that at least 25% of revenues from certain minerals on state lands go to the trust (see the home page of the Alaska Permanent Fund at www.apfc.org; see also Hickel, 2002). Much of the fund's revenue has come from oil drilled on the state's North Slope.

A noteworthy benefit of the fund's dividends, beyond their egalitarian distribution, is the economic fillip to the Alaskan economy. Instead of oil revenues being siphoned away by outside investors, the fund's dividends are used largely within the state, and so have a multiplier effect on the state's economy. In May 2004, the market value of the fund's investments was nearly $27 billion, making it one of the 100 largest investment funds in the world.

In designing trusts, it is important that they be structured to assure accountability to stakeholders. Besides requiring the utmost openness in deliberation and reporting, the creators of any trust must decide:

1) Who are the stakeholders/beneficiaries of the trust to which it should be accountable?
2) Who shall appoint the trustees?
3) What procedures and standards shall govern the activities of the trust?
4) Where do the trust's revenues come from?
5) What is the distribution formula for the trust's dividends (if revenue distribution is a purpose of the trust)?

The proper beneficiaries of most common assets ought to be the general citizenry, or the members of a defined community. Trustees could be appointed by the top elected officials or they could be elected by beneficiaries, but in any case they must have clear fiduciary responsibilities to stakeholders. The founding charter should stipulate the criteria and procedures for making decisions.

The Sky Trust as a model

The idea of harnessing common assets to generate revenues inspired Peter Barnes's ingenious idea to establish a 'Sky Trust' to generate revenues from the 'scarcity rent' of the sky. The scarcity is the sky's limited capacity to absorb carbon-based pollution. The potential rent to be earned from this scarcity would come from 'propertising' the sky and auctioning off the right to pollute specific units of carbon-based emissions. By assigning property rights to the waste–absorbing capacity of the sky, a new revenue stream can be created.

Congress took a small step in this direction in 1990 when it established a 'cap–and–trade' system for sulphur dioxide emissions, the chief cause of acid rain. The government set a steadily declining 'cap' on how much overall pollution could be emitted. Power plants were then given tradeable rights authorising them to emit sulphur dioxide into the atmosphere. This gave power-plant owners the discretion to use their free rights to pollute, or to sell them to others for a price and pocket the cash.

While this system of 'pollution rights' has been remarkably successful in forcing companies to reduce pollution in efficient ways, it contained a terrible flaw. It gave away the rights to pollute to companies for free. It assumed that existing polluters should pay no price for polluting a natural resource that, after all, belongs to all of us (Barnes, 2001; see also www.skytrust.org). But we all own the sky, and we all should be able to reap any financial benefits that may be available from giving property rights to polluters.

That is where the Sky Trust idea comes in. Barnes proposes that polluters be forced to *pay* at auction for their rights to pollute, with the money deposited into a stakeholder trust owned by all citizens. Every citizen would get one share. To assure that all citizens would benefit indefinitely, shares would not be transferable, but be associated with citizenship itself.

The Sky Trust model makes compelling economic sense on many levels. It forces polluters to pay a price for dumping wastes into the commons, and so encourages them to find innovative ways to reduce their pollution. In the short run, this is likely to raise the price of carbon-based products. But the Sky Trust also has the economic virtue of *returning* to consumers the extra money that they spend on carbon-based products, and in an equitable way: those who conserve fuel will recoup a greater proportion of their fuel expenditures than those who drive large, inefficient vehicles. As Barnes notes:

> Stakeholder trusts tied to waste sinks can penalize us when we pollute and compensate us when we are polluted upon. They can treat us as both sinners and victims, and keep track of the proportions, incrementally penalizing bad behavior and rewarding good behavior. In short, stakeholder trusts can be used to achieve two ends simultaneously: preservation of nature and greater equity among humans. (Barnes, 2001)

Developing a common assets strategy in Britain

How might a common assets agenda get started and gather pace in Britain? Fortunately, there are some precedents for using public policy to generate revenues from common assets. The biggest success story may be auctions for licences to use the airwaves for broadcasting and wireless services. The Radiocommunications Agency has determined that the value of the spectrum to the UK economy as a whole is more than £20 billion a year, and over 2% of the UK output. The use of auctions to wring maximum value from the airwaves was a singular innovation of the 1990s in both the US and the UK.

The sums deposited into the government treasury from these auctions are an important step toward reclaiming common assets. But it is worth enquiring how far the people really benefit from the sale of property rights in spectrum. There may be more efficient, remunerative or democratically appealing ways of capitalising on the spectrum. For example, as Yochai Benkler argues, the citizenry's interest in innovation, access to the spectrum and free speech interests may be better served by using the spectrum as a commons (see www.benkler.org/Pub.htm#Spectrum).

Natural resources are another type of common asset that British policy makers might wish to use to generate new revenues. The Alaska Permanent Fund may be the best guiding example. *Financial Times* columnist Samuel Brittan proposed in the late 1970s that state revenue from North Sea oil should be earmarked for citizen dividends that could be capitalised on the stock market (Brittan, 2003). Unfortunately, this opportunity was squandered.

But there are other opportunities. As well as a tax on land value, explored by Iain McLean in Chapter Five, it is worth exploring the potential of tapping into the scarcity rents of waste sinks – the Sky Trust model. The economic logic is compelling; the equitable distribution of revenues is attractive; and industrialised nations will need to take effective action sooner rather than later to curb carbon emissions. Why not inaugurate this new model now and learn how it might be replicated to address other types of pollution? In the US, a version of the Sky Trust proposal has been introduced in Senate legislation sponsored by Senators McCain and Lieberman. While it is not likely to pass during any Bush administration, support for it continues to grow, especially as national governments and corporations begin to take global warming more seriously.

One of the most innovative proposals for capturing revenues from common assets comes from German sociologist Joseph Huber and

British economist James Robertson, cofounder of the New Economics Foundation. Their 2000 report, *Creating new money*, notes that the British government has essentially forfeited the authority – and revenues – that come from issuing new non-cash money into circulation (Huber and Robertson, 2000). While the government pays for manufacturing banknotes and coins, banks are the more significant player in creating money by their ability to make interest-bearing loans, the cornerstone of their profits.

The right to issue new money, called 'seigniorage', was traditionally the right of monarchs and local rulers. But today, about 95% of new money in the UK is issued by private commercial banks, not governments. By failing to capture revenues from seigniorage, the British government loses an estimated £47 billion a year, Huber and Robertson estimate. Commercial banks enjoy 'a hidden subsidy in the shape of special, supernormal profits of the order of £21 billion a year in the UK. The government's abdication of the authority to create new money costs the public treasury the equivalent of an extraordinary twelve pence on income tax in the UK', they claim. 'In effect it has become a subsidy to the private banking sector – a nice little earner, but one that should always have been for public benefit rather than private gain' (Huber and Robertson, 2000).

Huber and Robertson urge that central banks should create the amount of new non-cash money and credit it to government as public revenue, which it will put into circulation by spending. Banks would function as credit brokers, essentially financial intermediaries. The case for seigniorage reform is a novel, unfamiliar departure, but it is intriguing and deserves consideration.

In a similar vein, it is worth contemplating how the taxpaying public might reap some revenues for its role in maintaining public financial markets. Taxpayers pay for the administrative agencies and judicial bodies that allow public markets to operate and be trustworthy. What is the value of this common asset? One indication is the premium that accrues to the investors and underwriters when a privately held company goes public through an initial public offering (IPO) of stock. This premium stems from the ability of the corporate asset to be turned into cash – made liquid – much more readily.

But this liquidity premium is not generated by the company itself, or from the chief executive officer, but from society – specifically, from the public stock market and the entire infrastructure of government, financial institutions and media that backs it up. Yet the people who profit from an IPO are private shareholders, who get large capital gains, and underwriters, who get fees. Why shouldn't taxpayers get a slice of the action – say 5% – which could be placed in a public trust resembling a mutual fund? Shares could be assigned to every citizen, along the lines of the Alaska Permanent Fund.

Conclusion

It is hoped that this chapter can begin to energise a larger set of players to move a common assets agenda forward in Britain. It is a fresh idea with sound economic backing and potentially enormous political appeal. It offers a feasible agenda for reducing inequalities of wealth without sparking familiar controversies over 'redistribution'. Certainly, many policy details must be worked out, but the overarching vision is clear and promising. Breaking the future challenge down, we can identify four key challenges:

1) Develop a commons discourse that reframes the political debate away from 'income redistribution' to a focus on reclaiming common assets.
2) Determine which commons are suitable for some form of assetisation.
3) Craft mechanisms to protect the long-term health of a given resource and allow efficient market use while assuring that the full benefits accrue to citizens.
4) Organise political campaigns to wrest control over common assets from government and markets and assign them to commons-friendly institutions such as trusts.

FIVE

Land tax: options for reform

Iain McLean

Introduction

This book aims to explore how the Child Trust Fund (CTF) might be developed in future, and, more generally, how a new, more egalitarian politics of ownership might be advanced. I shall assume that policy makers would like to progress beyond the modest CTF introduced in the UK 2004 budget to a more radical policy of giving each citizen a substantial endowment. Some writers believe that funding citizen endowments via inheritance tax (IHT) is not politically feasible. This may or may not be true. Those who, like me, believe that IHT can be an instrument for social justice may have been taken aback when the most left-wing British Sunday broadsheet, the *Observer*, launched a campaign in early 2005 to reduce the impact of IHT. However, even if the people cannot be persuaded that IHT is a just tax, land taxation could substitute for IHT in this role.

The structure of the chapter is as follows. Section 1 traces the normative argument for land tax in its most persuasive proponents since Tom Paine. It shows how some of the classical arguments for IHT also work as arguments for a land tax. Section 2 asks, 'Could land tax work?', while section 3 asks 'Could land tax fund a citizen's stake?' The answer is 'Yes' to both questions.

Classical arguments: Paine, Ricardo, the two Georges

Paine

Tom Paine produced the first clear proposal for a citizen's stake in 1797. The subtitle of his *Agrarian justice* (1995 [1797]) indicates that he had precisely the same idea as the one behind this book, although he also wished to endow an old–age pension entitlement. The title page reads:

> AGRARIAN JUSTICE,/OPPOSED TO/AGRARIAN LAW/AND TO/AGRARIAN MONOPOLY/BEING A PLAN FOR MELIORATING THE CONDITION OF MAN, BY CREATING IN EVERY NATION A NATIONAL FUND,

> To pay to every Person, when arrived at the Age of TWENTY-ONE YEARS, the Sum of FIFTEEN POUNDS Sterling, to enable HIM or HER to begin the World!

> And also,

> Ten pounds Sterling per Annum during life to every Person now living of the Age of FIFTY YEARS, and to all others when they shall arrive at that Age, to enable them to live in Old Age without Wretchedness, and go decently out of the World. (Paine, 1995 [1797], p 409)

Paine's political thought is equally rooted in the American and the French Enlightenments and reflects his friendship with the stellar figures of each: Thomas Jefferson and the Marquis de Condorcet. On the French side, Paine's thought derives from the Physiocrats, whose work he may have encountered through Condorcet or directly.

Agrarian justice is a short manifesto addressed to the Directory that then governed France. Like John Locke, Paine begins from the idea that in the state of nature all the earth is held in common. But, in contrast to Locke, Paine does not believe that labour can ever establish a title to the earth itself:

> Man, in a natural state, subsisting by hunting, requires ten times the quantity of land to range over, to procure himself sustenance, than would support him in a civilized state, where the earth is cultivated.... [B]ut it is nevertheless true, that it is the value of the improvement only, and not the earth itself, that is individual property. Every proprietor therefore of cultivated land, owes to the community a *ground-rent* ... and it is from this ground rent that the fund proposed in this plan is to issue. (Paine, 1995 [1797], pp 417-18)

Paine goes on to calculate national wealth and mortality rates, using data from Prime Minister Pitt the Younger's budget of 1796, plus some (heroic) actuarial assumptions about life expectancy. He assumes life expectancy of 30 at age 21, the age at which each would get their £15 citizen's stake to begin the world. (He notes also that fewer than half the babies born reach that age.) He therefore assumes that 1/30 of those over 21 die in any one year, and therefore that 1/30 of the (privately-held) assets in the economy change hands each year. The same proportion of national wealth is therefore available annually for redistribution, which Paine proposes to do by a 10% inheritance tax. He calculates that this would suffice both for his £15 endowment and his old-age pensions.

Thus the Paine scheme begins by being a land tax based on Lockean ideas, but ends up as an IHT on all assets, real and personal.[1] It is worth disentangling Paine's arguments, spending a moment on their Enlightenment forebears, and highlighting the parts that remain relevant to modern debate. There are three components to the argument.

1) *Land was originally an unowned common-pool resource. It is therefore legitimate for the community to tax it.* This argument itself comes in two varieties. One comes direct from Locke's *Second treatise of government*, chapter 5. Paine's argument that hunter-gatherers, lacking private property, remain poor echoes Locke ('And a King of a large and fruitful Territory there [among the Native Americans] feeds, lodges, and is clad worse than a day Labourer in England' – 1960 [1682]. *Second treatise*, § 41). It was also used, perhaps independently, by Condorcet, whose *Esquisse* ('Sketch of a history of the progress of the human mind' – 1988 [1795]) had been published posthumously, shortly before *Agrarian justice*. The *Esquisse* contains a sketch of a future social security system which is quite like Paine's and is likewise (more securely than Paine's) grounded on actuarial calculations of life chances. The second argument came from the French Physiocrats. The definition of their programme from the *Oxford English Dictionary* cannot be bettered: 'they maintained that society should be governed according to an inherent natural order, that the soil is the sole source of wealth and the only proper object of taxation, and that security of property and freedom of industry and exchange are essential' (*OED Online* s.v. *physiocrat*). Condorcet published furious pamphlets on free trade in corn based on the Physiocrats' ideas. Thus these ideas were in the air and Paine certainly absorbed them.

2) *There is no natural right to bequeath or inherit. Inheritance tax is therefore morally justified*. Land reform was a common theme of the French and American Enlightenments. Reformers in both countries tried to sweep away the old rules of inheritance after their respective revolutions. The most eloquent of these reformers was Thomas Jefferson. In a famous letter to James Madison, written from Paris in 1789 as Jefferson was completing his term as American Minister in France, Jefferson wrote:

> The question Whether one generation of men has a right to bind another, seems never to have been started either on this or our side of the water. ... I set out on this ground which I suppose to be self evident, '*that the earth belongs in usufruct to the living*'; that the dead have neither powers nor rights over it. ... Then no man can by *natural right* oblige the lands he occupied, or the persons who succeed him in that occupation, to the paiment of debts contracted by him. For if he could, he might during his own life, eat up the usufruct of the lands for several generations to come, and then the lands would belong to the dead, and not to the living, which would be the reverse of our principle. What is true of every member of the society individually, is true of them all collectively, since the rights of the whole can be no more than the sum of the rights of individuals. (Jefferson, 1999, p 593, Thomas Jefferson to James Madison, 06.09.1789)

3) *It is legitimate to levy capital taxes on personal as well as real property.* This is Paine's really original move:

> Personal property is the *effect of Society*; and it is as impossible for an individual to acquire personal property without the aid of Society, as it is for him to make land originally. Separate an individual from society, and give him an island or a continent to possess, and he cannot acquire personal property. (Paine, 1995 [1797], p 428)

In other words, personal property can only exist because of the norms and conventions of law and exchange. These are social constructs. Therefore the society that makes them possible has a right to tax them. We shall see below how this argument was most forcibly used in the UK between 1909 and 1914. It is time to revisit it.

Ricardo

David Ricardo (1772–1823) refined and formalised the ideas of the French Physiocrats. They had held dogmatically that the land was the source of all wealth, and that therefore only land should be taxed: a cranky inference that some followers of Henry George were later to take up. Ricardo was more sophisticated. In *On the principles of political economy and taxation* (1817 and 1821), Ricardo expounded his conception of rent with wonderful clarity:

> Rent is that portion of the produce of the earth, which is paid to the landlord for the use of the original and indestructible powers of the soil. It is often, however, confounded with the interest and profit of capital, and, in popular language, the term is applied to whatever is annually paid by a farmer to his landlord. If, of two adjoining farms of the same extent, and of the same natural fertility, one had all the conveniences of farming buildings, and, besides, were properly drained and manured, and advantageously divided by hedges, fences and walls, while the other had none of these advantages, more remuneration would naturally be paid for the use of one, than for the use of the other; yet in both cases this remuneration would be called rent. But it is evident, that a portion only of the money annually to be paid for the improved farm, would be given for the original and indestructible powers of the soil; the other portion would be paid for the use of the capital which had been employed in ameliorating the quality of the land, and in erecting such buildings as were necessary to secure and preserve the produce. (Ricardo, 1821, ch 2)

Later in the same chapter, Ricardo argues that *rent invariably proceeds from the employment of an additional quantity of labour with a proportionally less return*:

> The rise of rent is always the effect of the increasing wealth of the country, and of the difficulty of providing food for its augmented population. It is a symptom, but it is never a cause of wealth; for wealth often increases most rapidly while rent is either stationary, or even falling. Rent increases most rapidly, as the disposable land decreases in its productive powers. Wealth increases most rapidly in those countries where the disposable land is most fertile, where importation is least restricted, and where through agricultural improvements, productions can be multiplied without any increase in the proportional quantity of labour, and where

> consequently the progress of rent is slow. (Ricardo, 1821, ch 2)

Therefore, for Ricardo, as later for Henry George, land rents were inherently monopolistic. Landowners *as landowners* contribute nothing, unlike suppliers of capital and of labour, to the productive economy, and their rents rise inversely with prosperity. An abundant factor of production commands a zero rent. Under perfect competition, rents from capital and labour will tend to zero. Ricardian rents from land will not, because land is inherently scarce.

Ricardo's argument that there is an inverse relationship between prosperity and rent seems not to hold true today. Ricardo was thinking of farmland, which probably no longer carries a large Ricardian (= 'economic') rent. But nowadays, urban land where the value exists by virtue of the actions of people who do not own it, including public authorities, earns substantial economic rent. For Ricardo it was the lack of a productive contribution to correspond to the rent in his sense that justified a land tax (land might be productive, but the rent element came from a sterile scarcity). That part of his argument is as valid today as in 1817.

Henry George and David Lloyd George

Ricardo's theory of rent helped to mobilise the Anti-Corn Law League and the Repeal of the Corn Laws in the 1840s. But what seem to be the logical implications of Ricardian rent theory for taxation were not drawn until two generations after Ricardo. In 1871, Henry George (1839-97) was a journalist in San Francisco, which was then growing with astonishing speed thanks to the Gold Rush. Land and railroad owners were making conspicuous monopoly profits. The Central Pacific Rail Road controlled all overland traffic from the East, and its proprietors (including sometime Governor Leland Stanford) had extracted monopoly rents from the US people, via the US Congress, in the legislation empowering them to build the western end of the intercontinental railroad. George started to write what became *Progress and poverty* (George, 1911 [1879]).

As a self-taught Ricardian shaped by his experiences in California, George (1911 [1879], p 234) argued for the abolition of private property in land. However, his interim measure brought him far more fame than his fundamental policy. For *Progress and poverty* does not proceed with a programme of land *nationalisation*, but rather of land *taxation.* In a chapter headed 'The proposition tried by the canons of taxation', George observes:

> The best tax by which the public revenues can be raised is evidently that which will closest conform to the following conditions:
> 1. That it bear as lightly as possible upon production – so as least to check the increase of the general fund from which taxes must be paid and the community maintained.
> 2. That it be easily and cheaply collected, and fall as directly as may be upon the ultimate payers – so as to take from the people as little as possible in addition to what it yields the government.
> 3. That it be certain – so as to give the least opportunity for tyranny or corruption on the part of officials, and the least temptation to law-breaking and evasion on the part of the taxpayers.
> 4. That it bear equally – so as to give no citizen an advantage or put any at a disadvantage, as compared to others (George, 1911 [1879], p 290).

Note that these Georgeite principles of efficient and equitable taxation are directly derived from Adam Smith (1776, book V). They go beyond, and are detachable from, the Ricardian theory of rent. They are obviously compatible with Ricardo, but one could support George's principles of optimal taxation (as for instance do Kay and King, 1990, ch 12 passim, especially at p 179) without being committed to full-dress Ricardianism.

In the last decade of his life George became closely identified with what his followers have always called 'the single tax' (Barker, 1955, p 509). They argued, not just that land should be taxed, but that *only* land should be taxed. This was to regress from Ricardo to the Physiocrats, and has unfortunately given the followers of Henry George a cranky reputation that has prevented their ideas from being taken as seriously as they deserve to be.

George visited Ireland and Britain during the Irish land campaign and British agricultural depression in 1881–82 and 1884–85. His ideas spread throughout the British left: to the Liberal and Irish parties, and later to the Labour Party, having more influence than those of Marx (Pelling, 1965, p 10). They reached their apogee in Lloyd George's two budgets of 1909 and 1914. In the 1909 budget, Lloyd George introduced taxation of land values, to be implemented when a land valuation register was ready. Anticipating (and helping to provoke) the House of Lords' rejection of the budget, Lloyd George argued:

> The question will be asked 'Should 500 men, ordinary men chosen accidentally from among the unemployed, override the judgment – the deliberate judgment – of millions of people who are engaged in the industry which makes the wealth of the country?' That is one question. Another will be, who ordained that a few should have the land of Britain as a perquisite; who made 10,000 people owners of the soil, and the rest of us trespassers in the land of our birth[?] ... These are the questions that will be asked. The answers are charged with peril for the order of things the Peers represent; but they are fraught with rare and refreshing fruit for the parched lips of the multitude.... (at Newcastle upon Tyne, 10 October 1909, in Jenkins, 1968, p 94)

These are perhaps the most memorable words ever spoken by a chancellor of the exchequer, in direct line of descent from Paine, Ricardo and George. It was not only Lloyd George who took up the message in that administration. In reading the quotation below, note not only who first said it in 1909, but who revived it in 2003:

> Roads are made, streets are made, services are improved, electric light turns night into day, water is brought from reservoirs a hundred miles off in the mountains – and all the while the landlord sits still. Every one of those improvements is effected by the labour and cost of other people and the taxpayers. To not one of those improvements does the land monopolist, as a land monopolist, contribute, and yet by every one of them the value of his land is enhanced. He renders no service to the community, he contributes nothing to the general welfare, he contributes nothing to the process from which his own enrichment is derived. (Winston Churchill, 1909, in Barker, 2003, p 116)

In 1909 Winston Churchill was a Liberal minister. His Georgeite speech was made in the House of Commons in defence of his colleague Lloyd George's budget. In 2003 Kate Barker, a business economist and member of the Monetary Policy Committee of the Bank of

England, was commissioned by Chancellor Gordon Brown to report on the stickiness of the housing market in the UK and to propose remedies. The analytical chapter from which the quotation comes carries all the implications of an argument in favour of land tax, although in her recommendations Barker rejects land tax on the grounds that betterment taxes have always failed. So they have; but betterment taxes are not the same as land taxes. The next section of this chapter argues that land value tax could work.

Could land tax work?

The land tax campaign of 1909-14 failed. By 1914 the register of land holdings was still not ready. Lloyd George returned to land taxation in his 1914 budget, relying on his capacity for brilliant improvisation to work out the details. On a very complicated subject with powerful vested interests in opposition and no support from his own Treasury officials, Lloyd George failed. The outbreak of the First World War put paid to land tax in the UK.

However, in the summer of 2004, following on the heels of the Barker review, a government committee (the Balance of Funding Review) and the Commons' ODPM Select Committee both considered land tax (Office of the Deputy Prime Minister, 2004; Office of the Deputy Prime Minister Select Committee, 2004). Although they both rejected it, they both engaged (up to a point) with the arguments for it – something that no UK government had done since the Attlee government's abortive betterment tax of 1947. The Town & Country Planning Act of that year created a system of rationing land use by planning law, and a system of taxing those who benefited from this created scarcity – that is, holders of planning permission. The first limb of the Act is vigorously alive to this day. The second withered and was amputated when the Conservatives returned to power in 1951. Therefore, owners of land with planning permission, or land on which the market believes that planning permission for change of use will be obtained, derive far more economic rent from it than even Ricardo could have imagined possible.

The standard text on the UK tax system, one of the authors of which is now the governor of the Bank of England, insists that 'the underlying intellectual argument for seeking to tax economic rent retains its force' (Kay and King, 1990, p 179). Since 1947, land use in the UK has depended on its planning status. If a field is zoned for agriculture, it is worth a few thousand pounds per hectare. If it is zoned for business, it may be worth millions of pounds per hectare.

Land value taxation is efficient (because it does not distort the incentives to develop land) and equitable (because it returns some of the economic rent to the people who created it, namely the local authority and its electors). Henry George (see quotation above) recognised both of these properties. Tom Paine recognised the second. As Kay and King explain (1990, p 181):

> Suppose the award of planning permission increases the value of a plot of land from £5000 to £1 million. Then even if the resulting gain were taxed at 90%, the developer would still be better off by almost £100,000 using the land for housing than retaining it for agricultural purposes. Substantial incentives to bring projects forward would remain.

There are three main objections: the expectation that the tax would not be permanent; the costs of assessment; and the vociferous objections of likely losers – especially although by no means only the 'asset rich but cash poor'. Property interests have always seen off past attempts at land taxation. This happened not only in 1909 and 1914, but also, as Barker (2003, p 116, box 7.3) notes, in 1947, 1967, 1974 and 1985. On each occasion property owners had an incentive to delay transactions in the hope that their lobbying against the legislation would succeed. On each occasion, they did succeed. The inference to draw is not Barker's inference that land taxation is unfeasible. It is that any tax should be a tax on capital value, not a tax on transactions. That also argues for land tax over inheritance tax as a more truly Paineite basis for a citizen's stake, to which I return at the end of this chapter.

The second objection to land value taxation is the difficulty of assessment. This is less of a problem than it seems. The same difficulty faces both business rates and council tax, the two taxes that land value tax would replace (in whole or in part). Both of these taxes are linked to valuations that rapidly go out of date. Council tax bands are determined by houses' value in 1991. The next council tax revaluation is not due until 2007. The base for Uniform Business Rate is revalued only every five years. The more time that elapses between valuations, the more those whose assets have risen in relative value have an incentive to block revaluation. It was just such a revolt against rating revaluation in the 1980s that led to the poll tax disaster.

Enough houses change hands every year that the capital value of every house in the land could be calculated annually. Estate agents do it all the time, in their ordinary business. Therefore there is no reason why a public sector valuer (the existing valuation service or a successor) could not do the same. Oxfordshire County Council (2005) conducted a trial of land valuation, stripping away the value of the properties upon it, and found that the process was less laborious and resource-intensive than had been feared. Commercial and industrial property changes hands less often, so that annual valuation of every parcel of land may not be feasible. But this is not an insuperable objection. At worst a government could stick with the existing five-yearly revaluation, which could be updated whenever a sale took place. A good deal of detailed work would be required in order to calculate the correct taxation basis when land is leased rather than sold (and any prospect of a land value tax would give owners an incentive to sell leases rather than freeholds). So land value taxation is not an option for tomorrow. But it could be an attractive option for 2009, the centenary year of the People's Budget. A National Land and Property Gazetteer is already being constructed, by uniting databases from the Ordnance Survey, the Royal Mail, and local and central government. In principle it can identify every taxable hereditament in the UK. It is not a snooper's charter, because it contains information only about places, not about people.

A third objection, currently politically salient, is that any property tax including land tax penalises the 'asset rich but cash poor' – in current debate, the 'Devon pensioners'. The first, robust, answer, is that Devon pensioners should face the real opportunity cost of continuing to live in large houses. They have the options of taking in lodgers or trading down to smaller houses. A softer answer is that the tax liability on a freehold house could be deferred if the householder cannot pay, and become a charge on the estate when the house is sold. Local authorities would be able to borrow against this debt owed to them, and would therefore not be deprived of a cash flow.

Land tax would be a tax on land value, or more strictly on the economic rent deriving from land value. Therefore it should be levied at a zero rate at land that has no value above baseline agricultural use – a zero rate band up to £10,000/hectare has been proposed. Above that, it would not depend on whether land had planning permission, but on whether the market believed that it would get planning permission – thus it would catch speculative appreciation in land values on urban fringes. A fourth objection is, therefore, that if it is partly a local tax (which on balance I think it should be), land tax gives cash-strapped councillors an incentive to permit sprawling developments and US-style malls from which the 1947 system protects the UK. The answer to that objection is that councils, like Devon pensioners, should face the true opportunity cost of their decisions. And so should the people they represent. They should face the open choice: *permit development and face lower local tax rates, or refuse it and face higher local tax rates.* The ballot box should decide. This argument works both ways. If an authority proposes a development that reduces land values – say an incinerator or a tannery next to a housing estate – it is right that those who take the decision should face the true costs in a reduced land tax income flow.

Many of these objections could be rolled up into a single overarching objection: *there would be so many losers that land value tax would be politically unfeasible.* Policy makers could address this in various ways. In the first year, a reforming government could certainly ensure that the land value tax would bring in no more revenue than the taxes it replaced, and would damp the maximum gains and losses for any taxpayer by setting floors and ceilings. A cautious reforming government might restrict the scope of land value tax to non-domestic properties, conceding that the intellectual arguments for replacing council tax by land value tax were strong, but the practical implications of creating many losers (even while creating more gainers) were too scary. But land value tax would be more buoyant and more incentive-compatible than the taxes it replaced. Therefore over the years its yield would grow, so that it could fund all the things that the preceding taxes funded, and more besides. Some of this uplift would come from the increased economic activity suppressed under preceding taxes and suppressed no longer under land value tax.

It is an open question whether land value tax should be a local tax, a national tax, or a mixture. There is a tension between giving local authorities the incentive to develop, as a land tax would, and the principle of equalisation. Central government grants are designed to ensure that each local authority can provide the same level of service given the same tax rate and level of efficiency. So there is a trade-off between equity at a national level, and efficiency/equity at a local level. This should mean that only a portion of land tax proceeds would go to the local authority, thus reducing the incentives facing local authorities; or that the principle of equalisation would be undermined, with poor services for poor areas; or the grant system could be retained, but distributed in a way that allows the local authority the marginal increase in land tax revenues. However, this chapter proposes that some at least of the proceeds of land value tax should be used to fund the national objective of a citizen's stake. So in practice it would not hinder the smooth operation of an equalisation scheme that good central–local finance must include.

Finally, as a land tax would tax Ricardian rents, it must be a tax on that portion of the produce of the earth paid to the landlord for the 'use of the original and indestructible powers of the soil'. Therefore it is a tax on land, not on the structures that sit on the land. A future valuation regime would have to separate those two. In the case of houses that is both fair and uncomplicated. The value of every 'house' in the country can be calculated very quickly from estate agents' data. But I put 'house' in quotation marks because estate agents do, literally, sell estates not houses. They sell houses together with the plot of land that they sit on. A physical house – bricks, mortar and slate – also has a value, which might be taken as its rebuilding value in the house insurance. So the value of the land is just the difference between these sums. For commercial property, land value could be calculated by subtracting the value – annual or capital – of a given type and size of structure in the lowest-cost location (perhaps inner-city Liverpool or Salford) from the value of the same type and size of structure in higher-cost locations – say Westminster. The value of the land in the lowest-cost location would then be set, and taxed, at zero. Quite incidentally, that procedure would give a powerful incentive to redevelop brownfield sites in the inner city.

Could land tax fund a citizen's stake?

To get a feeling for the magnitudes involved, Table 5.1 reproduces from the 2005 budget the UK official estimates of the current yield of each tax.

Table 5.1 shows that tax proceeds on capital transactions are low, whereas even under the existing regime tax proceeds on (purported) land values are much higher. In the former class, IHT, capital gains tax (CGT), and stamp duty jointly yielded £12.2 billion (3% of receipts) in 2003-04. In the latter class, business rates and council tax jointly yielded £37.1 billion (9% of receipts). On the expenditure side, the CTF at its present level is estimated to cost £350 million (that is, £0.35 billion) in 2003-04, and slightly less in each of the next two years (HM Treasury, 2004, table 1.2).

Second, neither class of taxation comes anywhere near capturing the windfall gains of which Winston Churchill spoke in 1909, nor anywhere near recouping any of them for the public sector. Consider the case of transport improvements, for example. The Jubilee Line Extension in London, from Green Park to Stratford, was commissioned in the early 1990s for completion in time for the opening of the Millennium Dome, at its North Greenwich station. Because it was

Table 5.1: UK government: current receipts (£ billion)

	Outturn 2003-04	Estimate 2004-05	Projection 2005-06
Inland Revenue			
Income tax (gross of tax credits)	118.4	26.8	1138.1
Income tax credits	–4.5	–4.1	–3.9
National Insurance contributions	72.5	77.9	82.6
Corporation tax	28.6	34.1	43.7
Corporation tax credits	–0.5	–0.5	–0.5
Petroleum revenue tax	1.2	1.3	1.5
Capital gains tax	2.2	2.3	3.0
Inheritance tax	2.5	2.9	3.4
Stamp duties	7.5	8.9	9.7
Total Inland Revenue (net of tax credits)	228.0	249.6	277.5
Customs and Excise			
Value added tax	69.1	72.3	76.3
Fuel duties	22.8	23.5	24.6
Tobacco duties	8.1	8.1	8.4
Spirits duties	2.4	2.4	2.5
Wine duties	2.0	2.2	2.3
Beer and cider duties	3.2	3.3	3.4
Betting and gaming duties	1.3	1.4	1.4
Air passenger duty	0.8	0.9	1.0
Insurance premium tax	2.3	2.4	2.6
Landfill tax	0.6	0.7	0.7
Climate change levy	0.8	0.8	0.8
Aggregates levy	0.3	0.3	0.3
Customs duties and levies	1.9	2.2	2.2
Total Customs and Excise	115.7	120.4	126.5
Vehicle excise duties	4.8	4.8	5.1
Oil royalties	0.0	0.0	0.0
Business rates	18.3	19.0 1	9.4
Council tax	18.8	19.8	20.9
Other taxes and royalties	11.2	12.0	12.4
Net taxes and National Insurance contributions	396.8	425.6	461.9
Accruals adjustments on taxes	3.2	2.3	0.9
Less own resources contribution to European Communities (EC) budget	–4.6	–4.0	–3.9
Less PC corporation tax payments –	–0.1	–0.1	0.1
Tax credits adjustment	0.5	0.6	0.6
Interest and dividends	4.4	5.0	4.9
Other receipts	18.5	20.2	22.4
Current receipts	418.9	449.7	486.7
Memo: North Sea revenues	4.3	5.2	7.1

Source: HM Treasury (2005, p 250, table C8)

common knowledge that government credibility depended on its opening by 1 January 2000, suppliers of both capital and labour to the project extracted huge rents, and its costs overran hugely (for that and other reasons). Nevertheless, studies by Transport for London show that, even at the bloated costs incurred, the Jubilee Line Extension could very easily have been financed by a land tax. Property values adjacent to its stations rose hugely – by £2.8 billion at Southwark and Canary Wharf alone. Even at stations not on the Extension, property values rose by more than the general rate. People living near Stanmore station at the other end of the line had a new means of getting conveniently to other parts of London – not only to the Dome, but also to useful places such as Southwark and Canary Wharf.

Transport improvements cost money. The commonest source of land value gain, however, costs nothing except staff wages: namely, planning permissions for changes from a low-rent land use (such as agriculture) to a high-rent use (such as an out-of-town shopping centre). Here, the economic rent is created because planning law, for basically benign reasons, deliberately creates a scarcity. Left to themselves, market forces might produce a suburban Britain that looked like suburban America. Almost nobody at any point of the political spectrum wants that. Therefore, since 1947, there have been tight zoning restrictions on land-use planning in the UK. However, there has been too much sentiment and too little hard-headedness about the economic and social issues involved in the 1947 regime, which is still in place. The 1947 regime is very indulgent to farmers, which was appropriate after the blockades and food shortages of both world wars, but no longer is. It produced socially desirable policies such as green belts by command-and-control, not by price signals.[2] And, although nobody wants an unregulated market in land use, a regulated market would so far outperform the present command-and-control regime that an expanded citizen's stake could be financed as an almost incidental benefit, out of the small change.

At present the UK has a raft of bad land taxes. They include council tax; business rates; stamp duty; IHT and CGT to the extent that they catch increases in land values (which is not much, as those who benefit can pay for sophisticated tax advice); and Section 106 agreements. The last are agreements between a developer and a local authority whereby the developer agrees to contribute to some socially desired outcome (such as subsidising social housing or urban transport) to mitigate the impact of the development. Section 106 agreements are the worst sort of disguised taxation. They are supposed to be very closely linked to mitigating the impact of the development, rather than just being booty in return for planning permission. But booty is what they are in practice. They are extremely costly to both developers and local authorities; and the gains they produce are in no way commensurate to the cost. A simple auction of planning permissions would do far better. A tax levied on land value (and *not* on transactions, as IHT, CGT, stamp duty, and the abortive 1947, 1967, and 1974 land taxes all were) would be better yet.

Conclusion: implementing Paine

Tom Paine's argument is sound. Landowners accrue monopoly rents, which society has a right to tax for two reasons: first, that Ricardian rents should be taxed even if they arise without policy intervention; second, that policy interventions confer windfall gains, which it is appropriate for the community to tax. Paine assumed that the right tax was IHT, but this can be queried. It is unpopular; it is a tax on transactions, not on wealth; it is easy to evade. Death is an involuntary transaction, unlike those that trigger liability to CGT and stamp duty, but a taxpayer with foresight can give away assets before death in order to mitigate IHT liability.

Nothing in Paine's argument implies that IHT is the only appropriate tax, and Henry George succinctly gives the reasons why land tax is both the most efficient and the most equitable. It is efficient because it is hard to evade and because it minimally distorts economic activity. It would have beneficial effects on UK housing supply, as Barker's evidence shows, even although she shies away from that conclusion herself.

Admittedly, its transaction costs are high, but these have to be incurred already for the existing tax regime of council tax and business rates. Also, the formal incidence of land tax lies on landowners, whereas the formal incidence of business rates lies on occupiers. In economic theory, this difference matters not at all, for the reasons given by Kay and King (1990, ch 1 *passim*). In practice it would create considerable problems of transition, because UK business premises are typically let on long leases with upward-only rent reviews. A tax change that transferred liability from occupiers to freeholders would in the long run be neutral because rent agreements would change to accommodate it. But there would have to be some (perhaps messy) transitional arrangements.

The clinching argument for land tax, however, is that its net benefits are so great that it could fund an expanded citizen's stake almost on the side. The official numbers given in Table 5.1 show that the costs of the CTF are low, whereas the yield of the existing (bad) land taxes is high. Better taxes, which stimulated real economic activity where the present tax regime suppresses economic activity (in the case of Section 106 agreements) and encourages bubbles (in the case of council tax), could yield more while costing less (as a percentage of economic activity involving land). Policy makers have an opportunity to implement Tom Paine's dream. It is also the dream of David Ricardo, Henry George, and Lloyd George. What better way than that could there be to mark the centenary of the People's Budget in 2009?

In the interim, policy makers could do much to prepare the way. They could make council tax less regressive in its dying years by rebanding at the top and at the bottom, as evidence to the Balance of Funding Review, and the ODPM Select Committee, both recommended in July 2004. They could announce that at the revaluation in 2007 (which will provoke huge protests from those whose property has risen in value) that the government is committed to introducing a fairer system from 2009. They could scrap the overcomplicated schemes that either fail to achieve what they set out to, or achieve the opposite. Section 106 agreements, stamp duty exemption for non-domestic property transactions in 'deprived' areas such as Canary Wharf, and the Local Authority Business Growth Incentive scheme would all go. They would return business rates to local control. Without increasing tax rates, these moves to a more buoyant tax structure could endow the CTF more generously than now. Radical reform awaits its Lloyd George, and its ambulance wagon.

Notes

[1] In lawyer's parlance, *real property* (US: *real estate*) means immovable property such as land and buildings; *personal property* is everything else.

[2] Another telling citation from Barker refers to the late 1940s and early 1950s, when the green belt proposed by the 1943 Abercrombie Plan for green space in and around London had been implemented, but Abercrombie's idea of inner-urban parks on cleared bomb sites had succumbed to development pressures: 'Children playing in London's increasingly busy streets, and without most of the new local parks that [Abercrombie] had promised, could console themselves with the thought that 10 or 15 miles away there was a belt of agricultural land that they would never be able to spoil' (S. Inwood, quoted in Barker, 2003, p 36).

SIX

A capital start: but how far do we go?

Howard Glennerster and Abigail McKnight

Introduction

The capacity for individuals to make choices that, individually and collectively, affect their lives is one of the essential characteristics of a liberal democratic society. Its relative absence for some groups defines their social exclusion. As Sen (1999, pp xi-xii) says, 'the freedom of agency is inescapably qualified and constrained by the social, political and economic opportunities that are available to us'. Not the least of these constraints is the availability of credit or the possession of capital. Perhaps the single most distinguishing feature of the socially excluded in a society that has some kind of income safety net is their lack of assets and hence credit worthiness. This precludes risk taking, any feasible way of beginning a business, trading off between present and future income, investment in skills apart from those subsidised by the state, the capacity to overcome even minor disasters without becoming indebted to the state or local loan sharks. Peo███████████ped in a narrow range of choice sets that make their lives di███████gnificant ways from the lives of even working-class fam██████ steady, reasonably paid job. The capacity to chang███████tern of opportunities is highly constrained.

   Much of the discussion about giving children asse██ ██ birth has emphasised the behavioural advantages of educating fam███ into the ways of saving (Nissan and Le Grand, 2000; Regan, 2001; Regan and Paxton, 2001). For us, however, the starting point is the intrinsic importance of extending individuals' agency, especially that of the poor. The growth of owner occupation has given most people a significant asset that gives them an enhanced chance of borrowing, financing their old age, moving jobs and living arrangements, giving opportunities to their children to move into owner occupation and much else. The gap between the asset-owning and the non-asset-owning classes will grow and be self-reinforcing – unless we take positive steps to address asset deprivation.

The case for giving all citizens a more equal asset start can be traced back at least to Tom Paine (1987 [1797]). He argued that there should be a limit on the amount the aristocracy should be permitted to hand down to their descendants. Their wealth should be taxed and the proceeds used to give everyone a capital grant of £15 at 21 (plus a pension of £10 per annum for everyone aged over 50 and £10 per annum for the 'lame and blind' below that age). All citizens should begin adulthood reasonably equal in their capital assets and the freedom this brings. We may call this the redistributive asset model.

A quite different logic can be found in conservative writers and think tanks like the Adam Smith Institute (Butler, 1999). They see the welfare state as constraining individual choice and putting too much power in the hands of the state. They follow Milton Friedman (1962) here but wish to take his logic further. They argue that we should seek to fold as much /as possible of current welfare provision into a contingency fund: a 'Fortune Account'. This could cover long-term care, disability, health insurance, sickness and unemployment. On this model the government and individuals would pay into the fund sufficient to meet the likely costs of care or benefits that the individual would draw down as needed and add to as they wished. Sums could be paid in as regular contributions or, in part, up front as an initial asset. In its most extreme form a sum could be given to individuals at the beginning of their adult lives. They would then be 'on their own'. It would remove the state from any social policy function except redistributing capital: a libertarian redistributive model.

This model has parallels with American frontier history. Homesteaders were given plots of land in the new territories if they claimed and could farm them. There was no safety net but people began with a free capital gift from the state. It proved extraordinarily successful as a way of populating the west. There were losers too. Not the aristocracy in this case, but the indigenous Native Americans and those homesteaders who did not make it. There are more recent less extreme variants, notably the capital funds used in countries like Singapore (see Box 6.1) that forego a welfare state and in its place require compulsory savings paid into an individual capital fund.

A libertarian model should be contrasted with the notion of *adding* capital redistribution to the present forms of state welfare – complementing the *income* and service safety net we currently have with a *capital* equivalent financed by an estates tax, gift tax or wealth taxes (see Chapters Two to Five). Of course, the two models are not entirely mutually exclusive. Parts of the existing welfare state could be replaced by asset allocations as we shall see.

We need to be clear then: What is the rationale for extending a citizen's stake?

Should we seek to increase individuals' agency by removing the institutional and time-limited boundaries to state aid? Should we 'cash in' potential rights to free health care and schooling and combine all the equivalent purchasing power into a single cash sum given at one or two points in early life leaving individuals the right to spend it when and how they wished? Or should we merely add significantly more *capital* redistribution to the existing *income* redistribution undertaken by the state?

Box 6.1: Singapore's Central Provident Fund

This began in British colonial times as a central-funded retirement scheme to which employers and employees had to contribute. Each member amassed savings and the interest on them. This interest was not taxed. The scheme was rather like a compulsory national savings scheme dedicated to retirement. After independence it began to evolve into a broader savings and asset scheme.

First members could call on their deposits to help them buy public housing units for their own occupation. Then the scope of the scheme was widened to include funding for health care and higher education. The required contribution rate is now 30% of earnings – 20% from the employee and 10% from the employer up to a ceiling and up to the age of 55. After that the required contribution percentage falls but continues to be payable beyond 65. There are, in fact, separate personal accounts within the whole, notably for medical care.

There is a limit to what individuals can withdraw after the age of 55. A minimum sum has to be retained to ensure a minimum income in retirement. This can be left in the fund's retirement account and paid out as a fixed pension from the age of 60 until it runs out. Or the sum can be used to buy an annuity or put in an approved bank account. Apart from such restrictions capital in the fund can be used for house purchase or funding tertiary education for the individual or their children, or for investing in stocks and shares. On the sale of a house the principal borrowed plus interest has to be returned to the fund.

Some economic theory may help us think about the issue a bit more clearly. The case for one or both may be different with different kinds of state activity.

Economic theory and the case for asset-based welfare

The notion of wrapping up state aid into a one-off capital sum encompasses three distinct ideas. One is to give people greater choice between the institutions from which they can buy services. The second is to give people cash not services in kind and hence greater choice in how they make use of that spending power. The third, newer, element is to give them the option as to *when* to spend state aid. For example at the moment the state gives help with acquiring human capital – higher education. It does not give young people a sum of money to invest in a business or other form of capital investment. A cash sum unconstrained as to its use would enable the individual to make that choice. There is a literature about the limits and the advantages of the first two elements. We now focus particularly on the third element, although all, in practice, intertwine with the others.

Traditional economic theory suggests we should be careful. The reasons for much welfare provision are well grounded. Information and other failures in the market leave individuals in a poor position to make many choices over a lifetime.

Public goods and externalities

The obvious starting point is the theory of public goods and externalities. This theory suggests that, left to themselves, individuals will underinvest in certain activities because it is others who reap significant benefits not the individuals themselves. Children's schooling is one example of such an externality. The wider society gains from the child's education in ways that there is no reason for the parent to weigh. The parent will actually suffer if the child stays on at school when he or she could be working. The recent experiment with school maintenance grants suggests these negative financial incentives matter. Yet the child and the wider society benefit from an educated electorate and workforce even if the parents do not. Adam Smith certainly accepted the point, as did John Stuart Mill. Even those who advocate vouchers for schools favour tying them to schooling, requiring school attendance and keeping some kind of minimum school-leaving age. Simply to give parents a large sum of money at a child's birth would not necessarily lead to it being spent on the child's education without a set of rules about its use, which would lead one back to something like a voucher. Another example: the benefits of fundamental research undertaken by a university are not something individuals may be prepared to pay for when they buy a university place. The output of research will often be a pure public good not captured by any individual, certainly not the student.

In short, a key factor for politicians to consider in thinking about how far to take asset-based welfare is the extent to which there is a public good or social rate of return that derives from a particular kind of spending that would be unconsidered if individuals were left to make a set of choices about how to spend their capital sum. Where the benefits derived from a service are private the case for capitalising will be greater. Higher education is a good example here too. Why should university students be the *only* young people to gain what is essentially a capital allocation at the start of life?

Public choice

A somewhat analogous point arises from public choice theory. Electorates may support certain spending for morally approved purposes but not if they feel the money may be spent on other things. There is a marked difference in the approval ratings that the public give to health and education spending compared to cash benefits (Sefton, 2003). This is a long-standing result. In the US, voters are prepared to support food stamps but are much less supportive of general cash aid to poor families. Family allowances suffered from the same concerns in Britain (Land, 1969). It is precisely the restricted purpose to which the spending is tied that seems to sustain public support. The more morally approved the purpose, the more difficult it will be to generalise the benefit. The less morally approved the purposes on which the capital sum can be spent, the less support for the whole package. The problems of giving cash, not services in kind, are compounded by giving large sums of cash up front. One lifetime savings account spent on a holiday in the Bahamas reported in the press could jeopardise the whole programme.

The distribution of risk, uncertainty and cost

Where a service is largely provided on a uniform, equal basis across the country, cashing that service in as a lifetime capital sum seems, at least in principle, relatively straightforward. Schooling is a case. Yet even here individuals' needs vary from the average cost per pupil both over time and in relation to a child's ability and aptitudes. There are those who need special schooling and many would argue children from more deprived homes need more spent on them too. There is the possibility of some cross-subsidising within a normal school and adjusting the school's funding formula on the basis of the pupils' needs. Individualising those differential needs, translating them into a variable cash voucher as a child's needs become evident is, at least, a theoretical possibility. Doing so at the point a child is born, taking account of future school costs is a bridge too far.

This difficulty increases when we move to health care. Here the use of the service is highly variable in duration and cost between individuals. This is true on a yearly basis and even more over a lifetime. It is why private medical insurance excludes many individuals, including those with a prior poor health record or an existing condition, or it requires very high premiums from those who are least able to bare the cost. There is a classic American literature on this (Newhouse, 1984). The general practitioner fundholding experiment in England in the 1990s generated striking evidence (Matsaganis and Glennerster, 1994). In any one year just over a quarter of the patients of a large fundholding practice took the whole of the fundholding budget. Just 5% of the patients absorbed two thirds of the budget. Over time, some, but by no means all, of this variability evens out. Add in those with lifetime chronic diseases and the variability increases again. The smaller the numbers in any health scheme the greater the variability. An *individual* savings account has no 'risk pool' at all. Thus allocating every person a sum equal to the average health expenditure per person discounted over a lifetime would give some people a trivial sum compared to their medical bills. Others would have very large lifetime surpluses.

This variability would not pose a problem if we could predict individual medical expenditure with some reasonably high probability. Even if we could it would create political problems. Some people's savings account would be 20 or 50 times someone else's because of the predicted difference in lifetime medical spending. However, the fundamental technical problem is that we can predict only a very small part of the variance in medical expenditure at the individual level by associations with socioeconomic situation or parental medical histories. The earlier in life we try to do this the less good we are at it. Even the best studies can do no better than explaining about one seventh or one eighth of the variance. We can predict the demand for medical care spending for whole populations as small as 100,000 quite well – but even that is only about two thirds of the variance (Sutton et al, 2002). Future advances in genetic profiling could improve the accuracy somewhat but there would remain considerable variation in health expenditure needs unexplained by genetic factors.

A similar problem arises with long-term care. Perhaps only a quarter of people over 65 will need some kind of intensive care but the figure rises as people become older. Long-term care is very expensive. But predicting who would need such care at birth (or at 18) is impossible. Giving everyone the same capital sum to cover long-term care costs would run into all the above issues. The same would be true of ordinary sickness benefit.

The need for unemployment benefit over a lifetime raises comparable problems. Predicting unemployment levels for a society far into the future is immensely difficult. Predicting how far any individual will encounter it and for what length of time is essentially impossible. Thus, although giving everyone additional initial assets might reduce *general* unemployment by improving individuals' economic adaptability, there is no way of setting an appropriate sum that would meet an individual's lifetime chances of suffering unemployment. If someone had to spend their asset balance to cope with long terms of unemployment the sum left to cope with poor health or long-term care would disappear.

Time, cost, myopia and information

Welfare spending is strongly linked to age (see Figure 6.1). For people in their 30s, 40s and 50s the state spends about £2,000 a year on all welfare expenses except housing: education, health, social care and social security. Annual spending on people in their 70s is about £8,000, 80-year-olds £10,000 and 90-year-olds over £14,000. So the great bulk of any capital sum given at birth or at 18 would have to be saved up for a very long time. This poses two kinds of problem. First, how much will services cost in 60 years' time? How far will the technology of care and medicine have changed by then? How much will life expectancy have changed? In December 2004 the government actuary changed his estimates of life expectancy, increasing the predicted population estimates for the over-75s. He increased their projected numbers by a quarter at a stroke. It is this kind of *uncertainty* that makes insurance companies so wary of providing health insurance cover for older people or cover for long-term care insurance.

The second difficulty caused by the way welfare spending is skewed to the later years is myopia: peoples' fixation on the present, and the

Figure 6.1: Welfare spending by age

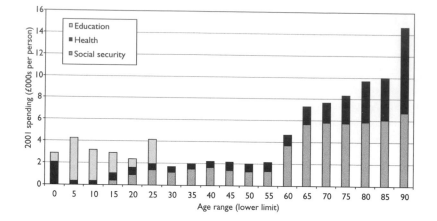

information complexity that there is attached to making investment and insurance decisions far ahead. American research (Aaron, 1999) suggests that individuals have very little grasp of the nature of the investment choices they need to make to generate an adequate pension in retirement. The Pensions Commission (2004, p xii) in Britain concluded that 'Most people do not make rational decisions about long term savings without encouragement and advice', and that is costly and by no means always successful. The further away the outcome the less people can grasp the issues or are interested in making what are key decisions. Responses to changes in government pension policy in the 1980s suggest that while older and better-off people responded quite rationally, people under 45 and poorer people responded very little, although the changes had large impacts on their lifetime pension wealth. The capacity of people to handle large capital sums concerned with outcomes 60 years hence may be much less than optimal overall and highly differentiated.

One possible way to cope with myopia (in regard to long-term care, for example) could be to pay out capital sums later in life. Thus a capital sum to encourage people to start saving for long-term care at the age of 50, say, might prompt awareness of an emerging problem at a time when the reality of old age begins to dawn. But significant uncertainties would remain.

Moral hazard

Finally, there is the well-known problem of moral hazard. If you give people a sum from which they are intended to save for retirement and they do not do so, is any government going to let them starve? The incentive will be for some people to engage in risky investment strategies in the knowledge that if they blow their savings the government will pick up the pieces. It is for this reason that even in Chile the government has required contributions to private pension schemes. But that is difficult to police and a significant percentage of the population are in informal jobs where this rule cannot be enforced. The same is true of health care. In the US many people do not take out health insurance as they think that in an extreme emergency a hospital will have to treat them.

Front loading and double tax burden

Any scheme that involved giving individuals a capital sum now would have macroeconomic consequences on top of the microefficiency issues raised above. Current pensioners would need supporting, as would those in middle age unable to amass pensions on the private market in time. Future state funding might be reduced but in the meantime the state would have to pay state pensions *and* give a capital start to young people. This is why schemes like those in Singapore have built up individuals' assets on the basis of regular compulsory saving.

Positive behaviour implications

So far, we have considered the caution economic theory implies if we contemplate capitalising the benefits of the welfare state. Not all the economic arguments are hostile to an initial capital inheritance, however. Experimental work with capital endowments suggests that people do undertake more saving of their own if they have had some opportunity to learn how to invest savings given to them by such schemes, they take longer perspectives and are more ready to take risks – 'asset effects'. Tax-advantaged savings accounts do seem to have had some effect in encouraging more saving for retirement in the US but not so much elsewhere. Even in the US a lot of the effect has been to divert savings from other purposes.

Knowledge that your savings wealth may be reduced if you do not look after your health may induce adoption of healthier lifestyles. If you part-own your social housing dwelling you may be a better tenant in ways we shall discuss later. Having capital available may enable people to be more entrepreneurial, to move jobs, to avoid debts. These are, indeed, part of the general case for spreading assets.

We have suggested that abolishing welfare as we know it to fund capital allocations at birth or on adulthood runs into economic difficulties. However, the strength of these negative arguments differs depending on the kind of welfare spending, the timing and the form such allocations take and how far the purposes on which the capital is spent are constrained. It would be possible to create separate funds on which people could only draw for educational purposes or health or housing. However, not only would this be difficult to police but it would defeat a major part of the attraction of a citizen's stake – giving individuals more free choice over their lifetime plans.

We now consider these issues on a case by case basis.

Weighing pros and cons

In Table 6.1 we produce a first approximation of the kinds of issues that would need to be addressed in seeking to capitalise particular kinds of welfare spending. Across the top are ranged the economic issues we have just discussed. Down the left-hand side we list the services that might be capitalised. We put a cross in the column where we think the economic case against is powerful.

Schools. School education provides externalities beyond the benefits parents may see in educating their own children. If a parent did not educate a child at all the state would have to require it. If parents chose to spend very different amounts on children social cohesion and equality of opportunity would be endangered. Since schooling is a generally approved activity electorates might be reluctant to put such spending into a general cash pot for parents to spend or not. We have therefore put a cross in each of the first three columns in Table 6.1 under schools.

Table 6.1: Risks and benefits of capitalisation

	Public good externality	Morally approved	Moral hazard	Myopia	Unequal uncertain risks	Complex market
Schools	x	x	x			
Higher education	x (part)	x				
Pensions		x	x	x	x	x
Sickness benefit		x	x		x	
Health care	x	x	x	x	x	x
Long-term care		x	x	x	x	
Housing						
Child benefit	x	x	x		x	
Unemployment		x			x	

However, schooling expenditure would come soon after the birth of a child, so issues of myopia do not arise at all seriously. Nor do the arguments about uncertain long-term risks or risk pooling as we saw in the previous section. Thus no crosses appear in those columns.

Higher education. Here the situation is different. Higher education is partially a public good – notably the research element and to some extent the benefits of teaching. But some gain is private and is captured in the higher incomes the graduate receives. Here we have the equivalent of a large capital sum granted to two out of five young people and not made available to others. What could an enterprising computer wizard or a young electrician or builder or plumber or secretary with an eye to opening a shop do with £30,000 matched with help from a bank?

Pure equity suggests that whatever sum the state advances to those entering university that brings a purely private benefit should be made available to all 18-year-olds. They would make the choice of spending it on university education or something else (Glennerster, 1982). Just how to calculate the private as opposed to the public benefit element from university teaching is a tricky point. In some ways the graduate contribution is seeking to do the same thing from the other end. It is reducing the scale of private benefit derived from this rather arbitrary investment in some young people and not others. How you decide the balance between the two methods is a political judgement.

There would be no moral hazard issues or long-term risk and uncertainty beyond those that exist today in the higher education private investment decision. There could be a problem with myopia with young people choosing to spend the lump sum at 18 rather than trade it for an uncertain stream of income over the lifetime. Moreover, those young people who have had most experience of handling savings or seeing their parents make long-term investment decisions would be at an advantage. This is a more general point to which we return.

Pensions. Much attention is paid in other countries, notably the US at the moment, but also Germany and Sweden, to the case for giving individuals the opportunity to contract out of the compulsory and generous state pension scheme and put their contributions into privately funded schemes. Germany and Sweden have done something like this at the margin. However, Britain has never had a generous state pension and has given individuals the right to contract out of state wage-related schemes since the 1960s. As a result we have one of the largest private pensions sectors in the world. British concerns are precisely the opposite – the difficulties that face those who thought they had secure assets in the private sector of pensions and the declining level of corporate and private savings in pensions (Pensions Commission, 2004).

The most obvious candidate for redirecting existing funds in Britain is the tax relief individuals now get when they contribute to a pension scheme. The value rises steeply with income and age. This is perversely redistributive. Nor is it clear that these provisions encourage more saving in total as opposed to redirecting it from other savings. Present arrangements could be phased out and replaced by tax credits that matched pension contributions by individuals but only up to a lower ceiling. With some of the increased revenue government could give 'pension starter packs' – a capital gift for those joining a pension scheme by the age of 30.

Sickness benefit. Statutory sick pay shares with pensions a certain political moral approval, tempered by accusations of cheating. Yet the state would find it difficult to let sick people starve even if they had spent their assets. It shares with health care all the same difficulties of predicting very different individual experiences of sickness. There might be more incentives to minimise periods of long-term sickness – perhaps a capital bonus for those who make fewer calls on the sick pay scheme. But that would go disproportionately to the better-off.

Health care. Health care raises problems across the board. Health care has both public good and externality properties. It is something where the actual type of institutional NHS spending carries a political bonus that might not carry over to the distribution of a cash sum. There are certainly big difficulties with unequal and unpredictable risks over a lifetime, problems with health insurance markets and the difficulty that the main spending comes at the end of life. There seems little case for switching health funding to a front-loaded capital basis.

Long-term care. Long-term care is similar in many ways, with moral hazard, myopia and uncertainty coming into play. Private insurers in Britain have largely withdrawn from long-term care insurance for these reasons. Yet it is also intimately tied to housing. Most people want to remain in their own homes for as long as possible. Adapting their homes for disability, linking the house to emergency cover, domiciliary care and ultimately having living-in care all costs money that could be gained from the capital tied up in an individual's or couple's house. Such capital can also provide a buy-in to a long-term care facility or extra care housing. There is considerable scope for mobilising such capital and using a range of benefits like the attendance allowance and pension credit.

A person's house is often their largest or only significant asset. Practical financial advice about using all the financial assets an old person has, the possibilities, and the stumbling blocks, could give many old people real independence and agency. Financial advice for older people ought to be encouraged as part of preventive care management.

Housing. Housing capital is now the largest accessible source of capital most people have and it does not suffer from the same kind of economic risks discussed above. That is to say it is not risk-free. Annual sales of equity release have grown from £127 million in 1998 to well over £1,000 million in 2003 and this looks likely to grow substantially. There are limits to the extent that individuals are prepared to use this to fund retirement, wanting to hand it on to their children, although bequeathing property is becoming less important to many younger people (Rowlingson and McKay, 2005). But a significant proportion of the population have no stake in owner occupation and hence access to this new freedom.

Giving *everyone* a capital start through enhanced baby or adulthood bonds could be helpful in getting first-time home buyers into the housing market, although prices would rise to mop up the gain in the short run. To do this on any scale universally would also be very expensive. Giving those who are social housing tenants some stake in their dwelling is preferable. It targets the poorest households and enables them to get onto the owner-occupier ladder. But it also can have a positive impact on tenants' attitudes to the accommodation they occupy. They have an interest in the good order of the estate and the block in which they live. They have an enhanced interest in participating in the governance of the housing association or cooperative, since the better ordered and governed the scheme the higher the value of the share they may be able to take out. This is the route down which the government has begun to move.

There are costs, of course. Giving a discount on the full market cost of a dwelling to help a tenant buy a share of a property is a capital transfer that will mean the state or a social housing landlord has less capital value at its disposal in the future but it does have the advantage of being a transfer targeted on the poor. The value of such property may fall if the estate or scheme is badly managed or if house prices in general fall. The tenant–part-owner then loses. This is a risk all asset ownership brings.

Child benefit. Given that child benefit is a flat universal cash allowance, turning it into an upfront cash baby bond poses fewer technical problems compared to other changes we have discussed. But it would cause substantial fiscal problems like all moves to capitalise. Done on any scale the costs would front load public expenditure. Today's chancellor would face a big cost but his successors would save.

Converting child tax credits into a lump sum would be more problematic as they are targeted at poorer families whose income can fluctuate over time.

Unemployment benefit. As we saw earlier, replacing the jobseekers' allowance by a capital sum at the beginning of life with which to see individuals through periods of unemployment poses real difficulties. It is not just the problem of forecasting the extent of unemployment likely in any economy for anyone in it over a lifetime, it would also mean calculating the individual differential risk an individual had of being unemployed in any given economic cycle. For all the reasons that make private insurance against periods of unemployment almost impossible beyond very restricted limits, this looks a non-starter. However, any scheme that encouraged saving and the pooling of families' assets would help the labour market. A larger savings cushion would mean households had more resources to job search.

Some academics have examined the case for having a combined social insurance fund for pensions and unemployment insurance. The more time you chose to be unemployed, the lower would your future pension be. Some kind of basic income to prevent starvation would have to be kept in place. The UK has gone down a different route, essentially limiting rights of access to long-term unemployment insurance and requiring job-seeking behaviour. These are more immediate incentives and more individualised than a threat to a person's pension that we know young people, especially, heavily discount. Moreover, as one study (Orsag et al, 1999) concluded: 'Merging the pension system and the the unemployment system into individual accounts would improve incentives but exacerbate ex post income inequality'.

Distributional consequences

There has been much controversy and analysis of the distributional impact of social expenditure. Brian Abel-Smith's (1958) and Julian Le Grand's (1983) work suggested that the middle class does very well out of the welfare state, at least in terms of the level of services in kind they receive. There was never any question that poorer people are the main recipients of cash benefits. As better data has become available we now know that the poor also receive more value from services in kind (Sefton, 1997, 2002). See Table 6.2.

There are several reasons for this benefit to the poor. One is that the poor are sicker than the rich and so use the health service, personal social services, social housing and special schools more. (It is still

Table 6.2: Distribution of benefits in kind by service: ratio of the benefits received by individuals in the bottom quintile group relative to the top quintile (not age-adjusted)

Health care	1.8
In-patients	2.2
Outpatients	1.4
GPs	1.5
Prescriptions	2.0
Dental services	1.0
Education	1.7
Schools (under 16)	2.6
Schools (over 16) and further education	1.6
Higher education	0.6
Housing	5.9
Personal social services	3.9

Source: Sefton (2002)

probably the case that the better educated get more than they 'should', given their health needs, because of their capacity to bring their education and confidence to bear on professionals involved.) The other reason the poor have more spent on them is that the very top income groups opt out of public services but go on paying tax. Thus, looked at on a yearly basis, the lower-income groups receive more social benefits in cash and kind than the higher-income groups. On the other hand the higher-income groups live longer, receiving more benefits but also paying more tax. The lifetime picture has also now been modelled (Hills and Falkingham, 1995). The net result is that on a lifetime basis the rich still end up paying more than they receive. The total effect of the welfare budget is redistributive towards the poor.

What all this suggests is that the lifetime redistributive effects of asset-based welfare could be very big depending on how it was funded and distributed compared to the present system. If everyone began life with the same sum of money and no access to welfare, those with low marketable talent and poor health would be potentially much worse off. If everyone had the same capital sum and no state support in old age, the poor might do better in accounting terms, especially if they had low life expectancy and this policy was financed with a capital levy on the rich. Cashing in higher education spending and extending the same sum to all young people aged 18 would have significant distributional effects (towards the poor). But all these crude social accounting calculations take no account of the differential capacity of the poor and the rich in handling investment decisions over a lifetime or the differential risks they face or the capacity to access capital markets.

Thus it is difficult to derive a priori conclusions about the distributional effects of capitalising welfare spending without knowing exactly which services would be 'cashed in' and modelling the impact in a lifetime context. Even then the differential behavioural responses of different groups are difficult to predict or even agree about the direction of change. The recent debate about the likely distributional impact of the graduate contribution is a case in point. The distributional implications of *replacing* existing service provision could be very important but also uncertain. Some of the capital conversions we have considered have involved giving lump sums to parents who are then charged with making potentially life-changing decisions for their children. There are likely to be both transitional and long-term implications in terms of variation in parents' interest and capacity to make optimal decisions on behalf of their children. Others have involved giving lump sums to young people at the age of maturity. Again, variability in young people's capacity to make optimal decisions, possibly with the support of their parents, will vary. While capital sums may reduce some forms of inequality, it is not clear, a priori, how these will evolve over the short, medium and long term. It is also not clear what impact capitalisation will have on society. Collective forms of provision with more or less equal access and variation according to need (such as through the NHS and state-funded education) can engender social solidarity. It is difficult to predict in advance what would be the impact of the possible 'sink or swim' mentality that could accompany capitalisation.

We have also not considered in detail the impact of restricting the use of capital grants to their intended use. Restrictions could limit problems associated with myopia if, for example, a capital grant intended for pension provision could only be put towards a pension. Yet we have seen that advantages flow from enabling individuals to trade future benefits for current cash support. Many of the problems we have discussed would remain even with restrictions and restrictions would incur additional administrative costs.

Conclusion

We began by contrasting two different political motives for creating a citizen's stake. One derived from Tom Paine and was driven primarily by the case for redistributing life chances and involved taxing the assets of the rich so as to secure capital for all, including the poor. All citizens should start life with a decent capital endowment. The other motive lay in reducing the scale of the state and the paternalistic allocation of aid into particular service forms between which people cannot now choose.

Responding to this second, libertarian approach, we have argued that the scope for capitalising existing welfare provisions is very limited. These provisions exist due to a range of market failures that make health care or long-term care insurance, for example, expensive or unavailable to many. These problems are compounded by trying to front load the value of the benefits or amalgamate a person's savings into an individual savings account. However, there is some scope for capitalising existing welfare provisions. Not surprisingly, both are already investments. One is higher education where some equivalent of the cash value of subsidies to those in higher education could be spread to all young people. However, there are distributional issues here that are also of general importance. Some families will have more capacity to make long-term investment decisions about the value of higher education than others simply because of their own personal experience. Social housing is another service where the capital involved might be partially unlocked. Indeed some steps down this road are already being taken.

Other measures are also possible. The large tax breaks now given to those contributing to private pension schemes, especially for those on high incomes, could be redirected to capital start-up schemes for those joining pension schemes by the age of 30. The whole issue of compulsory saving for retirement will be the subject of the Pension Commission's second report in autumn 2005. There are also Inland Revenue restrictions on the use of pension funds to finance long-term care that need looking at again. The state could encourage more innovative use of private housing capital in accessing long-term care. In short, there are ways in which individuals' existing capital – housing and pensions – could be freed from state limitations.

Part Two:
Forms of a citizen's stake

SEVEN

Attitudes of young people towards capital grants[1]

Andrew Gamble and Rajiv Prabhakar

Introduction

Asset-based welfare has provoked attention as one of the most innovative ideas in recent public policy. Policies to promote asset-based welfare can take a variety of forms (Kelly and Lissauer, 2000). One of the most prominent schemes centres on paying young people a capital grant once they reach a certain age. One reason why young people command attention is that they are the section of the population that have least access to assets (Banks and Tanner, 1999), and so tackling this points towards initiatives directed at the young.

However, there is as yet little evidence of the attitudes of young people themselves to this kind of policy. The attitudes of young people are important for the current and future design of this policy, since capital grant policies can be constructed in a variety of ways. Grants can differ over the amount of money that is paid out, the restrictions that are imposed on the use of such grants, as well as ways of funding the grants. The success of any scheme will depend on how young people choose to make use of their grants. Investigating their views helps anticipate which policies are likely to be a success and which issues need to be faced when revising and developing the policy.

This chapter presents findings from 11 focus groups held in Sheffield and London between 9 February 2004 and 16 June 2004 on the attitudes of young people to different models of capital grants. We seek to draw implications from these focus groups not just for the immediate development of policies like the Child Trust Fund (CTF), but also, more tentatively, for wider debates about the future of the welfare state. We find that young people react favourably to capital grant schemes, and like the idea of the CTF. Looking beyond the framework of current policy, our focus groups were in favour of a more generous CTF, although they wanted it to be a complement rather than a substitute for existing forms of welfare provision.

The chapter is structured as follows. First, by way of context we discuss how asset-based welfare appears to have been concentrated thus far in the US, Britain, Canada and Australia (countries sometimes referred to as 'Anglo-Saxon capitalism'), but why it may still have implications for other welfare states. Second, we briefly set out three prominent versions of capital grants that have been canvassed. Third, we outline the nature of the focus groups upon which our empirical research is based. Fourth, we indicate some of the important themes that emerged from these groups. We conclude by discussing what our findings reveal for the future of the CTF and relate the debate back to broader discussions about the future of the welfare state.

Assets and welfare regimes

Gösta Esping-Andersen's influential typology of welfare regimes identifies three main types (Esping-Andersen, 1990). In 'social democratic' regimes the state plays a dominant role in the finance and provision of universal and strongly redistributive welfare services. In 'liberal' regimes, individuals are expected to make provisions for much of their own welfare. The state provides a residual service for those who fail to make adequate provisions for themselves. In 'conservative' systems, the family provides the bedrock for the provision of welfare services, and less weight is placed on equality than under a social democratic system.

Most countries have hybrid regimes with a tendency to one type rather than another. All face challenges to adapt their regime to meet new problems, including ageing populations, affordability, quality of public services and choice. The British welfare model is more hybrid than most, because of the way it continues to combine universalist features, such as the National Health Service (NHS), with selective features, like social security. As a result the British welfare state is neither fully comprehensive nor entirely liberal.

Up to now, interest in asset-based welfare has emerged most strongly in countries with a relatively liberal welfare state: the US, Britain, Canada and Australia. This may be coincidental. But since asset-based welfare prioritises the role of the individual, it does perhaps appeal most naturally in countries where individual self-reliance is strongly emphasised. Moreover, the critics fear that asset-based welfare is another step towards making the welfare state entirely residual. It is said to represent another example of the subordination of welfare policy to the demands of the global market. Instead of welfare being understood as a universal entitlement of citizenship, it becomes a means to fit individuals to the requirements of work in flexible labour markets and to compensate in part for declining collective provision of higher education and pensions. Clearly, if the assets agenda were pursued on its own, and treated as a replacement for all other forms of welfare, rather than as a supplement to them, it would turn out to be a very regressive step, and Britain would end up with the most residual welfare state in the developed capitalist world.

But the fact that the CTF is universal is significant. It is the first new universal benefit in the British welfare system since child benefit was introduced in the 1970s, and so it breaks important new ground, reversing the trend over recent years in Britain towards increased means-testing. For its supporters on the 'centre-left', asset-based welfare is an essential part of attempts to create a social investment state, and, perhaps, part of a wider agenda on citizenship. It is not intended to replace the welfare state, but to complement it in ways that give people greater autonomy and independence within the framework of common entitlements and obligations (White, 2003).

Different capital grant models

Do the attitudes of young people give us any clues as to how asset-based welfare might evolve, as a substitute or complement to the existing welfare state? In our focus groups we probed this and other questions by presenting participants with three particular capital grant models that have been influential in the British debate: the stakeholder model; the Fabian model; and the Institute of Public Policy Research (ippr) model.

The first model is advanced by Bruce Ackerman and Anne Alstott in their book *The stakeholder society* (Ackerman and Alstott, 1999). They advocate paying a grant of $80,000 to all young adults at age 21. Those who want to use it to pay for higher education can access their grant before they reach 21. The grants would have tight eligibility restrictions. Those who receive a grant must have graduated from high school and must be free of a serious criminal conviction. The grant is a right of citizenship, but dropping out from school or committing crimes qualifies the right. The high-school graduation requirement is intended to help ensure that individuals have sufficient maturity to handle their stakes. The criminal conviction disqualification is partly to discourage criminality, and partly to bolster the scheme's legitimacy. Apart from these restrictions, Ackerman and Alstott argue that individuals should be allowed to use their grants as they please. Freedom requires that government should not interfere with the choices that people make.

Ackerman and Alstott propose two sources of funds for the grant. First is a 2% tax on wealth. Second, in the long term, the scheme would become self-financing through a form of inheritance tax (IHT). When the individuals who received the $80,000 grant eventually die, their initial stake will be repaid out of their estate into a fund that will be used to provide grants for the next generation.

The second model is advanced in a Fabian pamphlet written by Julian Le Grand and David Nissan, *A capital idea* (Nissan and Le Grand, 2000), Julian Le Grand having floated a similar idea for a 'poll grant' over 10 years previously (Le Grand, 1989). Le Grand and Nissan propose paying a £10,000 grant to all individuals when they turn 18. Le Grand and Nissan want a £10,000 grant because they argue that a capital grant needs to be substantial enough to make a difference to a person's life-chances. At the same time, they do not feel the need to propose a grant on the Ackerman-Alstott scale, in part because they assume a more extensive welfare state operating in the background to the scheme (such as a comprehensive NHS), an assumption that, given their US context, Ackerman and Alstott do not (and may not entirely want to) make.

Le Grand and Nissan propose that capital grants be financed by reforming IHT, calculating that a reform that raised the proportion of inheritances taxed to 15% could finance a £10,000 asset. They do not suggest any eligibility criteria of the kind favoured by Ackerman and Alstott, other than the requirement that people should be British citizens, but they do insist on imposing restrictions on how the grant may be used. This reflects concerns that public support may ebb from the scheme if there are high-profile cases of individuals 'blowing' their stakes. Le Grand and Nissan would limit use of the grant to fund investments in higher education, training, buying a home or starting a business. Individuals would receive their grant in a special account at a local bank or publicly owned savings institution. Spending would be overseen by a board of trustees. These could be employees of the institution that holds the account or could be drawn from panels of local business people or community leaders.

The third model is the CTF, developed initially by researchers at ippr – in particular Gavin Kelly, Carey Oppenheim and Nick Pearce – and substantially adopted by the Labour government in the form of the CTF. The CTF is backdated to all babies born from 1 September 2002, and the first accounts were opened in April 2005. Parents of newly born babies will receive a £250 voucher that has to be paid into an account with an approved provider. For children from low-income households the initial grant will be £500. Family and friends can make additional tax-free contributions into the CTF up to an annual limit of £1,200. The CTF is paid at birth rather than when a young person enters adulthood, but individuals only get access to their funds at 18. Paying the initial sum at birth is intended to promote financial literacy as the account holder grows up. There will be lessons at school on managing the CTF, and so the provision of this asset goes hand-in-hand with financial education. According to Inland Revenue illustrative figures, if no further savings were added to the accounts once the initial vouchers had been paid out, then the £250 would be worth around £500 and the £500 would be worth roughly £1,000 when the person is 18 (this is as a result of interest payments, so the exact amount depends on future interest rates or returns on equity). The Prudential Assurance Company estimates that if a family saved the maximum entitlement, then a CTF could be worth £30,000 when the child reaches 18.

The ippr model proposes no eligibility criteria, other than nationality, for children to receive the grant, and similarly it proposes no restrictions on the use of assets once they mature when the account holder turns 18 (HM Treasury, 2003a), largely because of the practical difficulties of policing what in many cases will be the spending of relatively small funds (see Paxton and White, Chapter Eight). While the other two models set out an ambitious vision for renewing citizenship through the assets agenda and developing a different kind of welfare state, the IPPR model is focused much more tightly on measurable social policy benefits that may arise from asset-based models. This feature undoubtedly helped it appeal to the government, and to the treasury in particular. For the treasury one of the main objectives of the CTF is to promote saving among young people (HM Treasury, 2003a).

The structure of the focus groups

The first CTF will not pay out until 2020, so definitive research of the impact of this policy on behaviour will have to wait. In the meantime, we can get some idea of the possible impact by looking at the attitudes of young people today to such policies. Focus groups were chosen as the most appropriate method for this, especially since there is evidence that young people often feel insecure when facing researchers on an individual basis and that this can be alleviated by a group setting (O'Toole, 2001). We targeted individuals aged 18 since this is the age that dominates most capital grant proposals for young people. The 11 focus groups were run at Sheffield and Walthamstow in London. These locations were chosen as typical urban locations with areas of high social exclusion. We wanted to test whether there were any regional differences in the responses, and focused on the north and south of England (a more comprehensive study would extend this regional base). Three sites were selected for the focus groups in each location: a sixth-form college; a further-education college; and a job centre. The aim here was to examine the attitudes of young people from different socioeconomic backgrounds. The sixth-form colleges were in relatively affluent areas, while the jobseekers tended to face the greatest socioeconomic challenges of the people we interviewed. We used the 2002 school-performance league tables to select sites for our study of sixth-form colleges and further-education colleges. Four main summary statistics are given in these tables: number of students; number entered for exams, average point score per student, and average point score per paper. In view of the fact that we want to study those individuals who are just about to leave the school or college, we focused on the measure that tells us something about the resources that each individual possesses as they enter the world of work or education. Accordingly, we used the average point score per student to select the sites. We selected sites that scored similarly between Sheffield and Walthamstow. For the job centres, we concentrated on sites in city centre locations.

John Bynner (2001) suggests that there are important gender differences in how assets affect life outcomes. In order to explore this, we organised two separate focus groups at each of the sites, one composed entirely of males and one of females, although in the case of the job centres it proved possible only to organise one focus group, covering both males and females. Each focus group had eight participants.

We structured focus group discussions using the three models of capital grants outlined above. The first was based on the CTF, assumed to provide a minimum sum of £1,000 at age 18. The second model was based on the Nissan–Le Grand proposal for grants of £10,000 at age 18. The third model was based on the Ackerman–Alstott proposal for grants of $80,000 at age 21. Slightly adapting the details, this gave us three proposals to put to the focus groups – universal capital grants of £1,000, £10,000 and £50,000, in each case to be paid at age 18 to all individuals. We began each focus group by asking if anyone had heard of the CTF (despite there having been considerable media coverage of the policy, almost nobody in our groups said they had) and we then sketched out the details of the policy. Next we asked participants to comment on the proposal for a capital grant of £1,000, and whether the grant should be subject to restrictions on use. We asked them to imagine the sum was £10,000, and then £50,000, in each case getting them to discuss how they would use such a grant, and whether they thought it should be subject to use-restrictions. This method of proceeding helped arouse the interest of the focus group, and led to lively discussions about how they thought they themselves and their contemporaries would react. Two handouts were distributed in the course of each focus group, the first giving brief details of the CTF and the second asking them to record their views on restrictions for the three different proposals.

Findings from the focus groups

Our main findings were as follows.

Merits of capital grants. Although very few participants had heard of the CTF, there was broad support for the idea of capital grants and for the CTF once it had been explained. The general view was that this was an interesting and potentially popular policy. We found no significant regional, class or gender differences (apart from one issue – childcare) in any of the responses of our groups.

Size of grants. Of the three capital grant models (£1,000, £10,000 and £50,000) the £10,000 model was the most popular. The main reason given for this was that most respondents felt that such a sum could make a real difference to their lives, and might change their behaviour, while the £1,000 would mostly be absorbed into current spending. The £50,000 proposal on the other hand was seen by most respondents as being too much for young people: 'It doesn't show you the value of money by getting 50 grand.… By just getting 50,000 you won't realise how hard it is to make that because you haven't made it' (female, sixth-form college, Sheffield). Paying grants at a later age than 18 did not change this broad conviction, although there was some support for the idea of paying the larger grant in instalments.

Although the £10,000 model was the preferred one, all the groups expressed broad support for the principle of the CTF as well as general approval for the additional £250 for low-income households. There was no inherent objection to the notion that different people will enjoy different levels of the CTF once the accounts mature. Some did express concern, however, that the design of the policy allows high-income families to save for their children through the CTF. But the more general view from these focus groups was that children of rich parents already enjoy substantial advantages and that the CTF would at least give something to everybody: 'Well, it's like that anyway.... At the moment there are some people who are coming to 18 and going to uni and have nothing. So it's better than nothing' (female, further-education college, Walthamstow).

Use of grants. In response to the question of whether there should be restrictions placed on the use of capital grants, the focus groups showed themselves strongly in favour of a principle of reciprocity. Most participants stated that if young people received a grant, then they should have a corresponding obligation to use it in an appropriate fashion: 'I think it should be directed somewhere, and people aren't just given a lump sum and say here you go, spend it' (female, further-education college, Sheffield).

The strength of this opinion was tempered somewhat by the size of grant involved. For the £1,000 model there was a division of opinion as to whether it would be worth specifying restrictions, given the relatively small sum involved. For the higher levels of grant, however, there were very few participants who thought that these grants should have no conditions attached to them. The most popular thing our respondents wanted to spend their grants on was higher education, followed by a car, starting a business or saving for a deposit on a home. The one notable gender difference was that the female groups much more frequently than the male groups raised the issue of using the grants to provide for childcare.

A number of observations can be made on these answers. First, most of the respondents said they would spend it in a responsible manner while also insisting on the importance of restrictions. But if individuals were in fact to spend the money as they suggest, then would not restrictions be redundant? In response, we note that although young people said that they would behave responsibly, they expressed doubt over whether others would do likewise:

> 'I think there would be a temptation for a large percentage of people to just go out and blow it, and not really achieve much. There would be a temptation for the money not to go to anything particularly appropriate, or alternatively people will come under pressure from their family to give it back to them.' (male, sixth-form college, Sheffield)

We suggest that this concern helps reconcile the declaration of responsible behaviour with an emphasis on restrictions. On responsibility, some commentators may believe that the true nature of the participant's likely expenditure plans emerge when they were asked in the focus groups how others, and not themselves, would probably spend their grants. Here, youngsters may not feel impelled to give what they regard as the 'right' answer. Although we do not share such scepticism, we note that if young people are in fact likely to 'blow' their grant themselves, then any restrictions they emphasise will apply as much to themselves as others.

Second, the respondents point to two areas of expenditure – namely childcare and cars – not usually mentioned in the policy literature when the menu of possible grant uses is laid out. Since women do the bulk of child-rearing in this country, it may come as no surprise that women raise the issue of childcare much more frequently than men do. We believe that the gendered nature of this response is itself a policy concern because it raises questions about whether child-rearing will be shared fairly among men and women in the future. Turning to the merits of the specific proposal, we suggest that even if one insists that capital grants be restricted to investment opportunities, then allowing expenditure on childcare is defensible. On the one hand, it may allow parents to spend more time at home with their child, and by doing so contribute to their child's early development. On the other hand, and working in the opposite direction, it may make it easier for parents, particularly women, to return to work by reducing the costs of childcare. We believe there is a case for exploring such issues further. We also record that this example shows how capital grants can be connected to a broader 'family-friendly' policy agenda (an issue that will be taken up in depth in Chapters Nine to Eleven). Similar points could be made about allowing grants to be spent on cars or driving lessons. In so far as possessing a car or being able to drive is important for employment, there are grounds for seeing car ownership as a form of investment.

Saving. Evidence on the likelihood of capital grants promoting saving was mixed. Some participants did think it would be valuable if the grants, particularly at the higher levels, were linked to lifetime savings accounts. It was also thought that the holding of a CTF would give young people valuable practical experience of how to save, supplementing and informing more abstract classroom instruction. The CTF was also praised for providing an important monetary incentive for people wanting to save. Matched savings models whereby government matches any funds saved by the account holder were given strong approval:

'If I'm going to give you £5 and you're going to give me £5 back, brilliant. If I'm going to give you £100 and you're going to give me £100 back, brilliant. I would give you my whole jobseekers' allowance to know I'm going to get that amount back.' (female, job centre, Walthamstow)

Contrary views were that providing people with high capital grants may prove to be a disincentive to save before 18 since individuals may anticipate the substantial sums that will accrue to them once they reach that age. In addition, some thought that holding an asset might not have any greater effect in motivating them to save than more financial education in school: 'It could make them lazy. It could work in the wrong way. If you know you're coming out of school or college and you're 18 and you get 50,000, you might not work as much' (male, sixth-form college, Walthamstow). Overall, however, there was mild support in our groups for the view that a model like the CTF will encourage saving.

Funding of grant. We asked our focus groups to consider the issue of how capital grants should be funded, in particular asking whether it should be linked to IHT (as proposed in some of the policy literature). The answer was unequivocal. There was deep resistance to the idea of using IHT for this purpose. Although participants did see the logic of taxing account holders at death so that the next generation of grants could be funded, most felt that a more important principle was to allow individuals to provide for their families. Echoing the findings from the workshops described by Lewis and White in Chapter Two, IHT was repeatedly described as 'double taxation'; it was regarded as unfair to tax someone at death if they had already been subject to taxation during their working life.

'That money was earned through a lifetime from one of the members of your family who has died. They've worked high and low for that, and then suddenly the government comes in and says, right, we'll take a piece of that, which is not really right ... I would scrap inheritance tax, but keep other taxes. Other taxes do do good, but inheritance tax does not belong on this planet as far as I'm concerned. It shouldn't have even been thought up.' (male, job centre, Sheffield)

Most participants had little or no knowledge about the actual structure of IHT. There was some movement once that information was given to them. But the common view expressed was that the 40% rate was much too high, even given the thresholds. Some favoured a lower rate implemented above a threshold of £100,000. The general sentiment, however, remained hostile to the use of IHT. There was a strong preference for relying on general taxation, specifically income tax, to pay for capital grants.

Conclusions: the future of the assets agenda

To review our focus group findings: very few of our participants had heard of capital grant models such as the CTF. Once the idea was explained, however, young people were generally supportive of this sort of policy. The Fabian model of a capital grant of £10,000 was most popular, and most of the participants in our focus groups also supported the redistributive element in the IPPR model, providing lower-income households with a higher initial endowment. There was only mild support for the proposition that measures such as the CTF will stimulate increased saving. Participants expressed some concern that grants might be misused, and were supportive of placing use restrictions on the grants to prevent this. They opposed the idea often floated in policy circles of linking the funding of capital grants to reform of IHT. While there is some movement of views once the beliefs of young people are explored in more detail, it remains that important barriers exist to the use of IHT.

So, what are the implications of these findings for the possible future direction of the assets agenda? First, the findings suggest that there would be support for grants that are larger than the current CTF, although clearly not for grants on the Ackerman–Alstott scale. However, second, the concerns over possible misuse of grants suggest that for the policy to command legitimacy there might need to be restrictions placed on how the grants can be used. This emphasis on restrictions is at odds with the majority of policy actors (such as politicians, civil servants and academics) whom we interviewed in a separate part of our study, who thought that restrictions are impractical. If there was a move to larger grants at some stage in the future then this discrepancy between popular and elite perceptions would have to be overcome (an issue explored by Paxton and White in Chapter Eight).

Third, although young people reported that saving would probably rise as a result of policies like CTF, the mildness of their support for this idea, and their perception that capital grant programmes could act as a disincentive to save, arguably throws some doubt on the strong emphasis on the promotion of saving in current policy. A broad citizenship ratio███████ital grants may give capital grants more legitimacy than ████████mphasis upon savings.

Fourth, our findings suggest that the assets agenda is more likely to evolve as a complement than a substitute for existing welfare policy (at least if policy evolves in a way that reflects popular preferences). Given the sort of sums that young people felt comfortable with, it is unlikely that capital grants will prove to be a practical alternative to the welfare state. Indeed, in the focus groups there was concern that an expanded capital grant model might be used as a way of curtailing other forms of public intervention. Several participants made a connection between capital grants and the debate over student tuition fees. Many thought the government might use an expanded capital grant as a justification for cutting expenditure elsewhere. There was no support for reining in other forms of welfare, and a general view that assets should be used alongside other forms of welfare provision rather than replacing them.

Thus, from the evidence of our focus groups it seems very unlikely that the welfare system could be reorganised solely (or perhaps even mainly) around a capital grant model, even if this was thought desirable. Our respondents liked asset-based welfare but did not want to see it replace traditional forms of welfare intervention. The hybrid nature of the British welfare model and the obstinate attachment of the electorate to it, suggests a continuing importance of social democracy in Britain and tempers the extent to which the universal features of the British system of welfare could be abandoned. The design of the CTF as a universal benefit is one of its most attractive features for our respondents. If the assets agenda is used in addition to other forms of welfare provision, and if the element of universality is retained, then there are prospects for deepening assets programmes in the future to make them a real tool of redistribution. It is the range of different life-styles and different statuses that a well-designed assets policy could help promote that makes it a potential new direction for the welfare state. Viewed in this way, forms of asset-based welfare may well prove attractive in other countries, such as Germany and in Scandinavia. The language of asset-based welfare may have particular liberal aspects, but it is part of wider discourse about the social investment state that has important social democratic as well as liberal strands (Esping-Andersen et al, 2002).

In terms of advancing the empirical material covered in this chapter, future research can be developed in a number of ways. In terms of funding, there is a case for exploring alternatives to IHT in view of the resistance it provokes (and for a discussion of some alternatives, see Chapters Four to Six of this volume). In relation to the forms that capital grants can take, it is worthwhile — particularly once the first CTF vouchers are issued — to gauge the attitudes of parents to these grants and their views on how they compare it to other policies.

Note

[1] This chapter draws on research undertaken for a project on Assets and Human Capital, funded by the ESRC (RES-000-23-0053). The support of the ESRC is gratefully acknowledged.

EIGHT

Universal capital grants: the issue of responsible use

Will Paxton and Stuart White

Introduction: the issue of responsible use

Critics argue that universal capital grants (CGs) are unlikely to make much long-term difference to economic equality or to personal freedom simply because many account holders will use them irresponsibly. Recent public opinion research on CGs reveals real concern over responsible use in the public at large. Chapters Two and Seven both provide evidence of this, as do some early media responses to the Child Trust Fund (CTF) (see, for example, the report in the *Daily Mail*, 11 January 2005). Unless we tackle the responsible use issue, the political (and moral) case for using scarce public monies to develop such policies further will be significantly weakened. This chapter explores how this issue might be addressed.

We proceed as follows. First, in Section 1 we distinguish three strategies for promoting responsible use: *complementary education*; *eligibility restriction*; and *use restriction*. The most frequently proposed strategy is that of use restriction. But it faces some tough questions. Is it wrong in principle to limit the freedom of citizens to how they may use their CGs? Which uses should be on the menu for people to spend their CGs on? Is it practical to limit the range of uses to which CGs can be put? Sections 2 to 4 consider these questions in turn. We argue that, while use restrictions are probably not wrong in principle, the practical problems are considerable. Section 5 therefore explores an alternative, more educationally based approach.

We conclude that it is best to encourage responsible use of CTFs through a version of this educational approach. However, in developing the citizen's stake policy in the future, one option is to complement the CTF with individual accounts that are tied to specific uses or contingencies, such as care responsibilities or training. If the administrative challenge posed by such schemes is manageable, then this approach, which clearly involves an element of use restriction, is also worth considering.

Three strategies

When we speak of responsible use of CGs we might mean one of two things. The first is *socially constructive use*, by which we mean making use of CGs in ways that contribute to the good of the community. Or we might mean *prudent use*, by which we mean using the CG in a way that improves or secures the asset position of the individual. Many uses of CGs will be responsible in both senses. For example, if Smith uses her CG to buy training that leads to a job, her use of the CG is, on the face of it, both prudent and socially constructive. However, it is possible for the two senses of responsible use to come apart. Imagine Smith uses her CG to engage in speculative trading that ultimately contributes nothing of real value to society, but which has the effect of making her much richer. This is prudentially effective, but it is not socially constructive. On the other hand, Smith might use her CG to subsidise unpaid educational work in low-income neighbourhoods. This is socially constructive. But as it leaves her with no financial assets at the end, it is not prudent. We shall assume that policy makers care about both socially constructive and prudent use of CGs. In thinking about how a government might tackle the issue of responsible use, at least three different types of strategy can be identified: complementary education, eligibility restrictions and use restrictions.

Complementary education. One possible strategy is to complement the CG with efforts to educate future grant holders in the responsible use of their funds. Educational efforts might focus both on financial literacy, and on questions of how the funds might be effectively used. This is the approach that the British government has adopted for the CTF. The government intends that the CTF be used to assist financial-capability education, arguing that the additional payment at age seven can be used to 'provide a useful starting point for involving children with their CTF accounts both in and outside the classroom' (HM Treasury and Inland Revenue, 2003, p 20). The government is to commission the development of teaching and learning resources related to the CTF that can then be integrated into different parts of the existing school curriculum. Developing the idea, one can imagine schools organising discussion sessions in which people talk about what one can do with a CTF. Representatives of universities, vocational training schools, small business associations and trade unionists could all contribute to these sessions. The educational approach is also in evidence in the Individual Development Accounts (IDAs) experiments pioneered in the US. In many of these schemes, individuals are required to attend financial education classes as a condition of receiving matching subsidies or withdrawing of their funds. These classes include a range of topics such as 'household budgeting, personal financial management, establishing and repairing credit, goal setting, and principles of investing' (Dailey, 2001, p 53). The public opinion research using deliberative workshops reported in Chapter Two produced some evidence that education of this kind would be valued. As one working-class male participant put it in one of the workshops: 'We need teaching, in school, how to invest, we're not taught anything like that ... we're not taught how to spend that money [from a CTF] ... You're not taught how to live' (male, 38, Stockport).

The educational approach still leaves young people free at the end of the day to misuse their CGs. Moreover, in the contemporary British case at least, relevant classes would have to compete against many other demands in a crowded curriculum. We also note that the first pilots of the Savings Gateway, a matched savings programme for low-income households akin to IDAs, experienced difficulty engaging clients with financial education – although engaging adults who have long left school may be tougher than engaging most children in the school environment.

Eligibility restrictions. A second approach is for the government to restrict eligibility for the CG, or to its full value, to people whose characteristics make it likely they will use the grant responsibly. A good example of the approach is provided by Ackerman and Alstott in their book, *The stakeholder society* (Ackerman and Alstott, 1999). Their baseline proposal is for a CG of some $80,000 for all citizens of the US on maturity. However, full access to this sum only comes when people are in their mid-20s. Prior to this, the grant can be used only for higher-education payments, and from the age of 21, access to the funds is phased in at $20,000 per year. Moreover, access to the capital sum, rather than the interest on the capital, is available only for people who have completed high school or an equivalent. Access to the full value of the CG is also forfeited if the individual acquires a criminal record before they reaches maturity, although entitlement can be regained after a sufficient period of good behaviour. Age, high-school education and the lack of a criminal record can all be seen as proxies for deeper characteristics that make for responsible use. In part the aim of the eligibility restrictions is *formative*. The eligibility conditions give young people an incentive to make the right, responsible choices early in their lives and, as they do so, they are formed as the kind of people who can then be trusted to make responsible use of CGs.

However, eligibility restriction risks compromising the universality of the CG in alarming ways. The impact of the kind of restrictions that Ackerman and Alstott propose will almost certainly fall disproportionately on young people from poorer backgrounds, precisely the people who potentially have most to benefit from the policy. Hence, any defensible scheme of eligibility restriction would offer citizens second and third chances to earn full entitlement. As said, Ackerman and Alstott themselves suggest that individuals should be able to earn back full entitlement to their stake through good behaviour. A more modest variant on this general approach is presented in this volume's final chapter. Here Pearce, Paxton and White suggest linking *top ups* to the basic CG to various kinds of responsible behaviour, such as volunteering, when young.

Use restrictions. The most obvious strategy for promoting responsible use is for the government to declare a range of approved purposes for CGs, and then to make release of funds conditional on showing that the funds are being used for an approved purpose.

The strategy of use restriction is favoured by most recent proponents of CGs, including Haveman (1988), Nissan and Le Grand (2000), and Halstead and Lind (2001). The typical list of approved purposes tends to include: higher education; vocational training, setting up a business; help with a house purchase. Use restrictions have also been a feature of the aforementioned IDA schemes that have recently been run in many parts of the US. As already noted, the participants in Gamble and Prabhakar's discussion groups (Chapter Seven) were amenable to this approach, as, to some extent, were the participants in our own deliberative workshops (Chapter Two).

However, the British government initially declared itself unsure of the case for placing use restrictions on the CTF and, in the final analysis, rejected them (HM Treasury, 2001; HM Treasury and Inland Revenue, 2003). One reason is that CTFs are partly intended to encourage saving, and use restrictions could reduce their attractiveness as a savings vehicle (although, if the use restrictions could be well designed, perhaps some parents might see them as an attractive form of security against the misuse of their hard-earned savings). But aside from this, the use restriction strategy faces some tough questions.

First question: wrong in principle?

Some argue that use restrictions are wrong *in principle* because of the limits they place on personal freedom. Ackerman and Alstott put this objection powerfully. For them, the point of a citizen's stake is to enhance personal autonomy. With a generous CG on maturity, it becomes possible for everyone to stand back a little when young and pose to themselves, in a meaningful way, the question: 'What do I really want to do with my life?' (see Chapter One, section 1, pp 2–4). However, if the point of the CG is to enhance autonomy, would we not undermine this by placing restrictions on how people can use their CGs?

However, there are at least two putative replies to this objection. The first is that it can be justified to restrict autonomy, paternalistically, to protect autonomy itself (the *paternalism argument*). The second is that it is legitimate to restrict individual freedom to meet the demands of justice, and that there is a demand of justice that constrains how people should use their CGs (the *justice argument*).

The paternalism argument. One threat to a person's autonomy is *dependency*: a one-sided reliance on some other person for one's basic material well-being. When you rely on someone in this way, they have power over you. They can use your dependency as leverage to control you. Now, if people use their CGs irresponsibly (imprudently), then they are more likely to be dependent for a living on the goodwill of another, whether it be an employer or a spouse. So, if we care about autonomy, what are we to do? Do we leave people with the choice to use their CGs however they like, knowing that they might use them in ways that compromise their autonomy? Or, to prevent this, do we limit how people can choose to use their CGs? Should we limit autonomy in order to help preserve autonomy? Merely invoking the value of autonomy gives no clear answer.

So far as adults are generally concerned, paternalism – limiting a person's freedom of action to prevent self-harm – is least controversial when the individual endorses the restrictions in question as a means of self-protection (for helpful discussion, see Dworkin, 1971). So perhaps one way of taking the paternalism debate forward in this context is to run some workshops in which young people are asked to reflect on the issues and consider what sort of self-protective use restrictions, if any, they would support placing on CGs. If a large supermajority comes out in support of self-protective use restrictions, then it would arguably be legitimate to impose them. The closest thing we have to such workshops are the focus groups with young people conducted by Gamble and Prabhakar (Chapter Seven). Although participants typically framed the issue in terms of preventing *others* from misuse of their CGs, rather than self-protection, these young people were strongly in favour of use restrictions. Their responses are certainly consistent with supermajority support for self-protective use restrictions. (For further discussion of this topic, see White, 2004b.)

The justice argument. According to Ackerman and Alstott, those taking up their stakes today share an obligation with other members of their generation to make similar stakes available to future generations:

> We must take the claims of equal citizenship for tomorrow's Americans seriously – as seriously as we take our own. If we wish to sustain a civic bond with our successors, we have no right to arrange the future for our convenience and let our successors fend for themselves … we have an obligation to provide them with the same fundamental rights that we have provided for ourselves. (Ackerman and Alstott, 1999, pp 81-2)

They call the idea expressed here the 'principle of liberal trusteeship'. From this principle they derive what they call the 'payback obligation': the obligation to pay a sum back at the end of one's life to help make an equivalent CG available for members of a future generation. This is not a strict legal obligation; some people might end up with insufficient funds to meet the obligation through no fault of their own. But it is a serious moral obligation.

However, if it is a serious moral obligation, why not design the CG scheme so that people are constrained at least to make a *reasonable effort* to satisfy it? Why not restrict the purposes to which the CG can be put to ones that make it likely the individual will have sufficient funds to meet the payback obligation – higher education, vocational training, buying a house, perhaps setting up a new business? These all involve the accumulation of assets that can be used to raise the funds to meet the payback obligation. The contrast is with using the capital of one's CG to finance extra consumption, leaving nothing to meet the payback obligation at the end of one's life.

Certainly, the restrictions limit freedom. But it is often appropriate to constrain people's freedom of action so as to increase the probability of their acting justly. That is what we are doing here. We are limiting the freedom of use of CGs to increase the probability that those receiving a CG will use it in a way that treats other members of their generation justly: that they do their share of accumulating funds for the next generation and not unjustly offload this responsibility onto others. In view of these two arguments, paternalism and justice, we do not think that use restriction is clearly wrong as a matter of basic principle. However, the arguments are certainly not conclusive, as Sections 3 and 4 will show.

Second question: what do we put on the menu?

If CGs do have use restrictions, however, what uses should be on the menu for grant holders to choose from? In this section we consider the following possible menu items: help with house purchase; house rental; higher education or vocational training; business start-up; and car purchase. House rental and car purchase do not usually appear on use menus for CGs, but we consider them because they are options that could be very significant to some young people, both subjectively (they would very much like to use CGs in these ways) and objectively (the uses may be important in achieving independence and becoming what Paine referred to as 'useful and profitable citizens' (Paine, 1987 [1797]). We examine these possible menu options against three criteria:

1) *Responsible use: prudence*. How well is the use likely to serve the individual's own long-term asset position?
2) *Responsible use: social desirability*. How well is the use likely to serve the wider interests of the community?
3) *Deadweight cost*. How far would a CG committed to this use be funding what people would choose to do anyway?

Ideally, we would want menu options to be ones that are responsible in both prudential and social senses, with low or zero deadweight costs.

House purchase. So far as the first, prudential aspect of responsible use is concerned, there is a clear link between house purchase and long-term asset accumulation, and there is some evidence that home ownership has a positive independent impact on life chances (Scanlon and Page-Adams, 2001). On the other hand, from the standpoint of social desirability, there is the danger that increased home ownership among young people will reduce geographical mobility and impair the efficiency of the labour market (Oswald, 1999). Deadweight costs are likely to be large, providing a subsidy to those who would have purchased a house anyway.

House rental. There is no strong link with long-term asset accumulation. There is also a weak direct link with social contribution, although it is possible that this use might ease the transition to independent adulthood in a way that facilitates social contribution. Deadweight costs, while difficult to measure, are probably very high; most people who want to rent already can and probably do so.

Education and training. Clearly, these uses are compatible with both senses of responsible use. A wide range of research establishes the link between educational achievement and later life outcomes (for example, Blundell et al, 2004). Investment in education and skills is of great importance for wider society, with implications for overall economic performance and levels of inequality or low pay in the labour market. So far as deadweight costs are concerned, the state already generously subsidises some forms of post-compulsory education, which raises the question of how existing subsidies to post-compulsory education should be integrated with a citizen's stake (on which see Chapter Six).

Business start-up. On the prudential level, there is a plausible link between spending on business start-ups and improved later life outcomes. However, levels of business failure remain high in Britain – one third of businesses that first registered for VAT in 1999, for example, were no longer trading three years later (Small Business Service, 2004). Although this is an imperfect measure of business failure, as some may have ceased trading for other reasons – such as owner retirement – it does illustrate the risks of starting a business, and these risks are likely to be higher for businesses started by young people. Setting up a business is also an obvious way of making a social contribution, although, again, the high risk of failure has to be set against this. We think deadweight costs would be low in this case. Only about 3% of working-age adults in the UK have any direct ownership interest in a business start-up at present.

Car purchase. Buying a car could be consistent with responsible use in both senses. For many young people, particularly those in rural areas, geographical mobility is important in terms of access to the labour market (see Performance and Innovation Unit, 2002b; Social Exclusion Unit, 2003, for further discussion). On the other hand, given environmental objectives, it might be better to promote geographical mobility through improvements to transport infrastructure, or to encourage more local retailing so as to reduce the need to travel. Deadweight costs are likely to be very high.

Clearly, the design of the menu for a use-restricted CG will be a matter of judgement based on the merits and demerits of these possibilities. (Of course, there may be other possibilities, such as allowing people to invest their CG in a pension.) From our brief, impressionistic review, education and training emerges as a clear winner in terms of the three criteria. All the other options have serious things to be said for and against them, with house rental looking like the least desirable option on balance.

That said, for young people from low-income backgrounds, using a CG to rent a house or buy a car could well represent an important means of achieving independence and becoming an economically active member of society. This is why we included these as possible menu options in our review. If we exclude such uses, as our review suggests we have some reason to do, then we will certainly be excluding uses that do make sense for some young people. There is an unavoidable tension here between keeping the menu short to reduce the risk of misuse and extending it to accommodate different circumstances and needs.

Third question: are use restrictions practical?

Suppose we have agreed on a menu of uses. We are still left with the key question: is restriction practicable? In Britain approximately 700,000 people a year turn 18 and when the CTF was developed between 2000 and 2002, neither the government nor the private sector was keen on the idea of having to police use restrictions for this number of people.

For a model of how use restrictions might work, we can perhaps look to the experience of the IDA schemes in the US. These operate use restrictions using the device of *dual signatures*. Each IDA has an account manager with authority to release funds. To release funds, the account manager must receive authorisation from both the account holder and from a registered provider of an approved good or service that the account holder wishes to buy. In the longer term, technological developments might also facilitate use restrictions. Some commentators believe that the banking system will make a transition to new 'smart card' technology over the next few years. By programming a smart card to access a CG, only certain purchases could be allowed from this account (Performance and Innovation Unit, 2002b). However, this would still require substantial coordination of suppliers to ensure that they accept and can work with smart-card technology.

However, whether we use dual signatures or computerised smart cards, two major problems would remain. First, there is the background problem of clearly identifying who counts as a legitimate provider of a given good or service. Second, there is the related problem of how to prevent people converting funds released for approved purposes into cash which they then spend as they like. The first problem emerged in Britain with the Individual Learning Account (ILA) scheme. ILAs provided financial support for courses of further education and vocational training, but had to be withdrawn very quickly because of problems of fraud. Bogus suppliers of educational services set up and encouraged people to apply for the ILA grants, which would then be shared with the people getting the grants with no real education actually taking place. The second problem can be illustrated by thinking about the use of CGs for business start-up. Someone might present a decent business plan and get approval to withdraw funds for the purchase of tools and equipment for the business. But they might then sell the tools and equipment and, say, take an expensive holiday. None of the menu options we considered in section 4 are wholly unproblematic in these respects.

Our conclusion is not that we should abandon wholly the idea of use restrictions. One possibility, for example, would be to complement a CG without any use restrictions, as the CTF is currently designed to be, with other accounts that are tied to very specific uses or contingencies that are significant but also reasonably easy to monitor. These might include education and training (notwithstanding the aforementioned problems that emerged with the ILAs, from which we can learn), the status of being a primary care worker, or sabbaticals from employment. In the latter two cases, there need not be any monitoring of how the funds are being spent, only a confirmation that the individual has a certain status – a requirement of a kind that we already use widely in the benefits system. Accounts of this kind would be akin to the 'social drawing rights' (SDRs) that many policy thinkers in continental Europe are currently discussing (see Supiot, 2001). In Chapters Nine to Eleven of this volume, Anne Alstott, Jane Lewis, Linda Boyes and Jim McCormick discuss the merits of some policy proposals that fit with this SDR approach.

However, in view of the difficulties discussed here, we do think it ill-advised to try to tackle the issue of responsible use in the citizen's stake entirely by use restrictions. We favour endowing young people with some capital that they are free to use as fully as they like. In the next section we consider how we might promote responsible use of this capital without resort to formal use restrictions.

Alternatives to use restriction: education, advice and mentoring

In this section we discuss three possibilities: linking a CG to *education and information* while the account holder grows up; the provision of *advice* (which could be structured in a number of ways with varying degrees of conditionality); and targeted support from *mentors* for some deprived groups. These options are not all mutually exclusive and could be combined in a number of ways.

General education and provision of information. Where a CG takes the form of a fund that builds up from birth, as the CTF does, there is a lot of potential for integrating the policy with education (Hind, 2002). As we noted above, the government intends to use the CTF as a vehicle for developing financial education in schools, forging links with subjects such as maths and citizenship education. This, combined with the sending of statements to children every birthday, and readily available information about the CTF through schools and the internet, can work to 'keep the account alive' in people's minds. Where CTF holders are reminded of the account more regularly, think more about it themselves, and talk more about it with family and friends, they are perhaps more likely to consider seriously how to spend the funds. However, we are not sure that basic education and provision of information alone, as the British government currently intends, will be enough to promote responsible use. There is a strong case for reinforcing this with a system of supportive advice and perhaps additional intensive mentoring for some children as account holders approach 18.

Supporting advice. We understand advice here to be one-on-one discussions with a professional adviser. It would be available before account holders access their CG, at some point in their late teens. The adviser could be a teacher or a careers adviser, such as those working in the Connexions service of local authority youth services in Britain. Indeed, Britain already has a comprehensive system of careers services that could be built on (OECD, 2003a). Trends in the nature of the advice profession are also helpful. Whereas in the past advisers used to specialise, the trend now is towards training more generic advisers. Careers advice for young people, for example, is no longer delivered through the Careers Service but through generic personal advisers, working with a general advice service for 13- to 19-year-olds, Connexions. We can imagine three models of supportive advice:

1) *Advice model 1: available but voluntary.* Under this model an interview, or sequence of interviews with an adviser, would be available to all CG holders, but access to the funds would not be conditional on attending any interview. With encouragement from teachers, parents and wider extended family, take-up could be fairly high. But take-up could vary, and there must be a concern that those who most need the advice might be least likely to volunteer for it.

2) *Advice model 2: access to CG conditional on advice.* A second model is to make access to CG funds conditional on attending an advice interview or sequence of interviews. If CG holders do not discuss their plans for the use of funds with a professional adviser, they would not receive clearance to access the funds. Under this model, some might attend the advice session without taking it seriously, but for most it would contribute to them becoming better informed about the options for spending the funds and help ensure that they think about how to use it as productively as possible. As part of the process, each CG holder could be required to draw up a plan that outlines how they intend to use the funds.

3) *Advice model 3: access to CG conditional on agreement of adviser.* A third, stronger model would be to give advisers a gate-keeping role. Access to the CG would be conditional not only on attending an advice interview, or sequence of such interviews, but on satisfying the adviser that one has responsible plans for how the funds will be used. Clearly, however, this model raises a lot of problems. Not least, it gives considerable power to the adviser, which could be used arbitrarily. How could government provide sufficient guidance to ensure fairness while simultaneously ensuring flexibility and necessary discretion for the adviser? Will there be an appeals process for CG holders to challenge advisers' judgments? Moreover, young people would surely learn to 'play the system', telling advisers what they want to hear, in order not to lose their funds. Under this model, with the threat of losing access to one's CG hanging grimly in the air, it is conceivable that young people will actually be less forthcoming about their real intentions to use the CG than under models 1 and 2. In addition, many professional advisers would feel uncomfortable with this gate-keeping role, perhaps seeing it even as contrary to their professional ethos.

Of the three models, model 3 strikes us as far too problematic. But models 1 and 2 are definitely worth consideration.

Targeted mentoring. The above policies we think of as universal, available to all CG holders. These universal policies could be complemented by more intensive support and guidance targeted at specific groups. This could be provided through existing long-term relationships that young adults have with professionals or through new mentoring relationships. Groups of young adults with long-term relationships with professionals include those leaving care, those in contact with the criminal justice system, and those with a social worker for another reason. These professionals could offer additional advice on use of CGs. Care leavers, for example, already draw up a 'care leaving plan', which helps this group think about their transition into independent adulthood. This could readily be modified to include a discussion of how to make use of a CG. However, there might be other young adults who could benefit from more intensive support. One option here would be to empower advisers under, say, advice model 2 set out above, to refer some CG holders to a mentor.

By mentoring we mean a long-term, usually one-on-one, relationship between a mentor and a mentee. In Britain the National Mentoring Network has over 1,600 members and there are likely to be many more unregistered providers. Local authorities could draw up a list of mentors in an area to which advisers could refer CG holders. Those referred would meet with the mentor voluntarily.

Two caveats need to be entered here. One is that for mentoring to work, the mentor and the mentee need to be well matched; training for the mentor is vital, throughout the relationship; and relationships need to be long term (Hall, 2002). Hence, mentoring will be very resource intensive and realistically can be offered only to a small fraction of those reaching 18. Second, given the costs involved, it is probably desirable that teenagers receive more from the mentoring relationship than just advice on how to use a CG. Indeed, the mentoring relationship may not be viable as a relationship if it is focused only on this one (albeit important) thing, rather than on the mentee's broader situation and needs.

It would be unrealistic to see intensive mentoring as the main way of promoting responsible use of CGs. But as part of a system in which all young people receive education linked to their accounts, and are required to attend at least one advice interview (model two above), targeted mentoring could help to address the issue.

Conclusion

Public opinion work to date suggests that CG policies, such as the CTF, receive solid popular support, but that this is tempered by a strong concern over the responsible use of the capital grants. If further public monies are to be directed towards such policies, this concern must be addressed.

We have identified three basic strategies for doing so: complementary education; eligibility restrictions; and use restrictions. Of these, we have not considered eligibility restrictions in depth (although we have noted one very modest variant on the idea under which children could earn top-ups to their CTF for volunteering and civic participation, an idea explored a little further in the conclusion to this book). So far as use restrictions are concerned we have expressed doubt that these are necessarily wrong in principle, but we have noted some practical problems with this strategy that count against relying heavily on it. With specific reference to the CTF, we have argued that a more plausible way forward rests on a deepening of the British government's declared educational strategy. This would involve creating a universal system of advice and targeted assistance from mentors for young people as they confront the question of how they will make use of their CTF accounts.

However, we have suggested that the CTF might be complemented by other individual accounts that focus quite narrowly on specific uses or contingencies, rather like the model of social drawing rights under discussion in continental Europe. In the case of some of the proposed accounts, the administrative challenges involved may not be insuperable, and precisely because the accounts are tied closely to specific uses and contingencies that are widely seen as legitimate by taxpaying publics, the accounts might not be subject to the same anxieties over responsible use as pure capital accounts. Proposals for more use- and contingency-specific accounts of this kind will now be considered in Chapters Nine to Eleven.

NINE

Caretaker resource accounts for parents

Anne L. Alstott[1]

Introduction

In this chapter, I propose asset grants to address a persistent inequity of modern society: the precarious economic position of those parents, mostly mothers, who sacrifice market opportunities to rear children. New *caretaker resource accounts* would give every parent who cares for a child under 13 an annual grant of $5,000, or approximately £2,500. The money could only be used to pay for one of three items: childcare, education, or retirement savings. All three would improve parents' future options and permit maximum flexibility in deploying resources over time.

The proposal for caretaker resource accounts reflects a normative commitment to individual freedom. One core claim is that an assets approach best supports each person's capacity to plan her life over time, with appropriate state support but minimal state intervention. A second central claim is that an assets approach can enhance the economic options of mothers in a wide variety of circumstances, from the poorest through the middle class.

Society can – and should – do more to protect mothers' life chances. In the US and Britain, mothers work less, earn less, and achieve less in public life than men or childless women. Although more mothers than ever work in jobs, many work part time or take years out, and even those who hold full-time jobs interrupt their working lives at higher rates than other workers. These patterns persist across income classes. To be sure, middle-class mothers are materially better off than their lower-class peers, but both groups face economic insecurity due to their limited earning power. Middle-class mothers are often only a divorce away from real economic distress.

Child rearing is intrinsically important to any society that aspires to greater equality of opportunity because enduring care by a parent (or a parent figure) is critical to children's development. While schools and other public institutions supplement parental care, it is the close and lasting relationship between parent and child that gives the child the emotional and social tools to take her place in the world. Parenthood is truly the last 'no exit' relationship left: marriages now come and go, but parenthood endures. Even when one parent exits, the other – typically the mother – remains. Ninety-five percent of children have never spent more than a month apart from their primary parent, usually their mother (Lugaila, 2003).

In developed societies, the parental role currently conflicts with employment. Preparing children for modern life requires care for 18 years (or more), and the work not only demands long hours but also limits life choices for the children's sake. Parents cannot choose jobs, partners or locations according to their whims; personal fulfilment takes a backseat to parental obligation.

The discussion draws on examples from the US, because I am most familiar with US data and policies. But while details differ, the policy landscape should be recognisable to readers from other countries, particularly Britain. As in Britain, many US mothers work part time (or not at all); paid childcare is costly relative to wages; and government subsidies are small. The proposal for caretaker accounts requires greater cultural and policy translation in other European countries, particularly those with already-developed public infrastructure for childcare. Yet it is worth thinking through the advantages of an asset approach, which could (among other advantages) complement efforts to enhance labour market flexibility by de-linking social welfare provision from employment.

Finally, a caveat: this chapter focuses on parents specifically rather than care workers generally. For example, it does not consider how asset accounts might assist people who care for older people or those with disabilities. This relatively narrow focus helps centre the discussion on one group (parents) who are relatively close in age and life stage and who share a task (rearing young children) that has relatively clear aims and time line. In contrast, the set of *all* care workers is quite diverse, ranging from young to quite old, and their relationships of care are quite variable, from the committed to the casual. An asset approach surely merits greater exploration for this broader set of care workers. But any analysis must take into account the variability of individual situations, as well as their commonalities.

Caretaker resource accounts compared to existing programmes for parents

Under caretaker resource accounts, each parent receives an equal grant of resources per year, which can then be combined in unique ways according to each parent's circumstances and plans. As the accounts aim to improve economic opportunities for parents who provide children with intensive and lasting care, the programme is limited to caretaker-parents, meaning parents who live with their children, and should not be available to absent parents. When both parents live with their children (either because the whole family lives together or because parents live apart but share joint physical custody), we could envisage the entire account going to the 'primary' caretaker, perhaps identified by lower earnings; or the account being split equally; or a combination of the two. These solutions are not perfect, but that should not be unduly discouraging: any large-scale public programme encounters similar administrative difficulties when it uses simple rules to approximate complex social facts (for example, the welfare system sets its benefits based on low income, even although poverty is complex in its causes and effects).

The caretaker-parent could spend her entire grant in the current year or save some, earning interest in the meantime. She could spend all $5,000 on one item or split it up among different uses. Because of this flexibility, the programme would be useful not only to parents who remain in paid work but also to those who leave paid employment or take part-time jobs and return to the full-time workforce later on.

Why $5,000? Simply to illustrate that a substantial, although not budget-busting, sum of money could make a significant difference in parents' life options. To make a difference, the asset grant should not be trivial; a few hundred dollars would provide only symbolic help. But an annual asset transfer similar to this value would mark a significant increase in the resources available to the average parent. Keep in mind that the typical family lives on about $50,000 per year and has little or no liquid savings. For these families, $5,000 would add significantly to the resources available to parents.

For example, suppose that Abigail is the caretaker-parent of a new baby. The government would establish an account in her name, on the books of a government agency or a private financial institution, and would deposit $5,000 once a year. Abigail's account would receive annual deposits as long as she remained the child's caretaker, until the child reached age 13. (This age is chosen as the age when many children no longer need paid childcare, but any cut-off is arbitrary.) Each year,

Abigail could spend up to $5,000 on childcare or on tuition for herself or she could make a deposit of $5,000 into a retirement account in her own name. If she spent less than $5,000 in any year, the unspent funds would accumulate with interest to be used in a future year. Abigail could not, however, withdraw cash or spend the money on other items (for example, living expenses for her family or school tuition for her child). This restriction would ensure that Abigail uses her resources to expand her own opportunities rather than to improve her family's short-term living standard. While this restriction is sensible given the aims of this programme, it does mean that caretaker resource accounts could supplement, but would not replace, anti-poverty programmes – an issue explored in more depth below.

The childcare subsidy implicit in caretaker resource accounts would be especially valuable to a moderate- or lower-income Abigail. For these caretakers, childcare costs are often high relative to earnings, and yet childcare is an important determinant of mothers' ability to work. A childcare subsidy of $5,000 may seem modest to an upper-middle-class family used to the price of nanny care or high-end daycare. But in fact, the $5,000 annual grant exceeds the average annual cost of childcare in the US even for full-time workers, for workers with small children, and for middle-class families.

The $5,000 voucher is more generous than existing US childcare subsidies in several respects. Most obviously, the dollar amount is larger. For example, federal tax subsidies for childcare provide at most $1,500 to $1,800 per year. Moreover, that programme assists only a subset of families – two-earner couples and single parents with earnings above the poverty line. Existing subsidies vary by family income, sometimes in arbitrary ways. Working-class families may earn too much to qualify for low-income childcare subsidies, yet too little to benefit much from tax subsidies for childcare.

Caretaker-parents with low and moderate incomes could also benefit from the options other than childcare. It may initially seem that such caretakers would need to use every dollar for childcare while working. But the need for childcare depends on the child's age and the family's circumstances: only about half of two-earner families with children under age 13 purchase paid childcare. School-age children require less childcare than infants and toddlers. In addition, in every income class, a substantial fraction of mothers do not hold paid jobs or work only part time, meaning they need less childcare. Some workers have cheaper sources of childcare: it is common for families of modest means to use relatives for care, or for husbands and wives to split shifts and purchase little or no paid care.

Parents who did not spend all their funds on childcare could use the remainder of their $5,000 to supplement their retirement savings. This option would be especially valuable to low- and moderate-income caretakers, most likely to work in jobs with no private pension benefits. It would also improve old-age security for the significant percentage of caretakers in every income class who spend time out of the workforce or in part-time work. In contrast, existing tax incentives for retirement savings are far less functional for caretakers and especially those of modest means. These subsidies apply only to savings by paid workers; they confer the greatest tax savings on higher-income workers, and they require workers or employers to make (in effect) a matching contribution.

The education option should also be valuable to low- and moderate-income caretakers, who often have less education to begin with and less disposable wealth for paying tuition to improve their education. The caretaker resource account would supplement, not supplant, present student-aid programmes, making existing grants more effective, and decreasing students' need to take out loans. The education voucher would not be restricted to university education but could also be used for vocational and technical training and community colleges. Most conventional student aid for higher education takes the form of loans rather than grants; existing grant programmes tend to provide small dollar amounts targeted to poor recipients.

This brief description raises many questions. For example, why shouldn't parents be able to use their funds for living expenses? And why shouldn't the programme be income-tested? I will turn to these questions, but before taking the programme to pieces, I would like to present it as a whole, in order to show more concretely what caretaker resource accounts could mean for parents in a variety of circumstances.

Three scenarios

Let's now consider three short, hypothetical scenarios which illustrate key advantages of caretaker resource accounts: their availability for different uses according to family needs; their portability as parents change or leave jobs; and their continuing availability over time.

> Beth has worked as a hairdresser since she was 19 and loves her job, even although the income is variable and the benefits nonexistent. She has a good chance to win a promotion to assistant salon manager in the next year. Her husband, Bob, works on a factory assembly line. The union

wage is pretty good, but he dislikes the repetitive tasks, and the commute is more than an hour each way. When Beth and Bob have a baby, Ben, they share responsibility for his care. During the day, Ben stays with a neighbour, who also cares for a few other children. Beth continues to work full time, but because she works nearby, she is more likely than Bob to take time off when Ben is sick or needs to go to the doctor. Both spouses agree that the caretaker resource account funds are best used to help defray the costs of daycare.

When Ben is three, the couple has a second child, and the family's world changes. Beth and Bob feel increasingly harried as they attempt to care for a toddler and a baby, getting children to daycare and parents to work each morning. They worry that their daycare arrangement is not stimulating enough for Ben, who is now the oldest of the four children the neighbour looks after. Bob and Beth would like to send Ben to preschool, but they can only afford a half-day programme and can't pick him up in the middle of the day. Their babysitter can't help out: she can't drive Ben to and from school while also looking after the other children in her care. The daily routine is also beginning to wear on the parents. Bob's long commute means that he leaves the house early and returns late, leaving Beth to drop off and pick up the children and make dinner too, most nights. The baby has chronic ear infections, and both Bob and Beth have nearly used up their sick leave. The last straw is a bout of flu that leaves everyone in the family exhausted. Something has to give.

After careful (and anguished) discussion, Bob and Beth decide that one of them should cut back their working hours for the next couple of years. Beth has just won her promotion and hates to give it up, while Bob has been more and more dissatisfied with his job. Although money is tight, the couple decide that they could manage if Bob takes a lower-paying sales job at the nearby mall, which offers variable hours and evening hours. With Bob at home several days a week, the couple can save money on childcare and send Ben to preschool a couple of mornings per week.

Bob spends more time with the kids; the kids spend less time in daycare; and everyone is a little less tired.

After three more years, Ben is in first grade, the baby has outgrown her ear infections, and Bob is itching to find a better job. Bob uses the accumulated balance in the caretaker resource account (as much as $15,000) to begin training as an electrician, taking classes at the local vocational and technical school. Going forward, Bob and Beth plan to use their caretaker account to pay for daycare for the younger child and after-school care for Ben. When the younger child goes to first grade, the couple's childcare expenses will fall, and they can use the extra funds to supplement their retirement savings.

For two-earner couples, the caretaker resource account functions like a flexible benefits programme, offering a menu of tuition assistance, childcare, and retirement contributions that supplement the benefits – if any – that employers provide. Caretaker accounts can also provide different benefits as family needs change. When Bob and Beth begin to work staggered shifts, so that they no longer need paid childcare (as 20 to 30% of working couples do), they can benefit from tuition assistance. Importantly, all of these options continue to be available even when Bob switches to a part-time job. Caretaker accounts also support partners as they shift roles over time, as in this example, when Beth and Bob, at different times, take on the primary caretaker role.

In the hypothetical example, Bob and Beth are neither particularly well off nor terribly poor. But their place on the economic ladder is not crucial: a Bob and Beth with similar concerns might be higher in the middle class, with Beth working to make partner at her accounting firm, and Bob leaving advertising for journalism. Or they might be far poorer, two high-school dropouts working at low-skilled jobs and hoping to earn their high-school equivalency diplomas. In any of these situations, caretaker resources would improve their options regarding education, childcare, and pension savings. The child-rearing years tend to be financially hard-pressed even for middle-class families because consumption needs are also high. Even middle-class families typically have little wealth until late middle-age, and then their wealth tends to be illiquid, tied up in pensions and equity stakes in cars and houses. Poor and working-class families often have zero or negative net wealth, even later in life. Childcare costs tend to be high relative to income for all these groups, and experts predict that childcare subsidies could improve employment opportunities and opportunities to purchase paid childcare. Many jobs have minimal or no private pension benefits: this situation is almost universal for low-paid jobs but also common for some higher-paying jobs.

One characteristic feature of any asset-based plan is that participants receive a fixed sum – here, $5,000 – and must make trade-offs. If Bob and Beth use their funds on childcare, they cannot also spend the money on tuition or retirement. That structure may seem unduly restrictive: wouldn't Beth and Bob be better off if they could simultaneously claim assistance with childcare, tuition *and* retirement?

The answer is that caretaker resource accounts, like other asset-based approaches, incorporate a normative judgement about the fair allocation of life-planning funds among participants and across different uses. To see the point, suppose that there are 1,000 eligible caretaker-parents, and a fixed, total budget of $5 million. Caretaker resource accounts have three features: they divide the total funds equally among individual caretakers; they permit each caretaker to choose how to allocate the funds among childcare, education, and retirement; and they allow caretakers to defer unspent amounts across years.

Caretaker resource accounts are thus *egalitarian*, *individualistic* and *decentralised*, compared to more familiar programmes. Traditional subsidies tend to allocate funds to different purposes in a centralised fashion (devoting, say, one third of the budget to childcare programmes, one-third to education, and one third to retirement funding). They may also adopt a use-it-or-lose-it structure: individuals who do not claim their subsidy in one year cannot ask for twice as much the next year. And they may ration resources unequally among claimants: only those who apply receive funds, and energetic applicants who seek multiple subsidies may claim more than their more passive peers.

> Carla left her secretarial job after the birth of her child. Although the loss of one pay cheque meant a tight budget for Carla and her husband, they decided it was worth it to have one parent at home during the preschool years. Carla ended up taking five years out of the workforce, working intermittently at part-time jobs during the Christmas season or in the evenings to help meet the family budget. Each year, Carla deferred all the balance in her caretaker resource account.
>
> Carla's marriage broke up when the oldest child was just five. In the divorce settlement, Carla received sole custody

of the children and modest monthly child-support payments. Carla decided to reenter the workforce, but to upgrade her skills to qualify for a better job. She used the accumulated balance in her caretaker resource account ($25,000 plus interest) to fund a two-year degree programme in human resources management at the local state college. The caretaker resource account funded tuition, books and childcare while she attended classes. Carla and her kids lived in a small apartment during those two years, making ends meet on child-support payments from her ex-husband and wages from part-time jobs. But at age 35, Carla accepted an entry-level job as a manager in the human resources department of a large firm.

Carla's interrupted work path is typical of a significant percentage of mothers. Even after children leave infancy, 35 to 45% of mothers in every income class are at-home mothers or part-time workers. Because caretaker resource accounts are independent of the caretaker's paid-work status, they provide benefits that workplace programmes do not. In Carla's case, she can save her grant for five years because she needs little or no paid childcare; later on, she can reenter the workforce with a new degree. The programme does not, of course, erase the effects of Carla's years out of the workforce; at age 35, she is an entry-level worker, in contrast to Beth, who remained in continuous full-time work and has already been promoted.

When Carla divorces, the caretaker resource account becomes especially valuable. The caretaker funds should be segregated in her name and exempt from property division in the event of a divorce. The caretaker grant should also be excluded in calculating alimony and child-support awards. Even if alimony rules were strengthened, as they should be, caretaker resources would provide a guaranteed capital grant that a divorced caretaker could count on to supplement her retirement wealth or to support her (through childcare and education) as she returns to work.

As a single parent of two children, Danielle needs steady work but also time to take care of the children when they're sick or to get them to doctor's appointments and after-school activities. Most recently, Danielle has worked in a commission sales job that offers flexible hours but some variability in income. In a good year, when sales are high, Danielle manages to save something. In other years, when the economy is depressed or the children are having a tough time, Danielle earns less, and sometimes her working hours drop to part time.

Over time, Danielle uses the caretaker resource account in different ways. For a few years, Danielle's cousin looked after the children during the working day. During those years, the caretaker resource account built up a significant balance. Later, when Danielle's cousin got sick, the childcare voucher eased the family budget a bit. When Danielle's hours drop to part-time, childcare costs also drop and the balance builds up again. Over time, Danielle has deferred about half the annual grant each year and intends to use the funds for retirement savings – a welcome boost, because the sales job has no pension benefits.

Danielle's situation demonstrates the adaptability of the caretaker resource account to changing circumstances. When she has a relative to provide childcare, or her hours drop to part time, the caretaker grant can be used for retirement savings instead. Importantly, Danielle can count on her resources regardless of the hours she works: she does not lose caretaker benefits when her hours drop to part time.

Caretaker resource accounts could make a dramatic impact on the economic situation of single mothers, who are an extremely poor group. Whether divorced or never-married, single mothers cluster at the lower end of the economic spectrum: in 1999, for example, 50% of single mothers had incomes of $24,000 or less (US Bureau of the Census, 2001, table 671).

Danielle also illustrates one situation that is particularly common for less well-off caretakers: she uses relative care rather than paid childcare. In general, poorer workers tend to use less expensive childcare than middle-class ones and are more likely to have their children cared for by a relative than by a stranger. This group could use caretaker resource accounts in one of two ways. Parents who are using relative care out of financial hardship could use the childcare voucher to improve the quality of childcare. But relative care is not always the option of last resort: studies suggest that many parents *prefer* relative care to commercial care.

These scenarios illustrate parents' different responses to caretaker resource accounts: Beth stays in the workforce, while Bob and Carla take time off, and Danielle's work hours vary over time. But how will the programme affect mothers' labour supply overall – is it possible that too many mothers will drop out of the workforce, worsening their long-term prospects? The question is of added importance in Britain, where the government's target of abolishing child poverty in a generation has led to an emphasis on increasing lone-parent employment.

But it is a difficult question to answer, because the empirical economics literature has typically studied programmes that differ significantly from caretaker resource accounts. At one extreme are welfare payments – small cash grants intended to supplement family consumption. At the other extreme are programmes that provide resources only to support work, or to reward it (for example, childcare subsidies and work subsidies, such as the earned income tax credit in the US or the working tax credit in Britain). Caretaker resource accounts fall somewhere in the middle. Unlike income support, caretaker grants would not directly support time away from work: one cannot use one's grant to pay the grocery bill. But unlike work-support programmes, caretaker accounts would enhance caretakers' non-work options, and permit parents more easily to defer employment.

The likely answer is that mothers would respond to caretaker resource accounts in different ways, but many would increase their work effort, either immediately or over time. Empirical studies of pre-1996 welfare programmes show reductions in work effort, but of relatively small magnitude. But these studies, as I suggested, are likely to exaggerate the negative labour-supply effects of caretaker resource grants, which do not provide current income support and which require funds to be deployed in some future-oriented way. In contrast to these pre-1996 programmes, the earned income tax credit and childcare subsidies have been shown to increase the labour supply of both single and married mothers.

Some mothers will experience caretaker grants as a work subsidy: they will choose the childcare voucher and will (re)enter the labour force or increase their hours of work. Mothers who do not respond in the short term may do so in the longer term, reentering the workforce sooner than otherwise or acquiring education to reenter at a higher level than they would have done in the absence of the programme. Over the long run, the programme could foster more complex and varied life patterns than we see today, in which (for example) early education and job experience tend to set the tone for the long term. In other work, I have explored the programme's likely effect on parents' educational attainment and savings and on dynamics within the family (Alstott, 2004, ch 6).

Note, however, that caretaker resource accounts are not designed to maximise short-run maternal labour supply. It should be counted as a success rather than a failure if some caretaker-parents use their new resources to work less, or to combine paid work and child-rearing in sequence, while others recommit themselves to paid work. Put another way, caretaker resource accounts would improve choice but largely within the context of existing market and family institutions. The accounts cannot, by themselves, achieve perfect gender equality in the marketplace or the home. No single policy can. Instead, we should understand caretaker resource accounts as a realistic, affordable programme that could improve mothers' situation in the short term *and* the long term, in combination with other measures – for instance, anti-discrimination policies in the workplace and in schools – that combat gendered patterns of socialisation, career preparation, and workplace segregation.

How do caretaker resource accounts stack up against alternative programmes of a realistic kind? The remainder of the chapter compares caretaker resource accounts to two familiar approaches: the citizen's stake (in its social inheritance mode) and income support for the poor.

Caretaker resource accounts compared to social inheritance

Social inheritance proposals typically (although not invariably) offer unlimited options, and in *The stakeholder society* (1999) Bruce Ackerman and I rejected state constraints on the use of asset stakes as unwarranted paternalism. Caretaker resource accounts, in contrast, may at first glance appear to provide an oddly limited menu of options. Why should parents be required to choose among just three options? And even if limitations are appropriate, why are these three uses – childcare, education and retirement – the right ones?

The answer, in short, is that caretaker resource accounts serve a social agenda different to that served by social inheritance. The citizen's stake ensures every young person a fair initial share of resources. *Every* person, including those who are (or will be) parents, steps up to her stake as an indicator of her social equality. Caretaker resource accounts, on the other hand, give some citizens a second bite at the apple – a second helping of society's resources – in light of a chosen life plan, parenthood. The purpose of caretaker resource accounts is to redress the conflict between society's interest in good parenting and parents' opportunity for employment. Because society demands that parents limit their own options for the children's sake, society then steps forward with additional resources to offset that limitation. The objective is not simply to give caretakers cash to spend. Instead, the goal is to enhance caretakers' long-term economic opportunities.

Accordingly, all three options involve investment in future-oriented activities. Childcare assists caretakers who wish to preserve their skills and opportunities by holding jobs. Education helps caretakers improve or maintain their skills. Retirement assistance is most obviously linked to the long term, assisting those who, in the shorter run, work for low wages, no benefits, or not at all. Caretaker resources should not underwrite current consumption or even future-oriented, altruistic projects unless they directly advance the caretaker's own fortunes. The point of preventing altruistic uses is not to squash parents' social commitments, but to require them to invest, in some way, in endeavours that build their own market experience and future opportunities.

For practical reasons, however, some parents may find that their grants cannot be used to support their preferred life projects, even although they have the requisite future orientation. For example, the programme (as I envision it) would not permit investments in entrepreneurship, even although that route could be quite productive for many. This is a bureaucratic difficulty rather than a matter of principle: the problem is that it can be difficult to distinguish entrepreneurship from misuse of funds.

The caretaker resource grant would be paid yearly, rather than in one lump sum like the social inheritance, for similar reasons. Paying the caretaker grants over time would provide a safety net for changes in plans: a child's ill health, a family move, a divorce, or simply a change in life objectives could motivate a caretaker to wish to change his plans for the future. Paying the grant yearly protects future caretakers, too. It would be inappropriate (and would invite strategic behaviour) if the caretaker–parent at birth could grab 18 years' worth of resources, leaving nothing to a later caretaker if the first one exits.

Of course, like any in-kind or voucher programme, caretaker resource accounts are vulnerable to the phenomenon of *cash equivalence*. Nominally, caretaker resource accounts grant $5,000 to every caretaker–parent and require her to use the money for childcare, education or retirement. But it is obvious that any caretaker who would in the absence of the programme buy one of the three services will find that caretaker resources free up extra funds in her general budget. This sort of substitution affects subsidy programmes of many kinds: a subsidy targeted to one good (say, retirement savings or childcare or education) may not increase net purchases, if consumers already buy that good and simply substitute the subsidy for their own funds. In that case, the subsidy redistributes wealth but does not change the consumption bundle.

Substitution may be more limited in caretaker resource accounts than in existing programmes, because caretaker accounts would assist many families who do not spend $5,000 on these items (Alstott, 2004, ch 6). But, in any event, cash equivalence does not fundamentally undermine the programme's aims. Caretaker resource accounts will ensure that caretaker-parents spend *at least $5,000* on future-oriented investments in their opportunity set, even if caretakers also have extra money in their general budget.

Caretaker resource accounts compared to income support for the poor

As well as not supporting present consumption, the caretaker resource accounts run counter to the usual impulses of social welfare provision (in the US) by not being income-tested. Why? I have considerable sympathy for income-support proposals; indeed, caretaker resource accounts share many of the normative commitments of basic income. Both would target resources to individuals to improve economic options while preserving room for choice. Both would enhance care workers' opportunities without privileging market workers over others.

But I believe that caretaker resource accounts better serve the cause of justice for parents. The critical point is that society faces two different problems, and different remedies are appropriate. Income transfers (and other consumption subsidies) address the problem of poverty due to low earnings capacity, whereas caretaker resource accounts tackle a separate social problem: how to alleviate the conflict between child-rearing and market pursuits.

Caretaker resource accounts therefore reject income testing, and aim for a net transfer to caretaker-parents *at every income level*, because family income is a poor proxy for mothers' economic opportunities. In principle, caretaker resource accounts could be 'opportunity tested', awarding extra resources only to those parents whose opportunity sets were significantly narrowed by child-rearing. But human beings unfortunately do not come with autonomy gauges, and income testing is a troublesome substitute for opportunity testing.

Income tests generally operate based on *family* income, both for technical reasons and principled ones. It is difficult in practice to allocate income to each member of a household, and usually unnecessary, because most income-tested programmes intend to boost family consumption resources. But family income may overstate the resources to which an *individual* caretaker-parent has access. Consider the hypothetical at-home mother of a middle-class family – a woman who has sacrificed her own career prospects to raise the children. She may live in comfort and yet have limited control over her husband's earnings, and little opportunity to invest money to expand her own options.

The caretaker role itself tends to reduce women's control over household assets and to reduce their power to bargain for a change in role over time. And the lasting nature of parental obligation adds uncertainty to the mix: even a mother who is doing well today will find that child-rearing limits her options should her circumstances take a turn for the worse – the loss of a job, or the death of a spouse. The economic consequences of divorce underscore this opportunity burden: a formerly affluent caretaker can find herself with severely limited opportunities when the marriage dissolves.

Conclusion: the uses – and misuses – of the asset approach

In the US, the last decade has been a dark one in social policy toward parents. Meagre, time-limited welfare benefits express the view that poor single mothers should not have children they cannot afford. Child benefits in the tax code provide small sums rather than real assistance to parents. Federal subsidies for childcare are small in amount and reimburse only a fraction (20-30%) of costs. Although the US tax code still confers major subsidies on the middle class, these take the form of benefits for the childless and parents alike. Deductions for home mortgage interest and retirement savings confer no special assistance to parents as *parents*. Asset-based policies have provided a little light in the gloom. Proposals to build individual wealth seem to have caught the spirit of the times, and programmes like Individual Development Accounts and, in Britain, the Child Trust Fund (CTF) have capitalised on the potential to redistribute wealth while helping build it.

But the strengths of the asset approach can become weaknesses if the device is ill-suited to the aim of the policy. Sometimes, the language of 'ownership' and 'private accounts' is code for a *lessening* of government's commitments to citizens. In the US, privatisation proposals for social security (public old-age pensions) fall into this camp. But, as pointed out by Glennerster and McKnight in this volume (Chapter Six), *nothing in the asset approach requires the abandonment of vulnerable groups to economic risk*. Caretaker resource accounts, for instance, can and should co-exist with income support that establishes a secure consumption floor for all children and for adults with low earnings.

In evaluating the citizen's stake as a model for social innovation, it is critical to bear in mind that wealth transfers can solve many problems but not all. For instance, caretaker resource accounts address primarily the situation of parents with ordinary childcare responsibilities. They cannot adequately address the special needs of parents whose children have serious illnesses or disabilities. In such cases, the economics of child-rearing will be especially challenging. And such parents will require greater, and more individually tailored, assistance than caretaker resource accounts can provide. In other work, I suggest how we might craft a complementary programme to address their situation (Alstott, 2004, chs 7 and 11).

What caretaker resource accounts can do is help parents provide continuity of care while pursuing lives of their own. They should not be the end of the story, but they are a good first step.

Note
[1] The material in this chapter is adapted from my book, *No exit* (2004), with permission of Oxford University Press. Further detail on most points raised in this chapter can be found in this book.

TEN

Carework: are care accounts the answer?

Jane Lewis

Introduction

Care occupies a complicated position in the welfare state. There are many groups that are commonly recognised to be to a greater or lesser extent dependent and in need of care – the young, the old (especially frail older people), and people with disabilities – but many would argue that all healthy adults require care, emotional if not physical. Care may be informal, with family members, kin or neighbours delivering it, or formal, with care taking place in an institutional setting; it can be paid – even neighbours and family carers may be paid – or unpaid (as is usually the case with informal care); and outside the family it may be delivered by the public, private or voluntary sector. There is no avoiding the issue that carework, wherever it takes place, in the family or institutions, is profoundly gendered. The responsibility for the vast majority of unpaid carework rests with women, and they also form the vast majority of what is in all western countries, to a greater or lesser extent, a low-paid formal care workforce.

Care is hardly a new issue, but it is new to the political agenda. This is in large measure due to the major changes that have been taking place in the relationships between families, labour markets and states (examined in Section 1). The changes are sufficiently dramatic to warrant new thinking about care and carework, and care accounts may have a part to play. But I argue that, given the nature of care and carework (Section 2) and the existing policy inheritances and logics (Section 3) it is unlikely that care accounts can be a major part of the answer (other than possibly in the US) (Section 4). In particular care accounts make two related claims that I call into question: first for the importance, possibly superiority, of cash provision over services, and, second, the opportunities that they present for exercising greater individual choice.

Why care has become a major issue for welfare states

It is perfectly possible to interpret the development of modern social policies as being centrally concerned with care needs (Jenson, 1997), whether for health care, or cash support in times of sickness or unemployment. However, this is ahistorical; provision for care has not been the stated aim of social policies in 20th century welfare states. Rather the central preoccupation has always been with the work – welfare relationship and the incentive effects of provision on the worker's inclination to search for employment. Care needs have not been prioritised and, in the UK case, social care services were the 'poor relation' in the post-war welfare state. Provision, whether in the form of cash benefits or services, has tended to be fragmentary, heavily means-tested and residual.

So, the fact that policies to address care are at the top of the political agenda in many western countries is something new, indeed, social care is one of the few areas of welfare provision to have expanded in most western European countries over the last decade (Daly, 2002) (particularly in respect of childcare services). The main explanation lies in far-reaching family and labour market changes, the nature of which may constitute a case for considering new approaches to social provision for care. Modern welfare states were built up in the early 20th century on the basis of full-time male employment and stable families. The core social programme – insurance against a range of risks – became part and parcel of the labour contract, with provision being made for 'dependants' (usually wives and children). This male-breadwinner model assumed men to be the primary earners and women to be the primary carers in the family. The model thus made provision for the support of women's informal care chiefly through men's contributions and benefits. Female economic dependence was inscribed in the model.

With the widespread entry of women into the labour market; the (much smaller) reduction in male labour-force participation (due mainly to early retirement); the much greater need for two incomes (particularly in relation to rising house prices); and the even more dramatic and rapid pace of family change over the last quarter of a century, assumptions as to the existence and desirability of a male-breadwinner model family could not hold. Dual-earner families have become the norm in most western countries, although the hours women work outside the home varies hugely. High and stable rates of divorce and high rates of unmarried motherhood, driven by increased cohabitation, have resulted in high proportions of lone-mother families in many northern and western European countries and in North America. It is difficult to combine paid and unpaid work, although in western Europe, where a one-and-a-half-breadwinner model family has become the norm, women continue to do a lot of informal carework. But it is very difficult for lone mothers to act as both an adequate breadwinner and a carer. In the US, where the vast majority of women work full time, there is, unsurprisingly, much more outcry about family stress and 'the crisis of care' (Hewlett, 1991; Hochschild, 1995; Heymann, 2000; Skocpol, 2000; Schor, 2001). In addition, population ageing, a major challenge for all developed societies, has increased care needs. Given these shifts, Heymann (2000, p 173) has suggested that 'what employment insurance was to families in which there was one wage earner and one homemaker, family leave insurance is to families with no adult at home'.

These major changes have coincided with a period of welfare state restructuring, the main feature of which has been an effort to shift the emphasis from rights to responsibilities and from so-called 'passive' to 'active' welfare provision, such that claimants on the welfare system are 'encouraged' into work and work is made 'to pay' (Lødemel and Trickey, 2000). Gilbert (2002) has characterised these trends in terms of a series of shifts from social support to social inclusion via employment, from measures of decommodification (that enable people to leave the labour market for due cause) to ways of securing commodification, and from unconditional benefits to benefits that are heavily conditional on work or training. These fundamental changes in ideas about social provision are driven in large measure by the aim of promoting competition and growth (Esping Andersen et al, 2002; European Commission, 2000, 2003) and justified in terms of widening the tax base and hence saving the continental European social insurance model.

However, they have also neatly piggybacked onto the erosion of the male-breadwinner family and have been underpinned by research findings that have swung away from condemning the effects of maternal employment on young children towards endorsing institutional provision, at least for three- and four-year-olds (Gregg and Washbrook, 2003). It is significant that the new principles have been applied much more equally to men and women. At the European Union (EU) level, targets for female labour participation have been set and as early as 1993, the European Commission identified the formal care sector as a source of new jobs (Commission of the European Communities, 1993), the implication being that women workers might trade the work of informal care for paid work in the formal care sector.

In this light, the shift in ideas and practices in regard to social welfare systems looks instrumental, but may also appear to be in keeping with greater 'individualisation' in terms of more female participation in the workforce, and more fluidity in family forms and intimate relationships. However, there is a danger that the new set of assumptions about the existence and desirability of an 'adult worker model family' (Lewis, 2001) are outrunning the social reality, for there are still profound gender divisions in both paid and unpaid work. Nowhere is there gender equality in the workforce, and time-use surveys show the small extent to which men have increased their contribution to the unpaid work of care and household labour (Gershuny, 2000). The determination to promote 'active' welfare has focused on the employment side of the employment/care equation and insufficient attention has been paid to the complicated nature of the issues around care. This becomes more significant given that other dimensions of welfare state restructuring in the field of service provision have relied on the introduction of market principles and the conscious promotion of a mixed economy of provision, particularly in the UK. These developments have been justified largely in terms of promoting greater choice of supply (see Jenson and Sineau, 2001), but, while the outcomes in this respect are at best mixed, reform has resulted in both more fragmentation and high turnover in services for older people and childcare. This in turn elicits the need for more rather than less informal carework (for example, to take a child from a daycare centre, where free part-time care is provided, to a childminder).

EU member states have given very partial acknowledgement of the fact that the shift to a set of assumptions based on an adult-worker model family raises problems regarding carework, and it is highly significant that in countries with historically short part-time working on the part of women (the UK, Germany and the Netherlands) there have been major initiatives in recent years to promote childcare services. Such policies are in line with the desire to promote adult employment because it is well known that services provide incentives to female employment, whereas care leaves – which are usually promoted by more conservative politicians – tend to promote female labour exit (Moss and Deven, 1999; Morgan and Zippel, 2003). In Germany, the archetypal social insurance welfare state, with a strong male-breadwinner family tradition, it is additionally significant that increased attention has been paid to family policies in general, over and above the longstanding preoccupation with social provision that preserves the labour market status of the (usually male) recipient (Bleses and Seeleib Kaiser, 2004). The reconciliation of work and family, and most recently attention to work–life balance (a term that is thought to have appeal for a greater proportion of the workforce, particularly men), has come onto the political agenda even in countries such as the UK, where it has never previously been thought to be part of the role of government to intervene in the 'private' care arrangements of families.

Care has never been the main focus for policy making; care policies have been harnessed to other policy goals. Recently this has meant policies designed to increase, above all, female employment (in the UK via tax credits and childcare services). As the levels of service change in a particular nation state, policies for care have again often been driven by other concerns (for example, social care reform in the UK can be seen to have been in large measure dictated by health care reform [Lewis and Glennerster, 1996]). Nevertheless, the development of care services has tended to have redistributive effects between men and women and may legitimately be conceptualised as part of a 'social wage', which in western and northern European countries historically moderated the workings of the male-breadwinner model.

There is therefore a case for looking in more detail at the nature of care and carework in order to establish which issues policy has to address. There is a case for arguing that care is effectively a 'new social risk' (Bonoli, 2004), emerging from the erosion of the male-breadwinner model family. In which case, there may well also be a need for new thinking and new policies to address it. Care accounts appear to offer an individualised cash solution that has the additional merit of facilitating choice at a time when standardised provision, particularly in the form of services, has become suspect, and when public services have proved difficult to reform. However, it remains to be seen which dimensions of the care problem they can address.

What is care?

According to Eva Feder Kittay (1999; and Kittay and Feder, 2000), care consists of meeting the needs of people who cannot meet them themselves. It therefore necessarily involves relations of dependence. Such a definition makes it easy to see the potential for tension arising in respect of the shifts underpinning welfare restructuring towards 'active' welfare and greater insistence on the economic participation of all adults. Kittay's formulation poses a rather stark opposition between relations of dependence and the 'independence' that comes from reliance (some might say dependence) on a wage. Her characterisation of care is undoubtedly accurate in the case of a profoundly disabled person, but may be less apt when it comes to describing the care needed by an early teenager, or indeed in respect of an non-disabled adult. Martha Nussbaum (2003, p 51) offers a larger definition of care and makes the case for care as a universal human need: 'Any real society is a caregiving and care-receiving society, and must therefore discover ways of coping with these facts of human neediness and dependency that are compatible with the self-respect of the recipients and do not exploit the care-givers'.

What this does is draw attention to not just the right of a dependent person to receive care, but also the right to give care (see also Knijn and Kremer, 1997). The human relations of care involve both the care giver and care receiver and may be as, or more, accurately characterised by *inter*dependence and reciprocity, as by dependence (which then tends to be pitted against the need to promote independence, defined in terms of wage-earning). This has particular purchase when it comes to the intergenerational aspects of care relations, which, interestingly, have been ignored in the debate over intergenerational accounting and whether we can afford pension provision in the future (Kotlikoff, 2003).

Joan Tronto's (1993, p 174) argument for an ethic of care suggests that it is the denial of interdependence that effectively devalues care, whether it is carried out in the public sphere as paid work, or in the private sphere of the family and (weakly) compensated by the state:

> Disdain of 'others' who do caring (women, slaves, servants) has been virulent in our culture. This dismissal is inextricably bound up with an attempt to deny the importance of care. Those who are powerful are unwilling to admit their dependence upon those who care for them. To treat care as shabby and unimportant helps to maintain the positions of the powerful vis-à-vis those who do care for them.

A disproportionate amount of care is given by women to women (because a majority of frail older people are female), whether formally or informally, and the reality of interdependence should not obscure either the power relations that may exist in the care relationship – which the addition of a cash payment in respect of one party to the relationship may disturb or reinforce – or in the relationship of both carer and care receiver to the wider society.

The relations of care may thus involve dependence, interdependence and power, as well as trust and love. Early analysis of the care relationship in the informal, unpaid sector insisted that care is embedded in personal relationships of love and obligation and the process of identity formation. Graham (1983, p 30) highlighted the conflation of care as exploited labour (with significant opportunity costs), and care as love rather than mere tending, and as such a key part of female identity: 'Caring is experienced as a labour of love.... The experience of caring is the medium through which women are accepted into and feel they belong to the social world'. Laura Balbo (1987, p 51) also stressed the emotional content of care – what she called women's 'servicing work':

> Unless something is added to material goods in order to link them to what a specific individual expects or wants, personal needs are not satisfied.... Being there to wait, to listen, to respond; to attend to the needs and desires of others; to worry when difficulties are anticipated; to deal with one's own sense of guilt when problems are not successfully resolved: this is servicing.

This means that caring is often a matter of 'passive' attendance (making sure that an old person does not fall, unpicking the knitting that has gone wrong, watching the children play), as well as 'active' tending. How much these dimensions of care can, do or should enter the arena of paid care is a matter of controversy (for example, in respect of the 'content' of nursing, see Davies, 1995; see also Himmelweit, 1995).

If care is a universal human need, then it has to be done and warrants a central place in policy making. The central issues for public policy become how it is valued in both the informal and formal sectors, and how it is shared, between men and women at the level of the household, as well as between family, market, state and employers. As Nussbaum (2003, p 51) has observed, given the human need for care and the gender inequalities in the responsibility for carework, care becomes 'a central issue for gender justice' (see also Moller Okin, 1989). There are also the vexed issues of what is considered to be 'best' for care recipients and what the preferences of care givers and care receivers might actually be.

Existing models of providing for care

Care policies can take very different forms, providing a range of services and cash benefits to carers and care recipients that may be designed to provide time to engage in paid employment or time to care. Policies have grown up in very different ways in different countries, in respect of their form, extent and concentration. For example, the UK has historically done somewhat more to provide for care for older people than for children, whereas in France, Belgium and Italy the reverse has been the case.

In short, different countries operate very different policy logics in respect of carework. Only the US and the Scandinavian countries have models based on the assumption that men and women will be fully engaged in the labour market, however, these models work in very different ways. In the US case, the obligation to enter the labour market is embedded in a residual welfare system that often borders on the punitive in respect of the non-disabled adult. In the Nordic countries, it is supported by an extensive range of care entitlements for adult workers in respect of both children and older people. The US operates a fiercely gender-neutral, equality-defined-as-sameness adult worker model, with substantial legislation regarding equal opportunities in the workplace, but very few public supports for carework, although the market provides good access to affordable (but not necessarily good-quality) institutional and home-based care (often using migrant workers, referred to as the reinvention of domestic service by Schmid, 2000). The Scandinavian model also uses gender-neutral language, but in practice has sought to help to reconcile work and family responsibilities mainly for women. It operates a gender-differentiated 'supported adult worker model', with high penetration of good-quality public services for the care of children and older people and cash transfers in respect of parental leave. As a result, high proportions of women work (long) part-time hours, exercising their right to work a six-hour day when they have preschool children, as well as leaving employment for up to three years if they have two children in rapid succession. As a result, the Swedish labour market is the most sexually segregated in the western world. Swedish women have more choice about combining work and care, but at the expense of equality in the labour market. The introduction of the 'daddy quota' in the Scandinavian countries, whereby men are obliged to take part of the parental leave allocation (usually a month) or lose it altogether, was aimed at changing the way carework is shared at the household level. But this has not been uncontroversial and the new Danish right-wing government abandoned the policy because of the way in which it explicitly tries to change behaviour in the 'private' sphere of the family.

The UK is not entirely without supports for care, but it has relied heavily on family-based care, and it is women's (short) part-time working that has made this possible. Perhaps in order to compensate in what remains relative to other western European countries a low wage economy, men work among the longest hours in the EU. Historically, services for the young were only made available for children at risk, and services for the old when there was no identifiable carer. Cash benefits have recently been made available via the tax credit system for the purchase of childcare, but 45% of childcare in the UK is funded by parents, compared, for example, to 23% in former West Germany. In respect of older people, the UK has attached cash benefits to the carer (via the invalid care allowance, now the carers' allowance), which were conceived as a compensation for lost earnings, and to the person-cared-for (via the attendance allowance for older people and the disability living allowance for people under 65). The disability lobby has been successful in gaining the right to opt for cash payments rather than standardised services, but the terms and conditions of care workers in the casualised private sector – who are the ones likely to be hired – are invariably worse than those of carers in the public sector. The welfare trade-offs and the politics of choice in respect of care are complicated, and have the potential to pit men against women, and carers against care receivers.

It is, furthermore, difficult to be sure of the preferences of care givers, or in the case of older people, care receivers. It is not clear whether British women would want to work full time, or even long part time, if good-quality, accessible and affordable childcare was to be introduced. The same probably goes for Dutch women. On the other hand, Norwegian women, who have historically been closer to their British and Dutch counterparts in their patterns of paid and unpaid work (Leira, 1992), have changed their attitudes towards employment, bringing them more into line with other Scandinavian women (Leira, 2002). Women experience stronger pressures to care than do men and may have more regard for their reputations as carers (Finch and Mason, 1993). In addition, the experience of informal care can bring positive emotional and relational rewards and may well be preferable to a low-paid, low-status, insecure job. Indeed it may be preferable to look after one's own children or mother than take a job looking after other people's. Catherine Hakim (2000) has stressed that a majority of British women are not careerist and prefer the kind of part-time work they have. But revealed preferences regarding carework are embedded in the choice sets available to carers, which are in turn dependent on the level of education and employment available; assumptions about what is the 'proper thing for women to do'; and assumptions about what is the 'proper thing for men to do'. In addition, if the historical experience of formal care services in the UK has been poor, reflecting their poor quality and high cost, then trust in such services is likely to be low.

Care policies involve choices and trade-offs – between men and women, paid and unpaid care workers, and public, private and voluntary sector providers. National systems have developed differently, which is important in considering what kind of solutions may be appropriate. In the US, where care issues have not been considered an appropriate concern for government, it would be very difficult for government to play a role in promoting service provision or indeed to intervene directly and explicitly in any way to secure provision. In EU member states, where for the most part there is a strong tradition of intervention in respect of care, compared to the US in terms of both cash *and* services, there are nevertheless important constraints in terms of the mechanisms that can be used in particular policy contexts. It would, for example, be very difficult to introduce a German or Japanese-style long-term care insurance for care for older people in the UK, where social insurance has dwindled dramatically as a form of provision since the mid-1980s. Both the UK and Germany have expanded the number of childcare places over the last decade, but in the UK this has been done relatively quickly by central government offering pump-priming money to (mainly) private sector bidders, whereas Germany has used the long-established system of local finance and local consensus between public and voluntary providers on the way in which services should develop. Service development has been slower than in the UK, but the places created have proved much more sustainable. Making provision for care is complicated by the needs and wants of carers and care recipients, and is further constrained by the nature of the welfare system.

What can care accounts do?

The tendency in care-related policies is to be over-optimistic about what can be expected from one type of policy. Thus in many western countries considerable hope has pinned on developing 'community' rather than institutional care for older people in the belief that it would prove cheaper and reflect the preferences of care recipients. However, good-quality community care is not cheap and the increase in older people's reliance on their kin is problematic in respect of the expectation that non-disabled adults will be in employment and at odds with the expressed wishes of older people 'not to be a burden' on their children (Arber and Ginn, 1991). The overarching direction of social policy in care over the past decade at nation state level and at EU level has been towards the 'commodification' of all forms of carework. Thus lone mothers might be encouraged to find employment in childcare services (Commission of the European Communities, 1993). This tendency has not been unambiguous: parental-leave policies have been further developed to target fathers in particular in Scandinavia; cash allowances have been increased in Germany alongside childcare services; while in the UK there has been much less concern about whether married mothers are in the labour market than lone mothers (Millar and Rowlingson, 2001). However, the emphasis in policy documents at national and EU levels has stressed the importance of labour-market participation, the implication in the UK being that care can then be bought, albeit with some subsidy from the state on either the demand or supply side.

Such a strategy is highly unlikely to be successful because it ignores both the meaning of care and the complicated nature of care needs. Care is more than tending, more than a task. It often involves emotional labour and relationship, and may be passive as well as active. The obligation to engage in unpaid carework is often strongly felt, especially by women. Women's reputations as carers are often important to them. Furthermore, even when care is commodified and put in the paid labour market, it neither fully substitutes for care in the family nor does away with the need to rely on the informal care provided by relatives and friends. Informal carers may actually see institutional provision – for example, respite care for an older person – as enabling informal care.

There are many groups of people who are dependent on the care of another, and whose needs vary, and there is also a good case to be made that care is a universal human need, in which case considerable thought is required about policies to encourage and enable all adults to care. What do care accounts offer? In the form favoured by Heymann (2000, that is, family-leave insurance, see above, section 1, p 153), they are comparable to the more extended parental-leave schemes now on offer in many western European countries and could be further extended to cover leave to care for older people. But this form of 'care account' represents a policy that is in direct opposition to the commodification of care. It assumes that informal care in the family is best. While it is neither possible nor desirable to commodify all care, the pressures for the development of an adult worker model family are considerable and, increasingly, other forms of social provision – notably pensions – depend on labour-market participation. It has long been noted that people outside the labour market tend to qualify only for 'second-class social entitlements' (Nelson, 1990) and this is more likely to be the case in the future. But given the strong argument for care as a human need, there remains a good case to be made for promoting the *real choice* to do paid and/or unpaid work, in which case the material disadvantage likely to be suffered by those opting for carework, particularly in terms of earnings and pension forgone, must be acknowledged and compensated.

Other forms of care accounts could conceivably hold out the promise of cutting through the complicated web of choices and trade-offs, as well as providing a good fit with increasing individualisation and the messy 'portfolio' careers and family-building patterns, which, taken together, involve multiple life-course transitions (Schmid, 2000). A dedicated sum for care allocated to the individual would in theory permit people to choose whether to care themselves or to buy care and what kind, and would have the advantage from the state's point of view of shifting the responsibility for decisions about the nature of care provision to the individual. Alstott's (2004) proposal for caretaker accounts would permit parents to spend the money on their own education, pension or on childcare. Similarly a Dutch proposal has been formulated to permit individuals to save money via tax deductions and to use it to take time off to care, or for sabbatical leave from paid work, or for pension contributions (Knijn, 2004).

However, there are major problems with these kinds of proposals. First, such a policy strategy is unlikely to make a genuine choice to care possible for all people. Parental leave was implemented from the 1970s in Sweden as an individualised benefit, but the rate of take-up on the part of men proved to be low, with concomitant effects on women's labour-market position. This is important because women's freedom to choose between employment and carework is restricted by the needs *and* choices of others. The perceived need to introduce a 'daddy quota' in respect of parental leave in the Scandinavian case, which does not force men to take care leave, but which does mean that the leave is lost if it is not used, demonstrated the extent to which significant changes in the way that carework is shared at the household level between men and women requires state intervention (Brandreth and Kvande, 2004). The Dutch government's policy of a 'combination scenario' has the aim of encouraging all adults, male and female, to engage in paid and unpaid work, which would effectively transform the one-and-a-half-earner model into a three quarters/three quarters one. However, no effective means of implementing such a radical scheme has been found. Nevertheless, in regard to the issue of sharing care, it is doubtful whether any great change will take place without state intervention. This has been shown to be the case at the level of the household and sharing between men and women, and also in respect of exhortatory policies in respect of employers to introduce 'family-friendly' policies (Lewis, 2002). Care accounts would privatise the issue to the individual account holder, who may not have the power to exercise genuine choice. In the case of the proposals on the table (see especially Alstott, 2004 and Chapter Nine of this volume), it is highly likely that women would use the money for childcare and men for their own education or retirement. Work on the household division of resources has long shown that childcare is considered a female responsibility in the UK, however it is provided.

Second, compensation for carework – the value attached to it – is never likely to be high. Alstott (2004) proposes $5000 per year, but the average weekly cost of a nursery place in the UK is £128, rising to £168 in inner London (House of Commons Work and Pensions Committee, 2003, p 10). When care is commodified the jobs are some of the lowest paid in western economies, which is why they also tend to be carried out by women. If the amount of money provided in a care account is modest, then it is likely to perpetuate low pay in the formal care sector, as well as providing an income for informal carers that will not permit economic autonomy. Furthermore, given that it is likely that under such a system care will be bought from low-paid private sector providers, there can be few guarantees as to its quality. In the US the privatisation of care to the family and the market has already resulted in what might be termed the reinvention of domestic service, and, as Ehrenreich and Hochschild (2003) have pointed out, has created 'care chains' between rich and poor countries, whereby poor women from developing or transition countries leave their families to look after the children or older people in the developed world. In short, the provision of cash to the exclusion of services is unlikely to permit a wide choice of care provision and may be to the detriment of the terms and conditions of the person who ends up providing the care. In particular, the neglect of service provision is likely to constrain women's choices.

The problem of care is too complicated to be solved by any one policy. Interestingly, those using Schmid's labour-market transitions approach reach the same conclusion from an analysis based on paid rather than unpaid work (Gautié and Gazier, 2003a). From the carer's point of view, the following dimensions are crucial to securing a genuine choice to engage in paid and/or unpaid work:

1) *Time.* Working time and time to care;
2) *Money.* Cash to buy care, cash for carers;

3) *Services for (child and elder) care*; and, in relation to both
4) *The household level* (in terms of the provision of cash and time for men and women);
5) *The collective level* (in terms of services and cash, and workplace-based changes).

Consideration of the care-recipient's view is more complicated still. In the case of young children, the research findings on 'what is best for children' based on different measures of the outcomes of different forms of care have undergone extreme pendulum swings, which have had much to do with ideas about the family and in particular mothers' role within it, as well as with the welfare of children (Bianchi, 2000). In the case of older people, we know something about their hierarchy of preferences regarding informal carers (Qureshi and Walker, 1989), and their preference for care at home rather than in institutions, but this is tempered by the desire not to overburden relatives.

Care accounts represent a highly individualised solution most suited to systems that are already heavily reliant on the private sector and the private sphere of the family. There is therefore good reason why much of the debate on this issue is American, where this may be the only form of provision that could prove acceptable. However, given that it cannot entirely address the issues raised by care, and given that western European countries, including to some extent the UK, have a policy inheritance regarding care that, while messy, is considerably richer than that of the US, it would surely be a mistake to put too many policy eggs in the care account basket. People want different things in respect of care, standardised services are problematic in increasingly pluralist societies, but an individualised financial payment is too crude an instrument to ensure real choice and high-quality provision.

ELEVEN

Having the time for our life: re-working time[1]

Linda Boyes and Jim McCormick

Introduction

How could working lives be reshaped to afford all employees greater choice in achieving work–life balance? The Scottish Council Foundation's 'Lifelines' study has considered this question, drawing on comparative findings from policy and practice in the UK, Canada and Australia and testing practical options for reform with public and private sector employees in Scotland (Boyes and McCormick, forthcoming b).

Two related dimensions for improvement emerge. One involves the context and culture in which work is performed, covering pay and conditions (for example, holiday and sick leave entitlements), employee representation and participation, and the balance between contribution and reward. Making progress towards more employees having a more fulfilling experience of work will involve a decisive shift from dominant measures of economic progress, such as aggregate employment rates, and a traditional agenda for health and safety at work, to a deeper understanding of the true determinants of job satisfaction, motivation and morale. The second set of issues is a sub-set of the first, with a focus on a 'whole career' approach to flexibility at work, including reform of time across working life. This chapter focuses on the second of these.

We have explored ways in which 'time assets' could be accrued, drawing on concepts of saving, borrowing and buying periods of leave. Employees can achieve greater integration between work and other aspects of their lives by accumulating assets in the shape of enhanced periods of paid leave (using deferral of both existing leave entitlements and salary) and by being enabled to take a phased approach to retirement. Specifically, we explore how greater flexibility in time use across whole working lives could help employees achieve better balance between time in and outside work, and improve potential to reach mid to later stages of career with lower risks of unmanageable stress and burnout, and higher levels of 'workability'. Our proposition is that by enabling employees to build up personalised time assets, warm rhetoric about work–life balance can become more of a reality.

Satisfaction with working life

Employment levels are relatively high and stable in the UK by OECD standards, despite significant geographical variations. The labour market is characterised by both continuity and rapid turnover. In 2002, while four in five employees had been in the same job for a year or more, and almost one in 10 had been in their current job for over 20 years, around one in 10 had been in their current job for less than six months (National Statistics, 2002). Moreover, a large minority of both men and women moving into work from jobseekers' allowance were claiming the allowance again within six months.

While more people are in work and some staying in work longer, job tenure is only a weak determinant of job satisfaction and workplace morale. Measures of satisfaction at work are a critical indicator of whether working experiences are sufficiently fulfilling. A range of other factors influence job satisfaction, including: job security; the balance between contribution and reward; personal control of workload, working hours and location of work; stimulating work; variety of tasks; prospects for career development.

Recent evidence suggests a significant number of UK employees believe work could be more satisfying. For example, the Work Foundation recently found that while two in three employees were satisfied or very satisfied with their work, 15% (equivalent to over four million workers) were dissatisfied or very dissatisfied with their jobs (Isles, 2004). Other significant indicators show that all is not well at work in Britain including the incidence of short-term sick leave (higher in public services than in the business sector) and the shifting composition of the flow into incapacity benefit, where a high proportion of new claims are now made by women on the grounds of poor mental health (such as stress and depression).

The desire for flexibility and work–life balance is reported to have grown in recent years, with an increasing interest among men as well as women in undertaking flexible working and achieving a greater balance between work and other aspects of life. Working flexibly is an important factor for many people looking for a new job, and those in employment who say they would be more motivated to stay with their current employer if they were more able to pursue outside interests in conjunction with their working life has increased (study commissioned by Lloyds TSB on behalf of Employers for Work–Life Balance, at www.employersforwork-lifebalance.org.uk/docs).

However, while there are indications that in some instances employers are coming to recognise the value of offering flexible working arrangements, practice is patchy. There may be a world of difference between well-evidenced policy proposals and effective practice from the perspective of employees and employers; and between options being made available in principle (for example, being negotiable but unwritten or referred to in staff handbooks) and proving to be accessible and attractive in practice.

The size of the workplace and characteristics of the workforce determine, in large part, the types of flexibility on offer. Flexible practices tend to be more common where the workforce is larger, consists primarily of women in couples with younger children, with lower or average earnings. Workplaces most resistant to any form of flexible working arrangements are smaller, or have a high proportion of male employees aged 25-40 who also tend to be higher earners and part of a two-income household (Dex and Scheibl, 2002). When opportunities for flexible working are offered, employee take-up is found to be generally low, explained by: perceived impact on career prospects; entrenched long hours culture; heavy work loads; and impact on earnings, particularly for below-average earners (Kodz et al, 2002).

Professional and managerial employees may be more concerned about the effect flexible working might have on career prospects (not so much work–life balance as the risk of 'career death'), while others tend to be disciples of the cult of presenteeism. For those on lower levels of the career ladder, the 'push and pull' factors such as affordability, workplace culture, ease of application, managerial and colleagues' views, and the impact on households are important elements of individual decision making (however constrained). Too often, well-intended policies have been developed without addressing how these will be actively promoted to both employees and managers, resulting in availability becoming confused with accessibility. Until more is done to encourage greater take-up of flexible working practices, it can be assumed that levels of take-up will lag behind latent demand.

If increasing demands from employment and care commitments are made on employees, time available may become even more compressed and over-committed. To attract and retain talented people, both now and in the future, government agencies, businesses and other organisations will need to offer greater flexibility over where, when and how employees work, most obviously by introducing a right to request flexible working arrangements to all employees with care responsibilities (not only parents with young children). Demand for time flexibility and greater autonomy over the shape of working life is likely to gain momentum across the workforce. We believe that the next phase of policy thinking and practice should move beyond flexibility within the working week to working–life flexibility, and begin to test further options to reshape working time more creatively.

Re-working time

The idea of enhanced leave from work is not new. A limited range of employers in the UK have offered paid sabbaticals as a reward for long service, usually for academics, senior medical staff and other securely tenured professionals, in order to pursue career development activities to benefit both the individual and their employing organisation. Unpaid career breaks of up to five years are becoming available in parts of the public sector, notably the civil service. For most employees not on high earnings and those facing high living costs, periods of enhanced leave would be unpaid and therefore of little advantage (New Ways to Work, 2002). With the exception of a pilot programme from the Department for Education and Employment (1998), for teachers working in 'more challenging' schools, policy makers and politicians in the UK have shown relatively little interest in encouraging this type of flexible working. Our 'Lifelines' study has explored the role of paid leave plans in other countries, notably Canada and Australia, where availability is growing in the public services. Some examples are provided below.

As part of most public sector agreements in Australia, employees are able to accrue annual leave credits. For example, the Department of Employment and Workplace Relations Certified Agreement has set a ceiling of 60 days accrued annual leave with the following safeguards to ensure employees balance their personal and professional time:

1) Where an employee has accrued 40 days' credit, any application for leave up to a maximum of 10 days must be approved; and
2) Upon reaching 60 days' credit, no further credits will accrue until the employee takes sufficient leave to fall below the limit (that is, they will be deemed to be on leave).

The Department of Education and Science and Training also offers employees the opportunity to *buy* additional annual leave. Employees can purchase up to eight weeks' additional leave and have their reduced salary spread across the year. An employee's salary for superannuation purposes continues to be their salary as if they had not purchased leave, effectively maintaining their superannuation contributions (Department of Education, Science and Training, 2002-05).

Time banks and time accounts systems have been piloted in Italy, France, Germany and Norway, offering employees a way of saving overtime, additional hours, bonuses, profit sharing and incentive payments to be translated into 'banked' time in most cases for up to one year, with some new proposals to create lifetime banks (Pillinger, 2001). Initiatives such as these were originally proposed to reduce the extent and costs of overtime, but increasingly are viewed as a means to allow time off to suit both employers and employees.

In the UK a small number of employers offer employees the opportunity to bank or buy annual leave. At present this facility tends to be limited to one year but there is no reason to suggest this could not be extended. Two related examples of contributory leave entitlements have been tested with case-study participants in four public and private sector organisations in Scotland. These are described in Boxes 11.1 and 11.2, suggesting how employees could accrue enhanced leave entitlements by deferring either existing leave or salary. A hybrid of both approaches is possible, depending on the most appropriate forms of deferral at any given stage.

Box 11.1: Banking leave (saving time) – option 1

Employees set aside a fixed amount of time, for example part of their annual leave, public holidays or overtime, over an agreed period, which is drawn upon at a later date by agreement between the employee and employer. By rolling up existing entitlements, employees can use this for whatever purpose they choose, for example, visiting family overseas, taking an extended break, learning or travelling. When banking annual leave, the amount set aside each year should not reduce that year's entitlement to less than the minimum set by the Working Time Directive (20 days for full-time employees and pro-rata equivalent for part-time employees).

For example, if an employee has 25 days' annual leave and chooses to bank five days each year over five years, by the sixth year they will have accrued 25 days plus their normal annual leave entitlement of 25 days, making a total of 50 days' leave. In addition the employee might choose to bank some public holidays.

Box 11.2: Deferring salary (saving money) – option 2

This option is based on the Deferred Salary Leave Program (DSLP) available to provincial government employees in Canada. Programmes were established in Saskatchewan in 1989 and British Columbia in 1991, for example. All permanent employees are eligible to participate following a qualifying period. In British Columbia this is two years' service. Programmes must conform to federal government legislation in Canada:

Participants must defer a proportion of salary for at least 12 months and no more than 72 months.

Employees in the British Columbia Public Service may defer between 10% and 33% of their gross salary to finance a future period of leave no less than six months and no more than 12 months.

Those who are approaching retirement cannot take a period of leave just prior to retiring, reflecting federal government tax rules in Canada. A 'return to service' commitment applies to all employees: participants are required to return to work for at least as long as the period of leave.

Federal income tax regulations provide the legislative framework within which the programme operates. Canada Life manages the investment for the deferred salary arrangements (with adequate insurance for contributors).

Employees contribute an agreed amount of gross salary to their trust account, which they draw on during their leave period. Deductions are made before tax. Income tax and Canada pension plan contributions are adjusted to reflect the reduced salary. Withdrawals from the fund are taxed.

Exit from the scheme is permitted should the employee terminate their employment, in the event of financial hardship or change to personal and/ or family circumstances. Money accrued is paid back to the employee. Accrued time/salary may be transferable to other departments of the public service by negotiation.

Case-study employees interviewed in Scotland believed that a contributory approach to taking additional periods of leave offered the following benefits:

1) A chance to 'recharge the batteries' with likely consequences of reducing 'burn out' and helping retention in the later stages of the career;
2) Increase leisure time, opportunities to travel or spend time with the family;
3) Quality time when people most needed it – at a stage when time has a higher premium (or when individuals are fit enough to benefit most);
4) Undertake learning, research or personal development;
5) Provide another element of choice in working life;
6) Improve employee–employer relations;
7) Improve motivation and retention of staff;
8) Improve productivity if people came back refreshed and ready to develop new skills;
9) Planning period would help employers plan and manage cover during time away from work (with opportunities to rotate/promote other staff);
10) Taken in the years leading up to retirement would allow employees to explore their options (although the DSLP model is clear that leave cannot be used immediately prior to retirement).

Employees identified the following conditions that would need to be met to make such approaches succeed:

1) Ensure adequate cover (quantity and quality) and continuity of work during the period of leave;
2) Alleviate any additional burden on colleagues;
3) Offer personal development for other employees either through a temporary upgrade or a move to broaden skills and experience while covering when someone was on a break;
4) Allow shorter periods of deferral and leave to help adapt to changing circumstances;
5) Enable 'borrow forward' of leave as well as saving in advance, and then pay it back in the same way;
6) Enable lower-paid employees to benefit and avoid creating further inequality at work through another perk for professionals;
7) Employers should be expected to accommodate requests unless in exceptional circumstances;
8) Levels of pay and conditions should be protected on return;
9) Safeguards should be built in to ensure the security of funds;
10) A systematic approach to reentry into the workplace should be in place.

Employees suggested that, depending on the period spent away from work and changes in the job, there might need to be a period of reinduction or additional training built in on returning to work, which might involve an additional cost that companies might not wish to meet. An alternative would be to build in a core number of days of 'contact time' when employees on leave come into work to update themselves on changes and developments.

Our research to date has identified consistent interest in such options from employees at various stages of their career, from senior NHS consultants to lower-paid social care employees. But we are in the early stages of the policy debate about working-life flexibility. There is very little published evidence identifying the scale and composition of take-up of deferred leave programmes in the Canadian provinces, or the impact of periods of leave of up to one year for participants, their colleagues and employers.

An overview of collective agreements suggested that leave options like those available to many public service employees in the Canadian provinces may be a useful means of helping older workers in particular to stay in the workplace:

> Although the existence of various leave of absence provisions does not in itself guarantee the elimination of work-related difficulties, these provisions do provide workers in general and older workers in particular, with the leisure time they need as a counterweight to an increasingly stressful work environment.... By accommodating the special needs of older workers, leaves of absence, among other measures, may be conducive to a reduction in early retirements, thus postponing any resulting loss of skills and experience. (Fourzly and Gervais, 2002)

A smaller study in Saskatchewan found that just over one in eight collective agreements included a deferred salary plan, covering almost 20% of workers (Saskatchewan Federation of Labour, 2000). Those agreements with a deferred salary plan covered public service agreements. The study identified the deferred salary plan as one way to improve work–life balance, but noted: 'It is clearly not an option for all workers [currently], as some families cannot afford the temporary cut in pay which could have an impact on the household's disposable income'. Current take-up rates of around 3% of eligible employees in Saskatchewan, in a programme first introduced in 1989, are believed to be lower than expected due to the relatively high rate of minimum contribution required.

Such examples of developing a new form of work-based saving require a high degree of commitment from employees. There are no direct costs for employers, but their active involvement is needed in negotiating when employees can draw upon accrued leave entitlements. Due to the extended contribution period for participants, employers should be able to plan well in advance how to cover for employees during leave.

Ideas into action: the policy challenge

We believe the benefits of enabling employees to take extended periods of paid leave across their working lives could be significant. Managed creatively, such approaches could enable employees to reach the later stages of their career with lower risk of burnout, better physical and mental health and higher levels of motivation. No less important may be a reduced sense of having missed out on having the time to spend with the family, to travel or to pursue a personal interest at a stage in life when it may be at a premium. The underlying principle here is to enable employees to make explicit trade-offs involving money and time across working life, rather than the only option being an extended period of working being followed by full-time retirement. Other positive consequences may include opportunities in job rotation, back filling of short-term vacancies and upskilling of other employees.

Accruing time in working life

Contributory leave options provide one way to establish a new culture of savings, where the currency traded could be either time or money. More time off will not be cost-free. One consequence of introducing approaches like these might be that some employees work a similar total number of years as they would otherwise, with time taken in leave added towards the end of their career in order to restore contributions notionally diverted from pension funds. In this way, the effective working life would be 'stretched' over a longer period. Alternatively, employees may decide to make an explicit trade-off by deferring their salary, enjoying more time out and retiring with fewer savings. In the context of ongoing concern (not to mention confusion at the heart of government) about long-term savings and occupational pensions, the scope to divert retirement contributions into other forms of short-term saving is unclear. Life-course leaves such as these can, of course, be used in gendered ways, with women often using them for care and men often using them for other activities such as training or leisure (Knijn, 2004). This may then have gendered effects on human capital or well-being. But the principle of offering employees the information and tools to make more explicit work/life trade-offs is, we believe, a compelling one.

Matched savings for the lifetime low-paid

What about inequalities in work? The lifetime low-paid may have enjoyed the least flexible working conditions, including the least generous leave entitlements, and remain in the workforce later than more affluent employees as a result of poorer second pension prospects. On the grounds of social justice as well as productivity and health, deferred leave plans should be accessible to all employees.

If our expectations as employees rise in relatively tight labour markets, we may see manual workers and some traditionally lower-paid employees coming to demand greater flexibility at work (Hutton, 2004). Access to enhanced leave would need to be incentivised to be effective. One approach would be to introduce a form of the Savings Gateway model, focused on life-stages. A matched savings scheme could be offered to employees, where low-paid workers contributing up to 5% from gross salary to a leave fund could receive a matching 5% top-up from government, and a sliding scale of matched contributions could benefit those earning up to the average. Alternatively, a non-contributory option might be appropriate for low-paid workers, with 'enhanced leave' credits banked and possible use of National Insurance records as a means of accruing time. Whichever options are offered, consideration must be given to portability, in the event that individuals move jobs, to ensure that their 'savings' remain intact.

Time-out accounts?

We believe taking a new approach to time across working life would open up a new front in the debate on asset-based welfare, linked to the emerging body of knowledge and practice around work–life balance and sustainability of work. The debate is now focusing on the pros and cons of pursuing an individual 'account' model to hold specific assets or a set of assets as they accumulate. There appears to be a strong case in principle for taking an *integrated* approach across various forms of asset accumulation, including the Child Trust Fund (CTF), Saving

Gateway and personalised forms of investing in learning, in order to avoid confusion and assist the goal of long-term equity. The role of 'care accounts' as a means of enabling care givers to invest in their own future prospects is considered in Chapters Nine and Ten of this volume, and well-developed arguments have been set out on the merits of introducing some form of personal development account or stake in a provident fund as multi-purpose savings vehicles.

Such ideas are being assessed on the grounds of equity, for example between income groups and the sexes, efficiency and transparency. If they score well on these criteria, we believe multi-purpose accounts may provide an important tool for resourcing personal autonomy. 'Time-out accounts' might then be integrated with other forms of asset holding. First, however, the contributory sabbatical model should be further tested in the UK, and in particular options for crediting the lifetime lower-paid. At the same time, we propose that all relevant information available through the workplace should be 'rolled up' in one simple statement of contributions paid and entitlements earned to date, annual leave records, regular retirement projections and information on getting appropriate advice and guidance. Such an approach would provide a more accurate and nore rounded picture of employees' assets, enabling them to make more informed trade-offs around their time, money and work.

Conclusion

While it is difficult to determine overall demand, evidence to date indicates employees in various sectors would seriously consider participating in deferred leave and salary sabbaticals if the conditions were right. Because we are discussing the potential benefits of such approaches in the UK, we can only suggest that offering them more widely would help employees better manage time across their working lives, with positive effects upon health and well-being. The pros and cons in practice remain to be demonstrated. The likely gains from such approaches will take time to emerge and will be variable depending on the commitment of employers in different sectors and by personal circumstances. Implementing the proposals outlined in this chapter will require both a culture shift and some hard choices on the part of policy makers, employers and employees. We believe the principle of offering employees the tools to make more explicit work/life trade-offs, retaining more control over their lives, is a compelling one and that comparative evidence and emerging local practice in the

UK offer grounds for policy makers to support the testing of various options to reshape working time more creatively.

Policies to reshape retirement across the public services provide an opportunity to introduce contributory sabbaticals. As an employer, government at both local and national levels is encouraging employees to extend their working lives. An integral part of this process will be to make work more satisfying and sustainable. Alongside reviewing working practices, we believe consideration should be given to testing this type of approach as a means of enabling employees to work longer if they want or need to, without significantly lengthening the total number of years spent at work. Piloting and learning from contributory sabbatical programmes would enable employers and government to build up a body of evidence on life-course flexibility – and could help to develop a set of affordable work–life balance policies with broader appeal than those experienced to date in the UK.

Note
[1] This chapter is based on the Scottish Council Foundation's study 'Lifelines: Re-working time and retirement', supported by Scottish Enterprise and Standard Life.

TWELVE

Conclusion: what is the best way forward for the citizen's stake?

Nick Pearce, Will Paxton and Stuart White

Introduction

As the principle of a citizen's stake becomes tentatively established in British social policy, and attracts attention from around the world, deep and searching questions inevitably arise. Three sets of questions may be distinguished:

1) *The underlying social ideal.* What broader social vision is the citizen's stake connected with? The basic idea of the citizen's stake is compatible with a wide range of conceptions of the good society. This is why it draws support across the political spectrum. But once the principle is established, further development of policies like the Child Trust Fund (CTF) requires a clear view of the specific conception of the good society we wish to advance.
2) *International relevance.* It has been argued that while asset-based approaches might have some relevance for nations of 'Anglo-Saxon' capitalism (such as Britain, the US, Canada, New Zealand and Australia), they have little relevance to continental Europe or other parts of the world. Is this fair comment?
3) *Immediate actions.* What immediate actions should policy makers take to shape future development of the CTF in particular and the citizen's stake more broadly?

We now look at each of these questions in turn.

Underlying social ideal

What kind of society is the CTF meant to help create? We begin by locating the CTF in relation to a currently influential conception of the good society centred on a *social investment paradigm*. We then outline three further perspectives that offer challenges or modifications to this paradigm: *libertarianism*; *post-productivism* (which we see as related to *civic republicanism*); and *egalitarianism*.

The social investment paradigm

A major theme in centre-left thinking in recent years is that the state should seek not merely to assist those in need, but, where possible, to help people build their capacities so that they can be more self-supporting. Spending to this end is not simply welfare, but a kind of investment. In Britain, this theme came into mainstream discussion with the report of the Commission on Social Justice in 1994, stressing the need to create an 'Investor's Britain' as opposed to a mere 'Leveller's Britain' based on income redistribution (Commission on Social Justice, 1994). A similar theme appeared in the writings of the then shadow chancellor, Gordon Brown, who wrote of 'a new economic egalitarianism which starts from the recognition that it is indeed people's potential – and thus the value of their labour – that is the driving force of the modern economy' (Brown, 1994, p 114). Some academics, such as Joel Rogers and Wolfgang Streeck, had developed similar ideas, calling for an 'egalitarian politics of production', a 'Left productivism', in which egalitarian goals would be pursued through constraining and enabling firms and workers to invest in skills (Rogers and Streeck, 1994). Thus, when Anthony Giddens identified a core idea of the Third Way to be the construction of a 'social investment state' (Giddens, 1998), he was describing something already well-established in the emerging philosophy of New Labour. Gösta Esping-Andersen's work has recently provided further intellectual support to this perspective (Esping-Andersen, 2002).

Many of the British Labour government's policies since 1997 can be seen as reflecting the social investment paradigm. When the government announced its aim of abolishing child poverty 'within a generation', part of the rationale it offered was that child poverty inhibits children's development, putting a potential drag on a productive and vibrant economy. An increase in spending on education as a percentage of GDP; the ongoing effort to develop childcare provision; growing recognition of the importance of the early years; maturing discussions about how the state can influence levels of 'social capital'; all these fit the social investment paradigm. The CTF, and asset-based welfare more generally, also fit comfortably into this paradigm. It is future-orientated – 'investment' for the long term – and it focuses on children – whom

Ruth Lister has described as having an iconic status in theories of the social investment state (Lister, 2004).

However, if we stand back for a moment, what kind of society is implicit in this social investment paradigm? Arguably, the underlying social ideal has three key features. First, it is *productivist*. It regards the good society as one with a very high level of participation in formal employment. 'Investing' in citizens is centrally about building capabilities for labour-market participation. Second, in most (perhaps not all) accounts of the social investment state, the emphasis is on *inclusion* rather than any strong notion of equality. Third, and finally, it sees asset-based initiatives very much as a *complement* to conventional welfare. Investment inclusion is sought through a range of policies that include, but are certainly not reducible to, capital grants like the CTF. More traditional welfare policies – cash benefits, in-kind benefits, regulation – remain as part of the social investment package.

But there are three alternative social ideals that respectively challenge these features of the good society as envisaged within the social investment paradigm.

Libertarianism

The libertarian perspective, first, regards asset-based policies like the CTF as substitutes for more conventional welfare policies, not as complements to them. The ideal for an asset-based libertarian is of a market society in which every person starts out with at least a minimally decent capital endowment, but in which other welfare supports have been removed or at least significantly curtailed. Health care is not provided by the state, free at the point of use. Rather, people are free to buy health care insurance out of their earnings and what they have made with their initial capital endowments. Similarly, labour-market regulations, such as minimum wage laws, are abolished or scaled back. The argument is that while these authoritarian interventions may be necessary to protect the vulnerable in a society where many people start adult life with no assets, they are undesirable in a society where everyone has a decent capital endowment to start with. Samuel Brittan's writings on the citizen's stake lean some way towards this libertarian perspective (see for example Brittan, 1983, ch 11, pp 258-61), although he envisages a continuing role for 'cash transfers to the poor' and 'non-monopolistic collective provision of services such as education and health'.

This, then, represents one possible future that might lie at the end of the road that starts with the CTF: the next stage the 'Thatcher revolution' against an overexpanded welfare state and labour-market regulation.

Post-productivism (and civic republicanism)

The post-productivist perspective challenges the productivism of the social investment paradigm. It embraces the idea of the citizen's stake. But it does so out of an ambition to give people greater 'real freedom' to limit their participation in the labour market. If people have capital, then they can derive income from this capital, and it becomes that bit more feasible for people to take time out of employment and devote themselves to other activities. A number of scholars have recently begun to challenge the social investment paradigm in the name of some form of 'post-productivism' (see, for example, Offe, 1992, 1996; Goodin et al, 1999; Fitzpatrick, 2003).

Post-productivism taps into a long-standing strain of left thinking that aspires to emancipate people from what is perceived to be the servitude of a life centred on wage labour. In its most radical, libertarian form, the emphasis is on freedom for its own sake: if people want to have more freedom to surf, rather than go to work, we should make that a more real possibility. (Recall the Situationist slogan: 'Beneath the pavement – the beach'.) For other thinkers the emphasis is on how people can (and should) use the time freed up from employment to engage in other socially useful activities, such as care, voluntary work or political activism. Indeed, we see here how post-productivism links with a *civic republican* critique of the social investment paradigm as putting so much emphasis on labour-market participation as to generate an imbalanced society in which people lack the time and energy to be citizens in a fully rounded way (White, 2004a).

Egalitarianism

The egalitarian perspective is grounded in the work of philosophers such as John Rawls and Ronald Dworkin (Rawls, 1999 [1971]; Dworkin, 2000). There is more to social justice than economic egalitarianism (for helpful discussions, see White, 2003; Miller, 2005). But the gap between rich and poor in societies like our own is, to some considerable extent, based on 'morally arbitrary' factors such as differences in class background and/or natural ability. In the egalitarian view, this undermines the claim that the inequalities are fundamentally 'deserved'; rather, to a considerable extent, they are inherently unjust. Moreover, political equality is itself a demand of justice, and it is essential to keep wealth inequality within certain limits in order to prevent this undermining effective equality in the political sphere.

From within this perspective, policies such as the CTF make sense as first steps towards a 'property-owning democracy'. A substantial welfare state would be complemented by CTFs and similar policies intended to sustain substantial equality in the background distribution of both human and financial capital (Rawls, 1999 [1971], 2001). The citizen's stake is then morally linked with tax policies that seek to spread the resources transferred between the generations and to appropriate for society as a whole the 'unearned increments' to asset values that otherwise fall as windfall gains into the pockets of some. James Meade's model of a property-owning democracy represents one attempt to think through in a systematic way what an economy grounded in these basic principles would look like (Meade, 1964, 1989). In Meade's model, equality is pursued through a mix of policies, in which a form of citizen's stake is combined with a reformed inheritance tax and with what Gerald Holtham has called a 'community fund' (the state owns a sizeable portfolio of assets and acts as a passive rentier, taking its returns on these assets to help finance public spending but without trying to run specific firms or industries; see Holtham, 1999).

Clarity of perspective

We have now outlined four perspectives that might all underpin a political project centred on a citizen's stake. Which of these social visions are we interested in?

Currently the most influential of these four perspectives is the social investment paradigm, and we are sympathetic to it. However, as should be clear from the Introduction to this book, we believe that this perspective needs to be deepened by engaging with the egalitarian perspective. From this standpoint, we should look to the CTF not simply as a *modification of welfare state policy* (the way it is presented in the social investment paradigm) but as potentially the first step towards a *new politics of ownership*, taking as an ideal the egalitarian property-owning democracy advocated by Rawls and Meade.

We could also be ambitious about the role of CTFs in promoting volunteering, care and political engagement, and for these civic republican reasons, we also support at least a modest reorientation towards the post-productivist perspective. Normatively, we have little sympathy for the libertarian perspective. That said, we should not be closed-minded about the possibilities of capitalising some existing benefits or services into an expanded citizen's stake (an issue to which we return).

International relevance

Is the CTF, and like policies, only relevant to nations of 'Anglo-Saxon capitalism'? What can other countries take from the discussion of the citizen's stake as it has developed in Britain? Does Britain have anything to learn from what is going on elsewhere?

The assertion that asset-based policy has relevance only in Anglo-Saxon capitalism has a superficial plausibility. Thus far, the most serious policy discussions about policies such as the CTF have been in Britain, the US, Canada, New Zealand and Australia. However, although the political economy of Britain is primarily liberal, it also has much in common with the 'social models' of continental Europe: social protection is more extensive than in the US, health care is free at the point of use, and there have been substantial redistributive measures to reduce child and pensioner poverty. The next decade presents an opportunity to forge a genuinely 'Anglo-Social' model (Dixon and Pearce, 2005). Furthermore, if we look a little more closely we can begin to see parallel discussions taking place in other countries. We can also see how these discussions might in future be brought into more explicit dialogue, from which all parties might learn.

To begin with, even if one thinks that policies like the CTF have a relevance only to the nations of Anglo-Saxon capitalism, this does not mean the broader, underlying idea of *asset-based egalitarianism* has no wider relevance. Asset-based egalitarianism is the pursuit of egalitarian economic objectives through efforts to render more equal the distribution of productive or marketable assets (Freeman and Rogers, 1997; Bowles and Gintis, 1998; White, 2001). Consider one contemporary example of a popular movement based around a philosophy of asset-based egalitarianism: the Movement of Landless Rural Labourers (MST) in Brazil. In a country where agricultural land remains a key productive asset, but is distributed in an extremely unequal way, the MST's objective is to secure a transfer of this asset from current landowners to the landless poor.

Turning to the nations of advanced capitalism in continental Europe, the picture is by no means as hostile to ideas like the CTF as critics suppose. As part of the project on which this book is based, the editors commissioned a review of the debate on 'asset-based welfare' in France and Germany. The study, undertaken by Alexandra Couto, found little direct reference to the CTF in the French or German press. However,

Couto also found academic discussion of some related policy ideas and some evidence that these ideas were moving into the mainstream of wider public debate (Couto, 2004). In the remainder of this section, we draw on Couto's helpful account of these ideas.

The first idea, developed by researchers such as Gunter Schmid, Klaus Schömann and Bernard Gazier, based at the Social Science Research Centre in Berlin, is that of *transitional labour markets* or TLMs (Schmid and Gazier, 2002). The premise behind TLMs is that it is both inevitable and desirable for people of working age to spend some time out of formal employment engaged in other activities such as training, carework or voluntary work. Given this premise, it is argued that labour markets need to be embedded within a framework of institutions that allow people to make transitions to and from employment to these other activities with income and pension security.

In exploring this objective, researchers have focused some of their attention on a second, related policy idea: *social drawing rights* (SDRs). Developed by the French legal academic, Alain Supiot, the idea is to create a set of individual accounts that people can draw on to help fund activities outside employment (Supiot, 2001). Accounts might be used, for example, to finance training (learning or training accounts) or to provide income during periods in which the individual is not earning (sabbatical accounts).

The specific idea of *sabbatical accounts* has also been taken up and discussed in Germany by researchers such as Claus Offe. For Offe, the aim should be to establish an individual sabbatical account that can provide up to 10 years of income support for time out from regular employment. This amounts to a temporary or time-limited form of unconditional basic income, and Offe explicitly defends the proposal as a possible intermediate step on the long road to the destination of a full-blown unconditional basic income (Offe, 2001).

TLMs have their equivalent in countries such as Britain, but there are clear differences in emphasis and language between continental discussions of TLMs, SDRs and sabbatical accounts, and debates within 'Anglo-Saxon capitalist' countries about asset-based welfare. Couto argues that explicit talk of 'assets' or 'capital' still runs counter to the culture of the left in continental Europe, and points out that a recent OECD report on asset-based welfare argued that policy makers would need to find a different language to talk about these policy ideas in a continental context (Organisation for Economic Cooperation and Development, 2004).

Some of the background assumptions are also different. In the nations of Anglo-Saxon capitalism there is perhaps a basic optimism about the ability of (relatively flexible, liberalised) labour markets to sustain high levels of full-time employment. In this context, as we noted above, ideas about asset-based welfare easily blend with a productivist philosophy that centres on building employment capability – the vision of the social investment paradigm. By contrast, in countries like France and Germany, there is arguably more pessimism about the capacity of labour markets to sustain high levels of full-time employment. There is a more acute sense of 'job scarcity' which, in turn, informs some of the thinking behind TLMs, SDRs and sabbatical accounts. The point of these proposals is not simply to free people up from the treadmill of full-time employment. Often, part of the declared aim is also to enable scarce jobs to be shared out more equally (see, for example, Offe et al, 1996). In short, the continental discussion is currently much more influenced by a certain strand of post-productivist ideas than is the debate in the nations of Anglo-Saxon capitalism.

However, while there are these differences, there are also some important affinities between proposals for TLMs, SDRs and sabbatical accounts, on the one hand, and ideas of asset-based welfare on the other. Looking to the future, we might reasonably expect to see a degree of mutual learning between proponents of the two sets of ideas.

Looked at from the vantage-point of asset-based welfare, SDRs can be seen as amounting to a form of universal capital characterised by a high level of use restriction: people get a capital endowment but the state sets strict limits on the purposes for which it can be used. However, it is possible that problems such as the administrative costs involved in sustaining a complex system of use restriction might in time prompt policy-thinkers in continental Europe to consider a weakening of use restrictions. SDRs would then start to look more like the capital grant programmes under discussion in the nations of Anglo-Saxon capitalism. This thought derives further support from the fact that some proponents of sabbatical accounts have been concerned to try to design the accounts so that they have some of the features that a pure capital account would have. For example, in the context of the academic discussion of sabbatical accounts, Jérome Gautié and Bernard Gazier suggest that people who use their sabbatical account to take a year out before the age of 30 might actually be debited two years from their accounts, while people in their 50s might be debited only 0.6 of a year for the same amount of real time out (Couto, 2004; Gautié and Gazier, 2003a, 2003b). This mimics the way that a pure capital account would work: by drawing less on the capital in one's early years one would allow the capital to accumulate, and could then use it to finance more time out of employment later in life. But one might then ask why we should set up a sabbatical account that mimics the way a pure capital grant would work, rather than just endow people with capital itself.

On the other hand, there is no doubt that proposals for pure capital grants generate strong anxieties among tax-paying publics about responsible use (see Chapters Two, Seven and Eight in this volume). The SDR model addresses the issue of responsible use precisely by connecting the individual accounts to specific socially useful activities. (Indeed, Supiot argues that this is central to their potential to command support from tax-paying publics; Couto, 2004.) Imposing restrictions such as these would mean a concomitant reduction in the autonomy of account holders. Nevertheless, it is possible that policy makers in the nations of Anglo-Saxon capitalism might come to see it as advisable to move somewhat in the direction of the SDR model as a way of addressing the responsible use issue.

In this book, we have already started the important process of bringing these two streams of thinking into dialogue (see also Gautié, 2003). Care accounts, discussed by Anne Alstott and Jane Lewis in Chapters Nine and Ten, constitute a form of SDR, as do the sabbatical accounts discussed by Linda Boyes and Jim McCormick in Chapter Eleven. As Paxton and White note in Chapter Eight, use-specific individual accounts of this kind could conceivably run alongside a CTF as part of an expanded citizen's stake.

Immediate actions

Informed by the foregoing discussion, we now consider some of the opportunities for immediate action concerning the CTF and the citizen's stake.

Reasonable equality of endowment on adulthood

If support for CTFs is grounded in egalitarianism, as we argue, then account holders should reach adulthood with reasonably equal endowments of capital. But consider the possibilities under the present system. On the one hand, a child in a low-income family could reach 18 with an account worth £2,300 after taking account of inflation. This would happen if they receive £500 from the government at birth, and (let us assume) at ages seven and 11, but their parents and wider family make no further contribution to the CTF. (We use the Inland Revenue illustrative figure of 7% nominal growth, and deduct

2% for inflation and 1.5% for management charges.) On the other hand, a child from a well-off family could receive £31,580 at 18: although they receive only £250 at birth, seven and 11, their family add the maximum of £1,200 into the account every year for 18 years.

In responding to this concern, it is important to be clear that, just because account balances will be unequal, CTFs as a whole will not add to inequality. Larger balances among richer families will in part just reflect existing patterns of saving, as wealthier parents redirect their deposits from private trust funds, on which data is poor, to CTFs, which will be more visible. Second, and more fundamentally, we need to distinguish between the *cash balance* of CTFs and the *benefits* that CTFs will bring. Even if the cash balances are higher for richer families, the impact on life chances could be greater for children from lower earners. CTFs might succeed in bringing financial engagement to those who are outside the mainstream, financial education to those currently unfamiliar with financial institutions, and possibly a lifelong savings habit to people who would otherwise assume that regular saving is for 'other people'. For poorer families, CTFs will make the difference between starting adult life with, say, £2,000, and starting it with nothing. There is evidence that indicates that it is this difference, between something and nothing, that has the most impact on later life chances (Bynner and Paxton, 2001). For all these reasons, CTFs, even in their present form, should be seen as broadly enhancing equality, not reducing it.

Nevertheless, more equal account balances would be desirable. As far as efficiency and the opportunity cost allow, we should be aiming to make the accounts of children from poorer families as large as possible. There are a number of ways this could be achieved.

More use of means-tested top-ups. At the moment, the government plans additional payments into the CTF accounts when the child reaches seven, and possibly a further top-up when they are at secondary school (11-16 years old). The size of the payment at age seven is currently planned to be similar to that being made at birth: £250 for most children, but £500 for children in poor families. One response to the problem of potential inequality in final endowments would be to have more top-up payments at later ages (such as 11 and 16), and to make these even more strongly weighted towards children in low-income households. For example at age 11, children in poor families could get five times instead of twice the payment received by other children. Clearly, however, there would be some downsides to this approach. It would create all the standard incentives problems with means-tested assistance. An alternative would be to vary top-ups according to the accumulated value of accounts at a given age. But this would create a disincentive for families to save into the CTFs, which is one of the major stated goals of the policy.

Government top-ups are an essential part of the CTF, and the existing deposits should certainly not be reduced or made less progressive. Further top-ups could make a substantial difference if focused on small groups in particular need, such as children looked after by local authorities (Maxwell, 2005). But the ability of top-ups to solve the problem of account inequality is limited.

Match parental contributions. Another possibility would be for government to match private contributions to CTFs. All families would be eligible to save up to a ceiling, similar to the current £1,200 per year, but low-income households would receive matching contributions from the government. For example, if the matching ratio were 1:1, then low-income households would need only to save £600 to get £1,200 for a child's account.

A match rate that starts high, but quickly declines as more is deposited, would reflect the idea that one of the main barriers to saving is inertia (Sunstein and Thaler, 2003). Providing a sufficient incentive to save something, even if a small amount, could then increase savings well beyond that level by breaking the inertia. The government is currently piloting a matched savings programme for low-income households, the Saving Gateway, and thought might be given as to how CTFs and the Saving Gateway could be integrated to boost the value of CTF accounts for children in low-income households. For example, parents could be given the option of directing all or part of their 'match' into their children's CTFs.

Matching is not without its problems. It would be expensive to match CTF deposits at the same rate as Saving Gateway deposits – lowering the match to 1:2, restricting the maximum to just £120 per year, and to the poorest 40%, would still cost £300 million per year. Targeting those who are closest to 18 also raises questions about efficiency: it would be surprising for 16-year-olds to be given artificial incentives to save for when they are 18, as their income is likely to be much higher when they are that much older.

Provide top-ups for civic participation. A third possibility, which connects with our civic republican as well as egalitarian commitments, would be for government to offer further payments into CTFs as a reward for civic participation or volunteering, by parents or the children themselves (Paxton, 2002; Stanley, 2004; Maxwell and Sodha, 2005). Relevant activities might include participating in a local community group such as a tenants' association, sitting on a citizens' jury, or being a school governor. All children might get a payment for their own or parental civic participation, but the payments could be larger for children in low-income families. Rewards for community engagement could be arranged through local authorities and social landlords, allowing them to be focused on those who are likely to have smaller accounts. In the case of the account holders themselves, namely the children, schools could play a role by awarding CTF credits for contributions to school life or the local community.

If, however, CTFs are to be linked to civic participation, central government must act as a catalyst, providing encouragement, support, and incentives for other agencies. Central government may have a role in making sure that other bodies, such as Sure Start Centres, schools or social landlords, lift their eyes above their own narrow performance objectives to the wider goals of civic participation and reasonable levels of wealth equality. Both leadership and funding are essential.

Responsible use

This issue is discussed at length in Chapter Eight, and we briefly review the main conclusions here.

Mentoring and educational programmes to complement the CTF. It is important to complement CTFs with educational programmes that cover not only financial literacy but effective spending and investment of CTFs. We would recommend that all children in their late teens have interviews in which the use of CTFs is discussed. For children who seem particularly at risk, a mentoring system might be developed to give further advice and support in the use of these funds, ideally through existing long-term relationships that young adults have with professionals.

Consider the use of SDRs alongside pure capital grants. A further response might be to consider the development of individualised accounts attached to specific needs or activities alongside pure capital grants such as the CTF. These accounts would be more like the SDRs currently under discussion in continental Europe. Possible accounts might be linked specifically to education and training; parental leave or other care responsibilities (such as Anne Alstott's carer resource accounts, discussed in Chapters Nine and Ten); or more general sabbatical accounts (ideas for which are discussed by Boyes and McCormick in Chapter Eleven). Under this proposal, a citizen's stake would consist of a pure capital element, like the CTF, but complemented by more use-specific individualised accounts.

We are confident that something like the mentoring and educational support needs to be taken up as the CTF is further developed. We are less sure that the use of SDRs is the best approach, but we think it worth further consideration.

Integration with wider policy towards wealth accumulation and distribution

A third challenge is how to integrate the citizen's stake policy with wider policy towards the promotion of capital accumulation and toward wealth redistribution.

The citizen's stake and wider savings policy. The CTF can provide the foundation for capital accumulation across the life-cycle. But this leaves open the huge question of how the state ought to support further capital accumulation. At present, the British government spends a lot of money supporting capital accumulation, particularly pensions saving, through tax relief, but the benefits of this expenditure are heavily skewed towards the higher-income groups (Agulnik and Le Grand, 1998). In the next stage of developing the citizen's stake policy, thought needs to be given as to how this support can be redesigned so as to support lifetime accumulation on a more equitable basis. In Chapter Six, Glennerster and McKnight make the suggestion of redirecting some of the existing tax relief to '"pension starter packs" – a capital gift for those joining a pension scheme by the age of 30'. This could be seen as another part of an expanded citizen's stake. (For further relevant discussion, see Altman, 2003.)

The citizen's stake and tax policy. There is some promise in linking citizen's stake policies, through soft hypothecation, to a reformed inheritance tax (IHT) (see Dominic Maxwell's discussion in Chapter Three). Moreover, even if one thinks that any direct linkage is unwise, there are good egalitarian reasons why we should nevertheless want to keep wider issues of tax reform and wealth ownership in view. Aside from the inequities that stem from inheritance, we should address the inequities that stem from the 'unearned increment' typically enjoyed by landowners in our economy. How can society take more of this increment, created as a result of society's cooperative activity, for the benefit of society as a whole? Land value taxation, discussed by Iain McLean in Chapter Five, is one possibility. Development of the 'common assets' principle, discussed by David Bollier in Chapter Four, is another way of widening claims on social wealth.

Being clear about the proper role of the citizen's stake

Finally, those who support the principle of the citizen's stake must expound a clear view of how far a mature stake should be seen as a complement, and how far a substitute, for traditional welfare provision. For social democrats, the initial instinctive reaction to this issue is likely to be against 'rolling up' important services and benefits into a personalised capital account. To some extent, as Glennerster and McKnight show in Chapter Six, this reaction is well-founded. There are good reasons why we should not go far in this direction.

However, as Glennerster and McKnight also show, in one or two cases there arguably is a coherent case for the rolling up of existing provision. Funding for higher education is one such policy area. Existing funding is regressive, favouring as it does higher education and middle-class students over further education and students from lower-income backgrounds. Over the long term, funding post-compulsory education through a citizen's stake policy should be considered an option (Piatt and Robinson, 2001). Some portion of current education funding could be put into special accounts that, after state-funded education ends at 18 or 19, could only be used for education and training. Such support would allow funding to follow the learner more closely, allowing them to choose the content and system that would be the most useful. Individual Learning Accounts, which provided government subsidies for education for a short period from 2000, were a lesson in how this should not be managed, with high fraud rates and poor-quality courses. But a closer attention to the standard of course providers, and a structure more similar to CTFs, could be successful.

Conclusion: ways forward

The citizen's stake is here and, we hope, here to stay. With every parent who opens a CTF for their new baby, the policy, and the underlying principle of a citizen's stake, is likely to become more embedded in popular thinking. In Britain, promoting the most promising mix of social visions (egalitarian, with elements of post-productivist and, more cautiously, libertarian) requires action at several levels.

Complementing CTFs, to ensure that society derives as much benefit from them as possible, we need:

1) top-ups for closely targeted groups, such as children looked after by local authorities;

2) further top-ups for civic participation, with central and local government acting as catalysts for other actors including schools and social landlords;
3) interviews and guidance on responsible use, with mentoring for those at particular risk;
4) active monitoring of account balances to see what patterns and levels of inequality emerge.

Tax and savings policies also need to be adapted in the light of CTFs:

1) Linkages should be made between CTFs and savings vehicles for low-income families, such as the Savings Gateway.
2) IHT should be reformed, both to address wealth inequality directly and to provide modest resources for CTFs.
3) Existing tax reliefs for pension savings should be examined with a view to creating a more equitable regime, possibly grounded in a 'pension starter pack' available to all.

Moving beyond CTFs:

1) Land tax and the 'common assets' framework should be developed, as ways of explicitly capturing the value of assets that properly belongs to the society as a whole.
2) Individual accounts that are more use- or contingency-specific such as care, sabbatical and learning accounts, might be developed to build on the CTF framework.

Together, reforms along these lines would build on the CTF, and start to deliver the full potential of the citizen's stake. They would help us to move closer to a society in which, in the words of John Rawls, 'all citizens [are] in a position to manage their own affairs and to take part in social cooperation on a footing of mutual respect under appropriately equal conditions' (Rawls, 1999 [1971], p xv).

References

Aaron, H. (ed) (1999) *Behavioural dimensions of retirement economics*, Washington, DC: Brookings Institution.

Abel-Smith, B. (1958) 'Whose welfare state?', in N. Mackenzie (ed) *Conviction*, London: MacGibbon Kee.

Ackerman, B. and Alstott, A. (1999) *The stakeholder society*, New Haven, CT: Yale University Press.

Agulnik, P. and Le Grand, J. (1998) 'Tax relief and partnership pensions', *Fiscal Studies*, vol 19, pp 403-28.

Alstott, A. (2004) *No exit: What parents owe their children and what society owes parents*, Oxford: Oxford University Press.

Alstott, A.L. (1999) 'Work versus freedom: a liberal challenge to employment subsidies', *Yale Law Journal*, vol 108, pp 967-1058.

Altman, R. (2003) 'Beyond tax relief: a new savings incentive framework', in W. Paxton (ed) *Equal shares? Building a progressive and coherent asset-based welfare policy*, London: ippr, pp 42-56.

Arber, S. and Ginn, J. (1991) *Gender and later life*, London: Sage Publications.

Atkinson, A.B. and Stiglitz, J.E. (1980) *Lectures on public economics*, Maidenhead: McGraw-Hill.

Balbo, L. (1987) 'Crazy quilts: rethinking the welfare state debate from a woman's point of view', in A. Showstack Sasson (ed) *Women and the state*, London: Hutchinson.

Banks, J. and Tanner, S. (1999) *Household saving in the UK*, London: Institute for Fiscal Studies.

Banks, J., Oldfield, Z. and Karlsen, S. (2002) 'The socio-economic position', in M. Marmot, J. Banks, R. Blundell, C. Lessof and J. Nazroo (eds) *Health, wealth and lifestyles of the older population in England: The 2002 English longitudinal study of ageing*, London: Insitute for Fiscal Studies, pp 71-90.

Barker, C.A. (1955) *Henry George*, New York: Oxford University Press.

Barker, K. (2003) *Review of housing supply: Securing our future housing needs: interim report – analysis*, London: HM Treasury.

Barnes, P. (2001) *Who owns the sky? Our common assets and the future of capitalism*, Washington, DC: Island Press.

Barnes, P. (2003) 'Capitalism, the commons and divine right', 23rd annual E.F. Schumacher lecture, Stockbridge, MA, 25 October 2003, available from the E.F. Schumacher Society, at www.smallisbeautiful.org.

Bianchi, S. (2000) 'Maternal employment and time with children: dramatic change and surprising continuity?', *Demography*, vol 37, no 4, pp 401-14.

Blackstone, W. (1942 [1769]) *Commentaries on the laws of England*, Chicago, IL: University of Chicago Press.

Blanchflower, D. and Oswald, A. (1998) 'What makes an entrepreneur?', *Journal of Labour Economics*, vol 16, pp 26-60.

Blescs, P. and Seeleib Kaiser, M. (2004) *The dual transformation of the German welfare state*, London: Palgrave.

Blumkin, T. and Sadka, E. (2003) 'Estate taxation with intended and accidental bequests', *Journal of Public Economics*, vol 88, no 1.

Blundell, R., Dearden, L. and Sianesi, B. (2004) 'Evaluating the impact of education on earnings in the UK: models, methods and results from the NCDS', London: Centre for the Economics of Education, London School of Economics and Political Science mimeo.

Bollier, D. (2002) *Silent theft: The private plunder of our common wealth*, London: Routledge.

Bonoli, G. (2004) 'Switzerland: negotiating a new welfare state in a fragmented political system', in P. Taylor Gooby (ed) *New risk new welfare: The transformation of the European welfare state*, Oxford: Oxford University Press, pp 157-81.

Boshara, R. (2001) 'The rationale for assets, asset-building policies, and IDAs for the poor', in R. Boshara (ed) *Building assets: A report on the asset-development and IDA field*, Washington, DC: Corporation for Enterprise Development, pp 5-14.

Bowles, S. and Gintis, H. (1998) *Recasting egalitarianism: New rules for communities, states and markets*, London: Verso.

Boyes, L. and McCormick. J (forthcoming a) *Rethinking retirement*, Edinburgh: Scottish Council Foundation.

Boyes, L. and McCormick J. (forthcoming b) *Taking time out*, Edinburgh: Scottish Council Foundation.

Bracewell-Milnes, B. (2002) *Euthanasia for death duties*, London: Institute of Economic Affairs.

Brandreth, B. and Kvande, E. (2004) 'Flexible work and flexible fathers', *Work, Employment and Society*, vol 15, no 2, pp 251-67.

Brittan, S. (1983) *The role and limits of government: Essays in political economy*, Minneapolis, MN: University of Minnesota Press.

Brittan, S. (2003) 'The logic of the baby bond', review of W. Paxton (ed) *Equal shares? Building a progressive and coherent asset-based welfare policy*, 3 August, available at www.samuelbrittan.co.uk/text159_p.html

Brown, G. (1994) 'The politics of potential: a new agenda for labour', in D. Miliband (ed) *Reinventing the left*, Cambridge: Polity Press, pp113-22.

Burger, J., Ostrom, E., Norgaard, R.B., Goldstein, B.D. and Policansky, D. (2001) *Protecting the commons: A framework for resource management in the Americas*, Washington, DC: Island Press.

Butler, E. (1999) *Beyond pension plus*, London: Adam Smith Institute.

Bynner, J. (2001) 'Effect of assets on life chances', in J. Bynner and W. Paxton (eds) *The asset-effect* London: ippr, pp 17-38.

Bynner, J. and Paxton, W. (2001) *The asset-effect*, London: ippr.

CEC (Commission of the European Communities) (1993) *Growth, competitiveness and employment – the challenges and ways forward into the 21st century*, Luxembourg: CEC.

Commission on Social Justice (1994) *Social justice: Strategies for national renewal*, London: Vintage.

Commission on Taxation and Citizenship (2000) *Paying for progress: A new politics of tax for public spending*, London: Fabian Society.

Condorcet, Marquis de (1988 [1795]). *Esquisse d'un tableau historique des progrès de l'esprit humain*, edited by A. Pons, Paris: Flammarion.

Couto, A. (2004) 'Asset-based welfare in continental Europe', paper prepared as part of the 'New politics of ownership' project, Oxford: Oxford University and ippr.

Dailey, C. (2001) 'IDA practice', in R. Boshara (ed) *Building assets: A report on the asset development and IDA field*, Washington, DC: Corporation for Enterprise Development, pp 51-64.

Daly, M. (2002) 'Care as a good for social policy', *Journal of Social Policy*, vol 31, no 2, pp 251-70.

Davies, C.M. (1995) *Gender and the professional predicament in nursing*, Buckingham: Open University Press.

Davies, J.B. and Shorrocks, A.F. (2000) 'The distribution of wealth', in A.B. Atkinson and F. Bourguignon (eds) *Handbook of income distribution*, North-Holland: Elsevier, pp 605-75.

Department for Education and Employment (1998) *Teachers: Meeting the challenge of change*, Green Paper, Cm 4164, London: Department for Education and Employment.

Department of Education, Science and Training Certified Agreement (2002-5) *Stay here and grow*, Australia: Commonwealth Government.

Dex, S. and Scheibl, F. (2002) *Smaller organisations and flexible working arrangements*, York: Joseph Rowntree Foundation.

Dixon, M. and Pearce, N. (2005) 'Social justice in a changing world', in N. Pearce and W. Paxton (eds) *Social justice: Building a fairer Britain*, London: Politico's.

Dowding, K., de Wispelaere, J. and White, S. (2003) *The ethics of stakeholding*, Basingstoke: Palgrave.

Dowie, M. (2003) 'In law we trust', *Orion*, July/August, pp 19-25.

Duff, D.G. (1993) 'Taxing inherited wealth: a philosophical argument', *Canadian Journal of Law and Jurisprudence*, vol 6, no 1, pp 3-62.

Duff, D.G. (2004) 'The decline and abolition of wealth transfer taxes: lessons from Canada, Australia and New Zealand', paper presented at University of Waterloo 'Tax policy research symposium: perspectives from law & accounting', 26-7 August.

Dworkin, G. (1971) 'Paternalism', in R. Wasserstrom (ed) *Morality and the law*, Belmont, CA: Wadsworth, pp107-26.

Dworkin, R. (2000) *Sovereign virtue: The theory and practice of equality* Cambridge, MA: Harvard University Press.

Economist (2003) 'Freeing the airwaves', *Economist*, 31 May.

Edwards, L. (2000) *Assets focus groups: Top-line findings*, London: ippr.

Ehrenreich, B. and Hochschild, A. (2003) *Global women: Nannies, maids and sex workers in the new economy*, London: Granta.

Esping-Andersen, G. (1990) *The three worlds of welfare capitalism*, Princeton, NJ: Princeton University Press.

Esping-Andersen, G. with Gallie, D., Hemerijk, A. and Myles, J. (2002) *Why we need a new welfare state*, Oxford: Oxford University Press.

European Commission (2000) *Social policy agenda*, COM (2000) 379 final, Brussels: EC.

European Commission, (2003) *Scoreboard on implementing the social policy agenda*, COM (2003) 57 final, Brussels: EC.

Financial Services Authority (2004) *Child Trust Funds: Consultation paper 2004/10*, London: Financial Services Authority.

Finch, J. and Mason, J. (1993) *Negotiating family responsibilities*, London: Routledge.

Fishkin, J. (1995) *The voice of the people*, New Haven, CT: Yale University Press.

Fitzpatrick, T. (2003) *After the new social democracy: Social welfare for the twenty-first century*, Manchester: Manchester University Press.

Fourzly, M. and Gervais, M. (2002) *Collective agreements and older workers in Canada*, Quebec: Human Resources Development Canada.

Freeman, R. and Rogers, J. (1997) 'The new inequality and what to do about it', *Boston Review*, December 1996/January 1997.

Friedman, M. (1962) *Capitalism and freedom*, Chicago, IL: University of Chicago Press.

Gamble, A. and Prabhakar, R. (2004) *Assets and capital grants: Interim findings on the attitudes of young people towards capital grants*, London: Political Studies Association .

Gates, J. (1998) *The ownership solution: Toward a shared capitalism for the twenty-first century*, Reading, MA: Addison-Wesley.

Gates, Sr W.H. and Collins, C. (2002) *Wealth and our commonwealth*, Boston, MA: Beacon Press.

Gautié, J. (2003) 'Recasting the 'work and welfare nexus': asset-based versus TLM capability based approaches', unpublished paper.

Gautié, J. and Gazier, B. (2003a) 'Equipping markets for people: transitional labour markets as the central part of a new social model', Paper given at the SASE Conference, Aix en Provence, 18 June.

Gautié, J. and Gazier, B. (2003b) 'Les marchés transitionnels du travail: à quel paradigme appartiennent ils?', Paper for the colloquium, 'Conventions et institutions: approfondissements théoriques et contributions au débat politique', Grande Arche de la Défense, 11–13 December.

George, H. (1911 [1879]) *Progress and poverty*, London: J.M. Dent.

Gershuny, J. (2000) *Changing times: Work and leisure in post-industrial society*, Oxford: Oxford University Press.

Giddens, A. (1998) *The third way: The renewal of social democracy*, Cambridge: Polity Press.

Gilbert, N. (2002) *The transformation of the welfare state: The silent surrender of public responsibility*, Oxford: Oxford University Press.

Glennerster, H. (1982) 'The role of the state in financing recurrent education: lessons from European experience', in M.J. Bowman (ed) *Collective choice in education*, Boston, MA: Kluwer/Nijhoff.

Goodin, R. (2003) 'Sneaking up on stakeholding', in K. Dowding, J. Jurgen Dewispelaere, and S. White (eds) *The ethics of stakeholding* Basingstoke: Palgrave, pp 65–78.

Goodin, R.E., Headey, B., Muffels, R. and Dirven, H.J. (1999) *The real worlds of welfare capitalism*, Cambridge: Cambridge University Press.

Graham, H. (1983) 'Caring: a labour of love', in J. Finch and D. Groves (eds) *A labour of love: Women, work and caring*, London: Routledge and Kegan Paul.

Gregg, P. and Washbrook, E. (2003) *The effects of early maternal employment on child development in the UK*, Working Paper, Bristol: The Centre for Market and Public Organisations.

Hakim, C. (2000) *Work-lifestyle choices in the twenty-first century: Preference theory*, Oxford: Oxford University Press.

Hall, J.C. (2002) 'Mentoring and young people: a literature review', in *SCRE Research Report 114*, Glasgow: University of Glasgow.

Halstead, T. and Lind, M. (2001) *The radical center: The future of American politics*, New York, NY: Doubleday.

Haveman, R. (1988) *Starting even: An equal opportunity program to combat the nation's new poverty*, New York, NY: Simon and Schuster.

HBOS (2004) *Historical data spreadsheet*, available at www.hbosplc.com/economy/includes/historicdata05_04_05.xls

Hedges, A. and Bromley, C. (2000) *Public attitudes towards taxation*, London: Fabian Society.

Hewlett, S.A. (1991) *When the bough breaks: The cost of neglecting our children*, New York, NY: Basic Books.

Heymann, J. (2000) *The widening gap: Why America's working families are in jeopardy and what can be done about it*, New York, NY: Basic Books.

Hickel, W.J. (2002) *Crisis in the Commons: The Alaska solution*, Oakland, CA: Institute for Contemporary Studies Press.

Hills, J. and Falkingham, J. (1995) *The dynamic of welfare*, Hemel Hempstead: Harvester.

Himmelweit, S. (1995) 'The discovery of 'unpaid work': the social consequences of the expansion of 'work'', *Feminist Economics*, vol 1, no 2, pp 121-39.

Hind, G. (2002) 'Financial education and the Child Trust Fund', paper presented at an ippr seminar on 'The role of financial education in asset-based policies', 25 February.

HM Treasury (2001) *Saving and assets for all*, London: HM Treasury.

HM Treasury (2003a) *Detailed proposals for the Child Trust Fund*, London: The Stationery Office.

HM Treasury (2003b) *Budget 2003: Building a Britain of economic strength and social justice*, London: The Stationery Office.

HM Treasury (2004) *Budget 2004: Prudence for a purpose: A Britain of stability and strength*, London: The Stationery Office.

HM Treasury (2005) *Budget 2005: Financial statement & budget report*, London: The Stationery Office.

HM Treasury and Inland Revenue (2003) *Detailed proposals for the Child Trust Fund*, London: HMSO.

Hochschild, A. (1995) 'The culture of politics: traditional, post-modern a cold-modern and warm-modern ideals of care', *Social Politics*, vol 2, no 3, pp 333-46.

Holtham, G. (1999) 'Ownership and social democracy', in A. Gamble and T. Wright (eds) *The new social democracy*, Oxford: Blackwell, pp 53-68.

House of Commons Work and Pensions Committee (2003) *Childcare for working parents: Fifth report of session 2002-3*, London: The Stationery Office.

Huber, J. and Robertson, J. (2000) *Creating new money: A monetary reform for the information age*, New Economics Foundation, available at www.neweconomics.org/gen z_sys_PublicationDetail.aspx?PID=81

Hutton, W. (2004) 'Got those old blue-collar blues', *Observer*, 22 August, p 24.

Inland Revenue (2005) Online statistics, available at www.ir.gov.uk/stats/index.htm

Isles, N. (2004) *The joy of work*, London: The Work Foundation.

Jefferson, T. (1999) *Political writings*, edited by J. Appleby and T. Ball, Cambridge: Cambridge University Press.

Jenkins, R. (1968) *Mr Balfour's poodle* (3rd edn), London: Collins.

Jenson, J. (1997) 'Who cares? Gender and welfare regimes', *Social Politics*, vol 4, no 2, pp 182-7.

Jenson, J. and Sineau, M. (eds) (2001) *Women's work, childcare, and welfare state redesign*, Toronto: University of Toronto Press.

Kay, J.A. and King, M. (1990) *The British tax system* (5th edn), Oxford: Oxford University Press.

Kelly, G. and Lissauer, R. (2000) *Ownership for all*, London: ippr.

Kittay, E.F. (1999) *Love's labour: Essays on women, equality and dependency*, New York, NY: Routledge.

Kittay, E.F. and Feder, E.K. (eds) (2000) *The subject of care. Feminist perspectives on dependency*, New York, NY: Rowman and Littlefield.

Knijn, T. (2004) 'Challenges and risks of individualisation in the Netherlands', *Social Policy and Society*, vol 3, no 1, pp 57-65.

Knijn, T. and Kremer, M. (1997) 'Gender and the caring dimension of welfare states: toward inclusive citizenship', *Social Politics*, vol 4 no 3, pp 328-61.

Kodz, J., Harper, J. and Dench, S. (2002) *Work life balance, beyond the rhetoric*, IES Report 384, Brighton: The Institute for Employment Studies.

Koenrer, B.I. (2004) 'The ambition tax: why America's young are being crushed by debt and why no one seems to care', *Village Voice*, 17-23 March, available at www.villagevoice.com/issues/0411/koerner.php

Kotlikoff, L.J. (2003) *Generational policy*, Cambridge, MA: MIT Press.

Land, H. (1969) *Large families in London: Occasional papers in social administration*, no 32, London: Bell.

Le Grand, J. (1983) *The strategy of equality*, London: Allen and Unwin.

Le Grand, J. (1989) 'Markets, welfare, and equality', in J. Le Grand and S. Estrin (eds) *Market socialism*, Oxford: Oxford University Press, pp 193-211.

Le Grand, J. (2002) 'Implementing stakeholder grants: the British case', Paper delivered at the 'Rethinking redistribution: universal basic income and stakeholder grants for a more egalitarian capitalism' conference at the University of Wisconsin, 2-5 May. Available online www.ssc.wisc.edu/havenscenter/LeGrand.PDF

Leira, A. (1992) *Welfare states and working mothers*, Cambridge: Cambridge University Press.

Leira, A. (2002) *Working parents and the welfare state: Family change and policy reform in Scandinavia*, Cambridge: Cambridge University Press.

Lewis, J. (2001) 'The decline of the male breadwinner model: the implications for work and care', *Social Politics*, vol 8, no 2, pp 152-70.

Lewis, J. and Glennerster, H. (1996) *Implementing the new community care*, Buckingham: Open University Press.

Lewis, S. (2002) 'Work and family issues old and new' in R.J. Burke and D.L. Nelson (eds) *Advancing women's careers: Research and practice*, Oxford: Blackwell.

Lister, R. (2004) *Poverty*, Cambridge: Polity Press.

Locke, J. (1960 [1682]) *Two treatises of government*, edited by P. Laslett, Cambridge: Cambridge University Press.

Lødemel, I. and Trickey, H. (eds) (2000) *An offer you can't refuse: Workfare in international perspective*, Bristol: The Policy Press.

Lowe, R. (1998) *The welfare state in Britain since 1945*, London: Macmillan.

Lugaila, T.A (2003) 'A child's day: 2000 (selected indicators of children's well-being)', *Current Population Reports P70-89*, Washington, DC: US Census Bureau.

Masson, A. and Pestieau, P. (1997) 'Bequest motives and models of inheritance: a survey of the literature', in G. Erreygers and T. Vandevelde (eds) *Is inheritance legitimate?*, Heidelberg: Springer Verlag.

Matsaganis, M. and Glennerster, H. (1994) 'The threat of 'cream skimming' in the post-reform NHS', *Journal of Health Economics*, no 13, pp 31-64.

Maxwell, D. (2004) *Fair dues: Towards a more progressive inheritance tax*, London: ippr.

Maxwell, D. (2005) *Child Trust Funds and local authorities: Challenges and opportunities*, London: ippr.

Maxwell, D. and Sodha, S. (2005) *Top tips for top-ups: Next steps for Chuild Trust Funds*, London: ippr.

McCay, B.J. and Acheson, J.M. (ed) (1996) *The question of the commons: The culture and ecology of communal resources*, Tucson, AZ: University of Arizona Press.

McLean, I. and Hewitt, F. (1994) *Condorcet foundations of social choice and political theory*, Aldershot: Edward Elgar.

Meade, J. (1964) *Efficiency, equality, and the ownership of property*, London: Allen and Unwin.

Meade, J. (1989) *Agathatopia: The economics of partnership*, Aberdeen: University of Aberdeen.

Mill, J.S. (1970 [1848]) *Principles of political economy*, edited by D. Winch, Harmondsworth: Penguin.

Millar, J. and Rowlingson, K. (2001) *Lone parents, employment and social policy*, Bristol: The Policy Press.

Miller, D. (2005) 'What is social justice?', in N. Pearce and W. Paxton (eds) *Social justice: Building a fairer Britain*, London: Politico's.

Moller, Okin S. (1989) *Justice, gender and the family*, New York: Basic Books.

Morgan, K. and Zippel, K. (2003) 'Paid to care: the origins and effects of care leave policies in western Europe', *Social Politics*, vol 10, no 1, pp 45-85.

Moss, P. and Deven. F (1999) *Parental leave: Progress or pitfall? Research and policy issues in Europe*, Brussels: NIDI/CBGS Publications.

Mulgan, G. and Murray, R. (1993) *Reconnecting taxation*, London: Demos.

National Statistics (2002) *Social trends*, London: National Statistics.

Nelson, B.J. (1990) 'The origins of the two-channel welfare state: workmen's compensation and mothers' aid', in L. Gordon (ed) *Women the state and welfare*, Madison, WI: University of Wisconsin Press, pp 123-51.

New Ways to Work (2002) *Breaks from employment: Flexible working factsheet*, London: New Ways to Work.

Newhouse, J.P. (1984) 'Cream skimming, asymmetric information and a competitive insurance market', *Journal of Health Economics*, vol 3, pp 97-100.

Nissan, D. and Le Grand, J. (2000) *A capital idea: Start-up grants for young people*, London: Fabian Society.

Nozick, R. (1974) *Anarchy, state, and utopia*, Oxford: Blackwell.

Nussbaum, M. (2003) 'Capabilities as fundamental entitlements: Sen and social justice', *Feminist Economics*, vol 9, nos 2-3, pp 33-59.

Offe, C. (1992) 'A non-productivist design for social policies', in P. Van Parijs (ed) *Arguing for basic income*, London: Verso, pp 61-78.

Offe, C. (1996) *Modernity and the state*, Cambridge: Polity Press.

Offe, C. (2001) 'Pathways from here', in P. Van Parijs (ed) *What's wrong with a free lunch?*, Boston, MA: Beacon Press, pp 111-18.

Offe, C., Mückenberger, U. and Ostner, I. (1996) 'Basic income guaranteed by the state: a need of the moment in social policy', in R. Offe (ed) *Modernity and the state*, Cambridge: Polity Press, pp 201-21.

ODPM (Office of the Deputy Prime Minister) (2004) *Balance of funding review: Report*, London: ODPM.

Office of the Deputy Prime Minister Select Committee (2004) *Local government revenue: Ninth report of session 2003–04, Volume 1: Report*, London: ODPM.

Olson, M. (1965) *The logic of collective action: Public goods and the theory of groups*, Cambridge, MA: Harvard University Press.

OECD (Organisation for Economic Co-operation and Development) (2003a) *Taxation of net wealth, capital transfers and capital gains of individuals*, Paris: OECD.

OECD (2003b) *OECD review of career guidance policies: Country note – United Kingdom*, Paris: OECD.

OECD (2004) *La constitution d'un patrimonie et la sortie de la pauvreté: Introduction à un nouveau débat sur la polique de bien-être*, Paris: OECD.

Orsag, J.M., Orsag, P.R., Snower, D.J. and Stiglitz J. (1999) 'The impact of individual accounts: piecemeal versus comprehensive approaches', Birkbeck economics working paper, available online at www.econ.bbk.ac.uk

Ostrom, E. (1990) *Governing the commons: The evolution of institutions for collective action*, Cambridge: Cambridge University Press.

Oswald, A.J. (1999) 'The housing market and Europe's unemployment: a nontechnical paper', Warwick: University of Warwick, mimeo.

O'Toole, T. (2001) 'Researching young people's political participation: towards a fuller understanding of the political', Paper presented to CANE conference, University of Sheffield, 17 November.

Oxfordshire County Council (2005) *The Oxfordshire land value tax study*, Oxford: Oxfordshire County Council.

Page-Adams, D. and Vosler, N. (1996) 'Predictors of depression among workers at the time of a plant closing', *Journal of Sociology and Social Welfare*, vol 23, pp 25-42.

Paine, T. (1987 [1797]) *Agrarian justice*, in M. Foot and I. Kramnick (eds) *The Thomas Paine reader*, Harmondsworth: Penguin, pp 471-89.

Paine, T. (1995 [1797]) 'Agrarian justice', in T. Paine, *The rights of man, Common sense, and other political writings*, edited by M. Philp, Oxford: Oxford University Press.

Park, A.C., Thomson, J.K., Jarvis, L. and Bromley, C. (2002) *British social attitudes, the 19th report*, London: National Centre for Social Research.

Pateman, C. (1988) 'The patriarchal welfare state', in A. Gutmann (ed) *Democracy and the welfare state*, Princeton, NJ: Princeton University Press, pp 231-60.

Patrick, R. and Jacobs, M. (2003) *Wealth's fair measure: The reform of inheritance tax*, London: Fabian Society.

Paxton, W. (2002a) 'Baby-bonds: bonding communities? Civic involvement and the Child Trust Funds', paper prepared for a joint IPPR/Global Service Institute seminar, 25 January.

Paxton, W. (2002b) 'The asset-effect: an overview', in J. Bynner and W. Paxton (eds) *The asset-effect* London: ippr, pp 1-16.

Paxton, W. and Dixon, M. (2004) *The state of the nation: An audit of injustice on the UK*, London: ippr.

Payne Watt, H. (1999) *Common assets: Asserting rights to our shared inheritance*, Washington, DC: Corporation for Economic Development and Redefining Progress.

Pelling, H. (1965) *Origins of the Labour party* (2nd edn), London: Oxford University Press.

Pension Commission (2004) *Pensions: Challenges and choices*, London: The Stationery Office.

Performance and Innovation Unit (2002a) *Geographical mobility*, London, Cabinet Office.

Performance and Innovation Unit (2002b) *Lending support: Modernising the government's use of loans*, London: Cabinet Office.

Pettit, P (1997) *Republicanism: A theory of freedom and government*, Oxford: Oxford University Press.

Piatt, W. and Robinson, P. (2001) *Opportunities for whom? Options for funding and structure of post-16 education*, London: ippr.

Pillinger, J. (2001) *Work/life balance findings: New ways to work*, commissioned by PCS, Inland Revenue and TUC, November, available online at www.tuc.org.uk/work_life/tuc-4022-f0.cfm

Qureshi, H. and Walker, A. (1989) *The caring relationship*, London: Macmillan.

Rawls, J. (1999 [1971]) *A theory of justice* (revised edn), Cambridge, MA: Harvard University Press.

Rawls, J. (2001) *Justice as fairness: A restatement*, Cambridge, MA: Harvard University Press.

Regan, S. (ed) (2001) *Assets and progressive welfare*, London: ippr.

Regan, S. and Paxton, W. (eds) (2001) *Asset-based welfare: International experiences*, London: ippr.

Ricardo, D. (1817) *On the principles of political economy and taxation* (1st edn) London: John Murray.

Ricardo, D. (1821) *On the principles of political economy and taxation* (3rd edn) London: John Murray.

Robertson, J. (2000) 'The alternative Mansion House speech', 9 April, available at www.wwdemocracy.nildram.co.uk/democracy_today/alt_mansion.htm

Rogers, J. and Streeck, W. (1994) 'Productive solidarities: economic strategies and left politics', in D. Miliband (ed) *Reinventing the left*, Cambridge: Polity Press, pp 128-45.

Rousseau, J.J. (1993 [1762]) *The social contract*, translated by C. Betts, Oxford: Oxford University Press.

Rowlingson, K. and McKay, S. (2005) *Attitudes to inheritance in Britain*, Bristol: The Policy Press.

Royal Commission on Long Term Care (1999) *With respect to old age: Long-term care – Rights and responsibilities*, London: The Stationery Office.

Sandford, C.T., Willis, J.R.M. and Ironside, D.J. (1973) *An accessions tax*, London: Institute of Fiscal Studies.

Saskatchewan Federation of Labour (2000) *Family friendly workplaces: A study of Saskatchewan collective agreements*, Regina: Saskatchewan Federation of Labour, with funding from the Women's Program, Status of Women Canada, available at www.sfkl.sk.ca/policy/Image8.gif.

Sax, J. (1970) 'The public trust in natural resource law: effective judicial intervention', *Michigan Law Review*, vol 68, p 471.

Scanlon, E. and Page-Adams, D. (2001) 'Effects of asset holding on neighborhoods, families, and children: a review of research', in R. Boshara (ed) *Building assets: A report on the asset-development and IDA field*, Washington, DC: Corporation for Enterprise Development, pp 25-50.

Schmid, G. (2000) 'Transitional labour markets', in B. Marin, D. Meulders and D. Snower (eds) *Innovative employment initiatives*, Aldershot: Ashgate.

Schmid, G. and Gazier, B. (2002) *The dynamics of full employment: Social integration through transitional labour markets*, London: Edward Elgar.

Schor, J. (2001) *The overworked American*, New York, NY: Basic Books.

Sefton, T. (1997) *The changing distribution of the social wage*, STICERD occasional paper, 21, London: London School of Economics and Political Science.

Sefton, T. (2002) *Recent changes in the distribution of the social wage*, CASE paper, 62, London: London School of Economics and Political Science.

Sefton, T. (2003) 'What we want from the welfare state', in A. Park, J. Curtice, K., Thomson, L., Jarvis and C. Bromley (eds) *British social attitudes: Continuity and change over two decades*, London: Sage Publications.

Sen, A. (1999) *Development as freedom*, Oxford: Oxford University Press.

Sharma, N. (2002) *Still missing out? Ending poverty and social exclusion: Messages to government from families with disabled children*, London: Barnado's.

Sherraden, M. (1991) *Assets and the poor*, New York, NY: M.E. Sharpe.

Sherraden, M. (2002) *Individual development accounts: Summary of research, research report*, St Louis: Center for Social Development, Washington University.

Skinner, Q. (1998) *Liberty before liberalism*, Cambridge: Cambridge University Press.

Skocpol, T. (2000) *The missing middle: Working families and the future of American social policy*, New York, NY: W.W. Norton & Company.

Sloan, H.E. (1995) *Principle and interest: Thomas Jefferson and the problem of debt*, New York, NY: Oxford University Press.

Small Business Service (2004) *Business survival rates*, available at www.sbs.gov.uk

Smith, A. (1776) *The wealth of nations*, New York, NY: Prometheus Books.

Social Exclusion Unit (2003) *Making the connections: Final report on transport and social exclusion*, London: ODPM.

Stanley, K. (2004) *Something for something: A national youth action programme*, London: ippr.

Steiner, H. (1994) *An essay on rights*, Oxford: Blackwell.

Steiner, H. and Vallentyne, P. (2000) (eds) *Left-libertarianism*, Basingstoke: Macmillan.

Sunstein, C. and Thaler, R. (2003) *Libertarian paternalism is not an oxymoron*, Washington, DC: Brookings Institute.

Supiot, A. (2001) *Beyond employment: Changes in work and the future of labour law in Europe*, Oxford: Oxford University Press.

Sutton, M., Gravelle, H., Morris, S., Leyland, A., Windmeijer, F., Dibben, C. and Muirhead, M. (2002) *Allocation of resources to English areas; individual and small area determinants of morbidity and use of health care resources*, Report to the Department of Health, Edinburgh: Information and Statistics Division.

Taylor-Gooby, P. (2004) 'Trust and the governance of risk: responses to the new pension settlement', Canterbury: University of Kent, mimeo.

Taylor-Gooby, P. (2005) 'Attitudes to social justice', in N. Pearce, and W. Paxton (eds) *Social justice: Building a fairer Britain*, London: Politico's, pp 106-30.

The Ecologist (1993) *Whose common future? Reclaiming the commons*, Philadelphia, PA: New Society Publishers.

Tronto, J. (1993) *Moral boundaries: A political argument for an ethic of care*, London: Routledge.

Unger, R. and West, C. (1998) *The future of American progressivism*, Boston, MA: Beacon Press.

US Bureau of the Census (2001) *Statistical abstract of the United States*, Washington, DC: Government Printing Office.

Van Parijs, P. (1995) *Real freedom for all: What (if anything) can justify capitalism?*, Oxford: Oxford University Press.

Watt, H.P. (2000) *Common assets: Asserting rights to our shared inheritence*, Washington, DC: Corporation for Enterprise, Development and Redefining Progress.

White, S. (2001) 'Asset-based egalitarianism: forms, strengths and limitations', in S. Regan (ed) *Assets and progressive welfare*, London: ippr, pp 4-16.

White, S. (2003) *The civic minimum: On the rights and obligations of economic citizenship*, Oxford: Oxford University Press.

White, S. (2004a) 'Markets, time and citizenship', *Renewal*, vol 12, no 3, pp 50-63.

White, S. (2004b) 'The citizen's stake and paternalism', *Politics and Society*, vol 32, no 1, March, pp 61-78.

Wilkinson, C.F. (1989) 'The headwaters of the public trust: some of the traditional doctrine', *Environmental Law*, Spring, pp 425-71.

Working Families (2002) 'Breaks from employment', *Flexible Working Factsheet*, London: Working Families.

Index

Locators in *italics* refer to boxes and tables.

Also available from The Policy Press

The glass consumer
Life in a surveillance society
Edited by Susanne Lace
Published in association with National Consumer Council

"The explosion of information in the Google age risks eroding our privacy faster than laws can be made to protect it. This book offers an incisive overview of the trends, risks and possible solutions to what may become the most critical consumer issue in the next century."
Chris Anderson, Editor, Wired Magazine

"A significant contribution to the ongoing debate on the important area of how best to protect individuals' personal data in an environment of increasing technological change."
Baroness Ashton of Upholland, Government Spokesperson on Constitutional Affairs

We are all 'glass consumers'. Organisations know so much about us, they can almost see through us. *The glass consumer* appraises the relentless scrutiny of consumers' lives. It reviews what is known about how personal information is used and examines the benefits and risks to consumers. The book takes the debate beyond privacy issues, arguing that we are living in a world in which – more than ever before – our personal information defines our opportunities in life.

Paperback £12.99 US$22.50 ISBN 1 86134 735 9
216 x 148 mm 272 pages June 2005

Remaking governance
Peoples, politics and the public sphere
Edited by Janet Newman

"This ground-breaking book provides many new insights into the social significance of governance. Drawing on relevant strands of social and cultural theory, *Remaking governance* provides a sustained critical analysis of unfolding governance-related ideas and practices at European and national level. It should move quickly into the canon of governance studies." *Professor Mary Daly, School of Sociology and Social Policy, Queen's University Belfast*

There has been an explosion of new forms of governance as societies adapt to economic, social and political change. This book highlights the dynamics of the social, cultural and institutional practices involved in 'remaking' governance. It is structured around three key themes: the remaking of peoples, publics and politics.

Paperback £23.99 US$39.95 ISBN 1 86134 639 5
Hardback £55.00 US$85.00 ISBN 1 86134 640 9
234 x 156 mm 232 pages September 2005

The right use of money
David Darton

"Money is a force for good or evil depending on how individuals choose to use it. This admirable book sets out multiple ways in which the human condition can be improved through the trading, giving, stewarding and multiplying of money." *Sir Paul Judge, Royal Society of Arts*

"The use of money to achieve social aims and objectives is a central concern to everyone who wishes to make a positive contribution to society. The high calibre of the contributors and the breadth of views expressed makes this book a unique contribution to public debate." *Lord Best, Joseph Rowntree Foundation*

The range of topics discussed is broad, from questions of economics and government policy, corporate and individual responsibility to how voluntary organisations can ensure that their money is used wisely.

Issues raised include:

- Does the way we use money betray the next generation?
- Is dishonesty within our financial systems making it too difficult for consumers to make informed decisions?
- Are we wasting money on good intentions that do not match real need?
- How can individuals, foundations and others with social concerns ensure that all their assets are used effectively?

The book concludes with suggested actions for government, business, financial institutions, voluntary organisations and individuals. Anyone concerned with issues of finance and social justice will want to read this book.

Paperback £9.95 US$20.00 ISBN 1 86134 616 6
216 x 148 mm 160 pages July 2004

To order copies of these publications or any other Policy Press titles please visit **www.policypress.org.uk** or contact:

In the UK and Europe:
Marston Book Services, PO Box 269,
Abingdon, Oxon, OX14 4YN, UK
Tel: +44 (0)1235 465500
Fax: +44 (0)1235 465556
Email: direct.orders@marston.co.uk

In the USA and Canada:
ISBS, 920 NE 58th Street, Suite 300,
Portland, OR 97213-3786, USA
Tel: +1 800 944 6190 (toll free)
Fax: +1 503 280 8832
Email: info@isbs.com

In Australia and New Zealand:
DA Information Services, 648 Whitehorse Road
Mitcham, Victoria 3132, Australia
Tel: +61 (3) 9210 7777
Fax: +61 (3) 9210 7788
E-mail: service@dadirect.com.au

Further information about all of our titles can be found on our website.

Policy & Politics

Policy & Politics plays a key role in the analysis and dissemination of policy studies and international political debate. It offers a unique perspective on critical policy developments by focusing on cross-cutting themes from accountability and regulation to evaluation; theorising the policy process to policy making and implementation.

Free online subscription

A subscription to Policy Press journals offers you easy online access to the full text of articles published. You can browse, search, download and print the latest published articles from your own office or from the library.

- Full text online for subscribers
- Easy searching, downloading and printing

To subscribe to Policy Press journals contact:

The Policy Press
c/o Portland Customer Services
Whitehall Industrial Estate
Commerce Way
Colchester CO2 8HP
UK
Tel: +44 (0)1206 796351
Fax: +44 (0)1206 799331
E-mail: sales@portland-services.com
www.portland-services.com